THE REFORMATION OF IMAGES

John Foxe, *Book of Martyrs*, 1640. The word of God vs popish superstition.

THE REFORMATION OF IMAGES:

DESTRUCTION OF ART IN

ENGLAND, 1535-1660

by

John Phillips

UNIVERSITY OF CALIFORNIA PRESS

BERKELEY   LOS ANGELES   LONDON

University of California Press
Berkeley and Los Angeles, California
University of California Press, Ltd.
London, England
Copyright © 1973, by
The Regents of the University of California
ISBN: 0–520–02424–9
Library of Congress Catalog Card Number: 72–97739
Designed by W. H. Snyder
Printed in the United States of America

Material in this book has been quoted with permission
of the following publishers: Harcourt Brace Jovanovich,
Inc., T. S. Eliot, "The Waste Land"; Harper & Row,
Publishers, Inc., Joyce Cary, *The Horse's Mouth*; Mac-
millan Publishing Co., Inc., C. S. Lewis, *The Screwtape
Letters* (© C. S. Lewis 1942) and Georges Bernanos,
Journal d'un Curé de Campagne; Princeton University
Press, José Ortega y Gasset, *The Dehumanization of
Art*; and Random House, Inc., André Gide, *Les Caves du
Vatican* and Katharine Anne Porter, *Flowering Judas
and Other Stories*.

The author wishes to acknowledge with thanks the individuals and institutions that made it possible to illustrate this book. Reproduced by courtesy of the Trustees
of the British Museum are figs. 2, 3, 4, 26, and 33. Reproduced with permission of the National Commission on
Historical Monuments are figs. 8, 14, 20, 22, 23, 24a, 24b,
25, 35, 36a, 36b, and 37. Figure 32 is reproduced with
permission of the Royal Commission on Historical
Monuments. Figure 15 is reproduced with permission of
the National Portrait Gallery, London; figure 11 with
permission of the Cambridge University Collection
(copyright reserved); figures 17a and 17b with permission of the Courtauld Institute; figures 18 and 31 with
permission of Rev. Canon Maurice Ridgeway; figure 38
with permission of the Ipswich Museum. The photos of
Nicholas Sapieha are reproduced in figures 5, 6, 7, 9, 10,
12, 13, 16, 19, 29a, 29b, 30, 34; of H. Felton, fig. 28;
of A. F. Kersting, fig. 21.

To my teachers

JERALD BRAUER   MARVIN LEVICH   JOSHUA TAYLOR

CONTENTS

PREFACE

THE PROUD abbey at Glastonbury was suppressed in 1539 and given over to pillage and destruction in the name of reform. When it came into the possession of the Lord Protector Somerset, he stripped the roofs of lead and arranged for a group of about two hundred Flemish weavers to take over the deserted buildings. Six houses were refurbished, but most of the buildings remained in great need of repair. Under Queen Mary the weavers left the country, and though there were hopes of restoring the abbey, little was done.

In the early seventeenth century, Glastonbury was quarried. Frequently, gunpowder was employed to hasten its demolition; the abbey's squared freestone, rubble core in the walls, and heavy stones of the foundation were tempting prizes for neighboring builders. It is possible that the solid foundation across the marshland which acted as support for the causeway to Wells was formed from the stones of Glastonbury.

Early in the eighteenth century, it seems that the abbey was tenanted by a Presbyterian who committed much havoc; every week, he sold a pillar, a buttress, a window joint or an angle of fine hewn stone to the highest bidder. Continued depredation throughout the eighteenth century and into the nineteenth reduced most of the remaining fabric. Today, Glastonbury's foundations have almost completely disappeared.

Yet these strange, desolate piles are still capable of moving us deeply, much as Antonio was moved:

> "I do love these ancient ruins:
> We never tread upon them, but we set
> Our foot upon some reverend history. . .
> but all things have their end:
> Churches and Cities (which have diseases like to men)
> Must have like death that we have."[1]

Much of Romantic painting and literature of the eighteenth and
nineteenth centuries was postulated upon an imagery of "natural"
landscape replete with such picturesque ruins—in fact the destroyed
fabric of the medieval church in England. It was the ruin of one art
in the service of other arts:

> "Where rev'rend shrines in gothic grandeur stood,
>   The nettle, or the noxious night-shade spreads;
> And ashlings, wafted from the neighb'ring wood,
>   Through the worn turrets wave their trembling heads."[2]

Englishmen acquired these sentiments only in later generations.
The destruction of images was seen by sixteenth- and seventeenth-
century contemporaries as a much sought-for victory of one mode of
salvation over another. Clearly, iconoclasm for the iconoclasts was an
act far different from our later understanding of it as vandalism. It
is thus necessary to try to understand the nature of the act in terms
that its perpetrators comprehended. I found that this history and fate
of one building like Glastonbury could reflect the broad social, political, economic and religious revolution that was taking place in
Reformation England. More profoundly, the same history revealed
the full range of human response and motivation as to why images
were either preserved, mutilated or destroyed.

In talking about iconoclasm, I have purposely not discussed the
question of whether or not the images treated were considered to be
works of art. I felt that in any case such considerations did not make
the objects more or less worthy of destruction in the eyes of their
destroyers. However, upon completion of this essay, I have been thinking whether this very question of art and images may be one of many
implicit distinctions that, through clarification, can be useful in de-
fining causes of destruction and attitudes that made destruction not
only possible, but acceptable.

1. John Webster, *The Duchess of Malfi*, V, iii, 9–18.
2. John Cunningham, "Elegy on a Pile of Ruins" *Poems chiefly Pastoral*, 1766.

It is widely acknowledged that images which can be identified as having evocative power can be distinguished, because of their totemic values, from images intended for purely representational or ornamental purposes. Such definitions are the stock-in-trade of anthropology, psychiatry, and a dozen other intellectual disciplines that have evolved since the Enlightenment. In cultures for which some objects may have totemic value, the difference between "nature" and "artifice" becomes exceedingly ambivalent. But in our culture, we have intellectual options that lead us to make such distinctions easily, even glibly, thereby avoiding the whole question of whether an object may itself represent or possess power. To state a complex of ideas simply, we can understand artifice as a condition generally unlike that of nature, without insisting that one condition is *ipso facto* better or worse (or of greater or lesser value) than the other.

During my reading of the image-breaker's documents, it became evident that the principals did not predicate their destruction of objects in terms of an identifiable aesthetic governing works of art/artifice, as we now understand such aesthetics and such works. The iconoclasts made their histories not in a broad confluence of intellectual currents, but in the exceedingly narrow channels that lay between God and the Devil—between salvation and hope of Heaven, or eternal damnation. Asserting the *a priori* virtue of God's handiwork as superior to man's was apparently the only aesthetic judgement a rightthinking Puritan could safely make. Outside such boundaries—themselves the proper province of religious dogma—lay the temptations of the world of artifice. Artifice was perilous not only because it might be merely extraneous to furthering the work of God—but because it might also be the work of the Devil or of Antichrist himself. The Antichrist was periodically awaited in a form not perfect—but *nearly* perfect.[3] The subversion by Antichrist of man would be accomplished through acceptance, because of man's fallible perception, of works of *seeming* virtue and beauty. Subversion by artifice has long served the motifs of art and has been the subject of countless literary forays. Spenser and Milton, contemporaries of the English iconoclasts, pos-

3. See J. B. Friedman, "Antichrist & Dante's Geryon," *Journal of Warburg and Courtauld Institutes* XXXV (1972) 111. For a systematic and comprehensive survey, see also Christopher Hill, *Antichrist in Seventeenth-Century England* (London: Oxford University Press, 1971).

sessed highly sophisticated concepts of artifice as a condition perilous
to man's eternal soul. The dangers of the Bowre of Blisse, a construction of great seeming beauty but wholly without natural leaf or
flower, and the sorry disorder of Pandemonium—the fallen angels'
effort to shape by artifice the perfect order of Heaven—are obvious
examples. They suggest the degree of intellectual involvement the
two poets had in the concept of artifice, as it was then understood: a
condition wholly contrary to the work of God on earth, and bearing
the hint that the very manifestations of artifice—the objects themselves—were perilous in themselves, full of the destructive power of
their always-suspect origins.

The Lollard argument (later to be the Puritan one) declared that
art should be true to earthly fact precisely because the human imagination was suspect; above all, it showed a clear preference for "real
objects" (good works) over simulated ones (works of art). Consequently much Puritan objection to religious images was expressed
in revulsion against man-made objects of beauty. While John Hooper
does not mention "art" as such, his Puritanism compelled him to advocate the ultimate superiority of nature (God's creations) over images (man's creations) that might be works of the Devil—of Antichrist.
If the late sixteenth and seventeenth centuries showed a developing
aesthetic consciousness for works of art (i.e. "artifice") among the
gentry and intellectuals, a Puritan "counter-aesthetic" developed at
the same time. It clearly rejected the view of man as independent
creator. Would not these Puritans have agreed (but only in part!)
with Paul Klee: "The artist neither serves nor rules—he transmits.
His position is humble. And the beauty . . . is not his own. He is
merely a channel."[4]

Artifice, in short, was dangerous, and may explain thereby why
images threatened so much of the institutional bases of religious and
political structures, and in what terms the subsequent, and conse-
quent, iconoclasm was justified and explained. Hence if this essay
might seem open-ended, perhaps it is incomplete in the direction of
exploring the specific content that came to form the so-called Puritan
aesthetic. But I must recognize that such a study would doubtless
further burden my argument and make still another book.

4. Paul Klee, *On Modern Art*, 1924.

Certainly any Puritan would agree with me that an inferior book can be just as difficult to write as a good one; the first can be as sincere in execution and as taxing in inspiration as the second. I have tried to avoid the pitfall of the first sort, and while there can be no substitute for what God holds back, sometimes the guidance of colleagues, friends and students can correct deficiencies, winnow the chaff and save the good wheat.

My appreciation for good counsel goes to Jock Weintraub and Charles Gray of the University of Chicago; Sears McGee of the University of California, Santa Barbara; Jon Westling of the University of California, Los Angeles; Fredrica Harris of the University of Illinois, Chicago Circle; William Smith, Richard Jones, Smith Fussner of Reed College; Richard Luman of Haverford College; Roy Strong of the National Portrait Gallery, London; Joel Hurstfield of the University of London; Peregrine Bryant of St. Catherine's College, Cambridge. I owe special thanks for her shared insight and encouragement to Frances Yates of the Warburg Institute; to Dorothy and Roger Phillips for understanding; to Aureen Mayne-Winter, Alice Worden, Marti Nakagawa, Fran Shaw and Martha Bergquist for many favors. A great debt goes to Lorna Price who was more than an editor. I also wish to acknowledge with thanks an Inland Steel grant from the University of Chicago, the Griffin Faculty Research Fund of Reed College and especially the Leopold Schepp Foundation and its secretary, Miss Josephine Hammond, for financial support. I dedicate this book to those three men who inspired me in more ways than either they imagine or this book represents.

INTRODUCTION

Au mur un assez vilain chromo, pareil à ceux qu'on voit dans
des salles d'hôpital et qui représente un Enfant Jésus bien jouf-
flu, bien rose, entre l'âne et le boeuf. Tu vois ce tableau, m'a-t-il
dit. C'est un cadeau de ma marraine. J'ai bien les moyens de me
payer quelque chose de mieux, de plus artistique, mais je préfère
encore celui-ci. Je le trouve laid, et même un peu bête, ça me
rassure.

GEORGES BERNANOS, *Journal d'un Curé de Campagne*

DURING THE YEARS 1535–1660 England's artistic heritage was sub-
jected to violent and extensive destruction. Religious painting
and sculpture were the most frequent, but not the only victims.
Bishop Joseph Hall experienced the full fury of this ravage when
his chapel in Norwich was attacked in 1647. "Lord, what work was
here!" he cried, having seen his walls beaten down, stained glass
smashed, carved pews pulled up, even decorative stone work broken;
while brass and iron were extracted from graves and windows, vestments and service books were thrown upon a bonfire in the public
square![1]
    This destruction in England extended from Henry VIII's dissolu-
tion of the monasteries in the 1530s to the Restoration of Charles II
in 1660. However, the questions raised thereby have a clear reference
far outside this temporal and geographical context. Christianity, for
instance, had long used representational art in its liturgy and in the
decoration of churches. Such images had served to teach men, lettered
or not, the fundamentals of their faith; but, almost more than anything else, they served as constant reminders of Christ's Redemption.
Images were the spiritual embellishment of the secular, the insistence
that men understand they were made in the image of God. Images
were the visual mandates that pursued men even to their graves.
    Subsequent ages' neglect of religious images in England is certainly
a result of the larger historical and theological development of Chris-

1. Joseph Hall, *Works* (Oxford: D. A. Talboys, 1837), I, liv.

1

tianity; but the absence of religious images is also due to the taint they assumed and their subsequent destruction during the Reformation. Religious art was not merely destroyed physically, but undermined ideologically. Yet even in a ruinous state the monuments provided a potent imagery in the service of another kind of art: Shakespeare's "bare ruin'd choirs where late the sweet birds sang" is a direct visual reference to the state of priories as a result of the Dissolution under Henry VIII, and the subsequent removal under Elizabeth of certain "popish" attributes and ornaments formerly revered in the churches of England. Almost three centuries later, the symbol of a ruined fabric and broken images still haunted T. S. Eliot:

> What are the roots that clutch, what branches grow
> Out of this stony rubbish? Son of man,
> You cannot say, or guess, for you know only
> A heap of broken images, where the sun beats,
> And the dead tree gives no shelter, the cricket no relief,
> And the dry stone no sound of water.[2]

If worship is the tangible form of individual and collective religious experience, it follows that sacred values will find expression in some concrete form.[3] And once this form is realized, controversy often results over its limits, its very definition. Consequently, iconoclasm has been as intense a religious phenomenon as iconolatry: the prohibition and destruction of images is as much a part of religion as the shaping and venerating of them.

History does not stand still. One age gives to another and misinterprets or misuses that which was previously proper and viable. Religious images had been regarded as dangerous by both early Christians and Jews primarily because of their identification with paganism. Implicit in this rejection of images was not only the distraction they could bring to the worshipper, but even more, the possible worship of them as idols. But as Christianity developed, most prohibitions against images were motivated by fear of anthropomorphism or "humanizing the holy."[4]

2. T. S. Eliot, "The Waste Land," *Collected Poems 1909–1962* (New York: Harcourt Brace, 1963).

3. Gerardus van der Leeuw, *Religion in Essence and Manifestation* (New York: Harper, 1963), p. 447.

4. Gerardus van der Leeuw, *Sacred and Profane Beauty* (New York: Holt, 1963), pp. 177, 179.

By the fourth century A.D., many of the early suspicions against the arts were temporarily laid to rest and some religious images were officially approved for churches. By the sixth century A.D., Christian images were being treated much like relics: both were understood as necessary adjuncts that helped to bridge the gap between sense and spirit. Since relics were believed to envelop sanctity, images were understood in much the same capacity. This was not far from the concept of talisman: a material object that is endowed with extraordinary powers, resulting from either its own nature or an external force.[5] The suspicion of idolatry and magic associated with images thus came to be confirmed. Consequently, such objects would be theologically attacked and physically destroyed in the eighth and ninth centuries.

But religious images have been destroyed for reasons other than their religious character. The image could be the object of loot or victim of sport, or both. Such acts of iconoclasm differ from religious acts in that the destruction of the image is frequently not the stated purpose or intention, but a by-product of the original impetus. He who chips noses from statues or robs the precious stones of the adorned saints probably does not intend the destruction of the whole work; yet the practical result is very frequently precisely that.

There are also conscious acts of destruction due to indifference to the fate of the object; the object is not despised, but simply destroyed because it is in the way. Many medieval interior church fittings were destroyed not out of religious indignation but out of practical considerations that such adjuncts were simply no longer needed in contemporaneous religious services.

Taste or fashion have sometimes dictated the removal and impairment of works of art either because of morality (prudishness) or because of aesthetics (reconstruction). When Charlemagne decorated his palace in Aix-la-Chapelle, he used sought-after classical marbles stripped from the temples of Rome and Ravenna. The remains of antiquity provided foundations for superstructure of the age that was to follow.

5. A fetish, on the other hand, is a talisman wherein dwells the spirit that gives it its force. An idol is a fetish representing the supposed form of the spirit or force living inside it.

Association also plays its part and images suggestive or representative of despised ideas or institutions have always been objects of the iconoclast's zeal. When the social, religious and political values in the art of the *ancien regime* were considered "untrue," the objects embodying them were destroyed by zealots of the French Revolution.[6]

Often there is a lack of evidence to indicate what attitudes impelled the iconoclast to act. The human motive itself is often complex; many factors can be combined in any one act of destruction. Unconscious forces always exist but in this historical inquiry they cannot be analyzed. In practice, categories break down, divergent purposes coalesce, the context is created and the act of destruction results. Reform, greed or caprice can impel men to the same end; even their actions belie their purpose.[7] Gibbon, in the last chapter of *The Decline and Fall of the Roman Empire*, illustrates the complexity of assigning responsibility and assessing motivation for acts of destruction.

After a diligent inquiry I can discern four principal causes of the ruin of [the city of] Rome, which continued to operate in a period of more than a thousand years. I. The injuries of time and nature. II. The hostile attacks of the barbarians and Christians. III. The use and abuse of materials. And, IV. The domestic quarrels of the Romans.[8]

Equally important is the complex task of qualifying the terms used in this essay. Iconoclasm in the conventional sense is the destruction of paintings, sculpture and other images. As the chapter on the use of such images in the Middle Ages will show, adjuncts to worship included the buildings which contained and displayed such elements and the ceremonies themselves which were performed inside. Indeed, the Roman Catholic Mass was more than a representation of the historical event of Christ's sacrifice. Adjuncts employed in this service were all basic to the theology of the sacrament and were intimately

6. Stanley Idzerda, "Iconoclasm during the French Revolution," *American Historical Review*, LX (1954), 13–14.

7. Louis Réau has written a history of iconoclasm whose definition is excessively inclusive. While his essay affords an insight into the wider spectrum of motivation, it is perhaps confusing on the important distinction of conscious and unconscious behavior. Louis Réau, *Les Monuments détruits de l'Art Francais* (Paris: Libraire Hachette, 1959), I, 16–19, 20–23.

8. Edward Gibbon, *The Decline and Fall of the Roman Empire* (New York: Modern Library, n.d.), II, 1441.

tied together in their use. Insofar as the Reformation's assault on medieval iconolatry was theological (and to a considerable though by no means exclusive extent it was theological), to pry apart these various elements of painting, building, relic and so forth would do violence to precisely that historical process which I propose to portray. Likewise it will not be my concern to question if all these objects ought to be considered works of art.

This application of "image" is made with the assumption that such representation had far-reaching implications for many levels of English society in the sixteenth and seventeenth centuries. As previously stated, the history of iconoclasm in England reflects the perennial and yet practical question of the proper role of images in religious worship. At the root of this question is the profound inclination of some men to see a sharp dichotomy between nature and spirit, to reject earthly life as means to knowing the divine. Therefore, if images by their very nature were held to reflect a "gross spirituality," or the needs of men to materialize the divine, it is logical that those Englishmen who sought to reform or purify Christianity cried out for their removal. But removal to what degree?

Historical Christianity was built, in part, on pre-existing Roman and Judaic cultures. The problem of images reflected the old question of the degree to which the trappings of paganism should be allowed the sanction of Christian toleration. A variety of old practices still existed in Tudor England; it was believed that the medieval church had left the door open to much that could be considered superstitious. Controversy had always burned over the question of the focus and limits of the sacred; images came to play an increasing role in this dissension.

On the other hand, concrete images whether in paint, glass or stone have mirrored the devotions of the past along with obsolete political ideas and institutions. Frequently such symbols continue to live long beyond the experiences which had brought them forth. It was natural, then, that the associations with hated institutions and ideas would bring down the fury of Englishmen on the material forms which symbolized these practices. For many Catholics, a rood screen might suggest a liturgical device that appropriately separated the altar from the congregation; to Protestants, it spelled out the sacrifice of the Mass and an identification with Rome. Again, the gold that adorned the shrines of the saints might prove tempting enough to the mind to threaten the veneration of their images; even war and social expediency might create the context for destruction. Images meant different things to different people; the acts which brought them down sprang from a variety of motives and circumstances.

If iconoclasm is a possible symptom of the great changes taking place in England, an inquiry into the forces behind the destruction itself is, in part, a story of English life and thought. And it is only through an attempt to fathom the role these religious representations played in medieval cultural life that we can understand their destruction in sixteenth and seventeenth century England. For if the material and spiritual values of society had changed by 1500, it was small cause for wonder that many Englishmen would be impatient to change outmoded forms of religion as well. Lollardy of the late fourteenth and fifteenth centuries had rejected images, relics and saints as excessive; some English humanists of the fifteenth and sixteenth centuries had ridiculed them as unnecessary. Both views helped to prepare the ground for the reformation of images that, in most instances, spelled iconoclasm.

My intent is to view iconoclasm in a larger context and responsive to varied forces and contradictory influences, and yet continuous and tempered by previous historical periods. Most work on English iconoclasm, however, has not responded to the complexity of the problem. Traditionally, iconoclasm has been identified, if not equated, with Puritanism. A Puritan is thought to be representative of a recurrent type of mind which is incapable of accepting anything from the life of the world as bridge to the divine.[9] Englishmen could be called Puritans, it is claimed, if their rejection of the sensuous seemed natural, not only when they objected to the presence of images in wor-

9. Matthew Arnold, *Culture and Anarchy* (Cambridge: University Press, 1960), pp. 129–144; 145–164. Edward Dowden, *Puritan and Anglican* (London: Kegan Paul, Trench, Truebner & Co., 1901), pp. 6, 9–11. Ernst Troeltsch, "Renaissance und Reformation," *Historische Zeitschrift*, CX (1913), 519–56. Joseph Crouch, *Puritanism and Art* (London and New York: Cassell, 1910), p. 37. E. N. S. Thompson, *The Controversy Between the Puritans and the Stage* (New York: Henry Holt & Co., 1903), pp. 9–26. G. Nuttall, *The Puritan Spirit* (London: Epworth Press, 1967), pp. 11–21.

ship, but also when they stressed the ethical element over physical beauty.[10]

An analysis that identifies iconoclasm with Puritanism would articulate the controversy over images as a theological argument, showing that the iconoclasts of the sixteenth and seventeenth centuries were quite aware of the arguments against images mounted by the early fathers and of the iconoclasts of the eighth and ninth centuries. Such a study might depict these reformers as unoriginal or conservative.[11]

It is not my purpose, however, to use the Puritan "type" to explain iconoclasm. While theological and scriptural attitudes tell us much about the correlation between external acts and internal values, iconoclasm itself is too complex a phenomenon to be identified simply with a type of religious thinking.

The historian who seeks to discover not only processes of thought, but also its practical consequences, cannot allow any idea or historical phenomenon to be divorced from the environment which gave it birth and configuration.[12] Under Henry VIII, Archbishop Thomas Cranmer, who sought to re-establish the English Church on a greater scriptural foundation, was able to argue theologically to certain con-

10. M. M. Knappen (ed.), *Two Elizabethan Puritan Diaries* (Chicago: American Society of Church History, 1933), pp. 1–16. John New, *Anglican and Puritan* (Stanford: University Press, 1964), pp. 34–6; 103–4.

On the various interpretations of Puritanism, see Basil Hall, "Puritanism: the Problem of Definition." *Studies in Church History* (London: Thomas Nelson and Sons), 1966, II, pp. 283–96. Leonard J. Trinterud, "The Origins of Puritanism," in Sidney Burrell (ed.), *The Role of Religion in Modern European History* (New York: Macmillan, 1964), pp. 56–65. C.H. and K. George, *The Protestant Mind of the English Reformation 1570–1640* (Princeton: Princeton University Press, 1961), pp. 397–411. The arguments of New and the Georges and reviewed by Patrick McGrath, *Papists and Puritans under Elizabeth I* (London, Blandford Press, 1967), pp. 31–46 and by F. Smith Fussner, *Tudor History and Historians* (New York: Basic Books, 1970), pp. 121–23. Professor George supports his arguments in "Puritanism in History and Historiography," *Past and Present* XXXXI (1968), pp. 77–104; and New, in "The Whitgift-Cartwright Controversy," *Archiv fuer Reformationsgeschichte* (1969), 203–211.

11. Arthur Lovejoy's "unit-idea" itself is understood in the biologist's sense of isolating "beliefs, prejudices, pieties, tastes, aspirations" and then studying the fortunes of these ideas as they in turn influence other ideas. *The Great Chain of Being* (New York: Harper Torchbooks, 1960), pp. 3, 19.

12. Johan Huizinga, "The Task of Cultural History," *Men and Ideas* (New York: Meridian, 1959), p. 38. Yet see Lovejoy's discussion on this point: "Reflections on the History of Ideas," *Journal of the History of Ideas*, I (1940), 23.

clusions; his attitude towards iconoclasm was tempered by the variety of forces operative at that time. However, with Henry's death, and with his young son, Edward, on the throne, Cranmer could think and act in ways that reflected a new and different configuration of forces. Not all these forces were religious. The ability to accept new ideas and reject old ones—an inner iconoclasm—can help provide the context for outer or external iconoclasm; but the phenomenon of destruction in England will be shown to be too complex and contradictory to be equated only with a way of thinking called Puritan.

Another approach to the study of iconoclasm might lie in investigating extant parish records such as church wardens' accounts, as well as a photographic survey of images remaining in churches, in order to show the extent and nature of destruction. Certainly such statistical and archaeological information would help temper what generalizations a historian might make about iconoclasm. Yet three obstacles immediately confront this "parish by parish" approach. Most inventories of church furnishings are not so descriptive or specific as they might be; much that was hidden, sold or destroyed was simply not reported at the time or later. Added confusion results from the tremendous amount of reconstruction and remodelling of the physical fabric in the nineteenth century; there is no defineable continuum between what exists in the churches of today and those of Reformation England. Last, it must be stressed that even if complete church records and relatively untouched churches were at our disposal, it might be possible to measure the extent of the removal of objects, but still not know the purposes of those who modified the appearance of the church and its furnishings.

This is not to deny the value of knowing when and in what counties of England the greatest amount of destruction took place. I have attempted such an investigation in Suffolk with incomplete information and unsatisfying results. Possibly other historians will seek this information in other counties and their findings may lead to a new appraisal of our resources and a tempering of our conclusions. This essay, however, seeks to trace more generally the interrelations between complex exigencies in English life and the destruction of images. I will allude often to the "fact" of destruction as it occurred; my concern, however, is not with the recitation of these facts, but with the complex interplay of social, political, economic and theological forces along with simple human greed and cantankerousness. In no period do all these various forces play equal roles in the destruction of images; in each segment of the sixteenth and seventeenth centuries, the weight of the forces varies and the interplay changes with repercussions leading to different consequences.

Consequently, the illustrations do not catalogue the dissolution of English art, but are used to exemplify the various forms iconoclasm took in the sixteenth and seventeenth centuries; I selected them to show a distinct, but wide variety of buildings, paintings, sculpture, glass and brasses which fell victim during the Reformation in England.

The greatest burden of a method which seeks to clarify the various patterns and interactions of men over the role of images is that it is ruled by the special complexity of its material. Thus, in evaluating the general configuration of forces operative, I cannot measure the exact degree of motivation prevailing at any one time. But in detecting common trends to men's thinking about images, I wish to point out that the actions which follow from such thoughts are inevitably tempered by changing historical contexts. It will thus be seen that iconoclasm itself results from many varied forces generated by these contexts. I conclude by showing the impact of iconoclasm even on the nature and subject matter of English art: an artless Church helping to create a churchless art.

The basis for the destruction of the English art under discussion begins in the Middle Ages; it is nurtured by Lollardy in the fourteenth and fifteenth centuries and by humanism in the fifteenth and sixteenth centuries. But the real beginnings of any discussion of iconoclasm must comprehend the very special role these tangible signs played in medieval life and thought.

I. THE MEDIEVAL FABRIC

For Thou dost abide where speech, sight, hearing, taste, touch,
reason, knowledge and comprehension merge in one.

NICHOLAS OF CUSA, *The Vision of God*

OVER THE CENTURIES, Christianity evolved stories and legends of
saints and martyrs. The graphic description of both their martyrdom and beatification lacked neither storyteller nor a pliant Church
eager to use painting and sculpture for the purpose of edification.
Rich shrines and magnificent images were built to honor the saints'
memory, but with the Church's vigorous furthering of their histories
—whether in picture or legend—multiplication escaped control. It
proved difficult to restrain men's minds; the very conditions of communication, control and verification encouraged abuse.[1] The sacred
uses of the arts were endless and legends soon became interwoven
with the fabric of daily life. For the miraculous was not understood
to be far removed from this earth and present time, but rather to be
dwelling continually in the present and future. The ever-increasing
number of saints and images of saints bridges all gaps of temporal
and spatial existence, revealing the divine in utmost immediacy.[2]

The medieval fabric was not simply a cloth of delicate workmanship; it was an attitude and a way of life that found embodiment in
images supported by Christian doctrine. Admittedly imprecise as a
term, the "fabric" of medieval Christianity is used in this essay to
provide the reader with some understanding of the forces sustaining
images in the English Church. It is the task of this chapter first to
chart the history of the doctrine of images from the early church

1. Helen C. White, *Tudor Books of Saints and Martyrs* (Madison: University
of Wisconsin Press, 1963), pp. 22–23.
2. Beverly Boyd, *The Middle English Miracles of the Virgin* (San Marino:
Huntington Library, 1964); Walter Hilton, *The Scale of Perfection* (London:
John M. Watkins, 1932), pp. 287–89; R. Morris (ed.), *Legends of the Holy Rood*
(London: Early English Text Society, 1871); Johannes Herolt, *Miracles of the
Blessed Virgin Mary* (London: George Routledge, 1928).

through Thomas Aquinas; and then to describe how medieval Englishmen used these images in daily life.

The Christian use of images sought to lift the visible and earthly to the dignity of reflecting the invisible or eternal. Because of Christ's Redemption, it was believed that man could be free from the present world and yet live within it. The power that could make him independent of nature likewise gave him power over nature. The thoughts of medieval men did not always dwell on their salvation, "but when they did, it was with deep intensity and above all, with the aid of vivid and very concrete images." [3]

The second commandment of Moses maintained "Thou shalt not make unto thee a graven image, nor the likeness of any form that is in heaven above, or that is in the earth beneath." With this passage went a variety of kindred quotations. "Thou shalt worship the Lord thy God, and him only shalt thou serve" (Deuteronomy 6:13). "Confounded be all, they that worship carved images" (Psalms 97:7). Such passages as these could be supplemented with others from the New Testament wherein the spiritual character of God was emphasized. "God is a spirit, and they that worship him must worship him in spirit and in truth" (John 4:24). "Blessed are they which have not seen and yet have believed" (John 20:29). The actual use of images in the early church, however, suggests that there were practical as well as philosophical reasons for their employment. Christians were part of a Mediterranean civilization borrowing from prevailing art forms. The practical impetus was, of course, the competition for men's souls, the need to acquire new followers and to secure their allegiance through images. [4]

Theologically, however, it was the Incarnation of Christ that had justified the use of images in Christian argument. God Himself through Christ had taken on human form and thus revealed the earthly world to be capable of bearing the Divine. [5] If Christians were

3. Marc Bloch, *Feudal Society* (Chicago: University Press, 1956), p. 86. Jean Seznec, *The Survival of the Pagan Gods* (New York: Harper, Bollingen Library, 1961), pp. 16–17, 84.

4. Elias J. Bickerman, "Symbolism in the Dura Synagogue," *Harvard Theological Review* LVIII (1956), 137, 145; Erwin R. Goodenough, "Catacomb Art," *Journal of Biblical Literature* LXXXI (1962), 133f.

5. G. B. Ladner, *Ad Imagem Dei* (Latrobe, Pa.: Archabbey Press, 1965), p. 1.

to depend on the Old Testament and yet remain consistent when they made images, the defense of religious representations would have to be based on the Scriptures sacred to Jew and Christian alike. It could be proved by Scripture that God commanded Moses to fashion two cherubim in gold (Exodus 25); and God showed Ezekiel a temple ornamented with palms, lions, men and cherubim (Ezekiel 41). "If you wish to condemn me," wrote Leontius, seventh century Bishop of Neapolis in Cyprus, "on account of images, then you must condemn God for ordering them to be made." Idolatry is not the issue for Christians make obeisance neither to wood nor stone but only to God.

> We do not say to the Cross nor to the icons of the saints 'You are my God.' For they are not our gods but open books to remind us of God and to His honour set in the churches and adored . . .

> If we worshipped the wood of the image, should we not burn the icon when the representation grew faint? When the two beams of the Cross are joined together I adore the figure because of the Christ who on the Cross was crucified, but if the beams are separated, I throw them away and burn them.[6]

The Jews made obeisance to the book of the Law, but no one would claim they did honor to the paper and ink. As Jacob kissed the bloody coat of Joseph and imagined he held him, so Christians holding the image of Christ could imagine they held Christ Himself. Thus, basic to the Christian defense of images is the general acceptance of things of this world as necessary bridges to the next.

There were also important traditions in the early church that existed to defend, define and interpret Christian truths in the light of contemporary pagan practice. Even in the realm of pagan mythology, these traditions had associated sibyls and prophets with the foreknowledge of Christ's coming. The result was to endow pagan gods with real virtues, to regard them as symbols of the physical world, to gain moral lessons from their lives and at times even to bestow on them supernatural characteristics.[7] Reconciling Christianity with pagan culture and natural history was for St. Augustine one step toward a fuller understanding of divine things. In his view, when the Jews

6. Norman H. Baynes, "The Icons before Iconoclasm," *Harvard Theological Review* XLIV (1951), 98, 99, 101.

7. Seznec, *Survival of Pagan Gods*, p. 44. Erwin Panofsky and Fritz Saxl, "Classical Mythology in Medieval Art," *Metropolitan Museum Studies*, IV (1933), 228–280.

left Egypt, they carried with them the gold and silver treasures of
their enemies; with such precedent, Christianity might do likewise.[8]

Though many of the early Fathers condemned the influences of
pagan culture, it could not be denied that many elements of Christianity were products of that Mediterranean culture which had nurtured the myths, parables and images of the pagan world. A conflict
had existed since the early church, for Christians could not rid themselves of methods and ways of thinking which, though dubbed pagan,
were merely human. This tension, reflecting the contradictions of a
historical religion that moves in the realm of spirit, periodically reap-
pears in the history of Christianity.

By the sixth century A.D., the Christian defense of images was tied
up with the educational and emotional effects of the image on the
beholder. It was one step from here to the claim that the end of the
image is chiefly to exist as a ladder, or channel of communication, for
the worshiper to approach God. But it was another step entirely
when in the sixth and seventh centuries, the beholder was left out
almost completely. Concern soon centered on bridging the gap between the materiality of creation and the realm of the spirit through
a true cosmic relationship of image and archetype.[9]

When the image had achieved a status perhaps incompatible with
the word of Scripture and had clearly wrought a breakdown of the
distinction between image and archetype, concerted opposition burst
forth in the Byzantine Empire of the eighth and ninth centuries. The
Iconoclastic Controversy (as it is called) attracted pious men on both
sides. In view of latent iconomachy in the nature of religion, the Jewish prohibitions against images, as well as the strong early opposition
to Christian art by many Fathers, it is surprising only that the controversy was so late in coming.

In 725 A.D. the Emperor Leo moved against images and initiated
a policy of destroying them in the Empire. It appears that his motives
were many and partly undefined. That such motives were influenced

---

8. Exodus 3:21–22; 12:35, 36. St. Augustine, *On Christian Doctrine*, II, Chapter
18, 25, 40. H. Marrou, *St. Augustine et le fin de la culture antique* (Paris: E. de
Broccard, 1938).

9. Ernst Kitzinger, "The Cult of Images in the Age before Iconoclasm," *Dumbarton Oaks Papers*, VIII (1954), pp. 137, 139. See his remarks on the parallelism
of images with relics and their mutual magic producing effects (pp. 118–119).

by religious fear of superstition and abuse is indisputable. Less sure was Leo's sympathy with Eastern heresies which rejected the idea of representation of the deity owing to the iniquity of matter. At the same time, political motivation played a part in the attempt to do away with the cult of images, in order to rebuild and raise the general tenor of society. "With these qualifications the motive of Leo is to be explained as a combination of Asiatic monotheism with a strong reformative social policy, working on conservative lines."[10]

After the Iconoclastic Controversy of the eighth and ninth centuries, the Mosaic prohibition of images was qualified by maintaining that the Old Testament had forbidden idolatry because God is not visible, but that the coming of Christ had revealed the physical nature of God. The theological objection that Christ, being God, is uncircumscribed and therefore not to be depicted, was refuted by Nicephorus. Christ was circumscribed because of his incarnation: therefore he could be portrayed. The theological basis of iconolatry became the incarnation and the ennoblement of nature.[11]

The final settlement of the Iconoclastic Controversy resulted in the Church's position on images being formulated by a general ecumenical council at Nicaea in 787. This council concluded that images were to be lawfully enjoyed in churches because they served to bring back the memories of their archetypes and awakened men to a contemplation of the Divine. While true worship belonged only to God; salutation, veneration and reverence might properly be directed to images. The Council declared that the honor paid an image is passed on to its archetype (or he who venerates an image venerates him who is portrayed). Sacred images continued to be considered as effective channels from the material world to the divine.[12]

This defense of images rested on a theory of knowledge which postulated that an understanding of universals is derived from par-

10. Edward J. Martin, *A History of the Iconoclastic Controversy* (London: S.P.C.K., n.d.), pp. 27–28. Gilbert Cope, *Symbolism in the Bible and the Church* (London: S.C.M. Press, 1959), p. 42.

11. Paul J. Alexander, *The Patriarch Nicephorus of Constantinople* (Oxford: Clarendon Press, 1958), pp. 22–53, 189–213; Gerhart Ladner, "The Concept of the Image in the Greek Fathers and the Byzantine Iconoclastic Controversy," *Dumbarton Oaks Papers*, VII (1953), 5–221.

12. Gervase Mathew, *Byzantine Aesthetics* (New York: Viking Press, 1963), p. 105. Martin, *Iconoclastic Controversy* pp. 94–109.

ticulars. Since images exist as a similitude of a corporeal thing (the material on which the intellect works), then it is through these impressions of corporeal things that man is led to higher truths. And because men, being weak, remember material more easily than spiritual things, one is advised to identify and to understand such spiritual things through signs and images. Scripture itself speaks of spiritual truths under the similitude of the corporeal "because it is natural to man to reach the intelligibilia through the sensibilia because all our knowledge has its beginning in sense." [13] Thomas Aquinas's defense of images was not the only one in the Middle Ages; however, since it repeated many of the traditional arguments from the Council of Nicaea and later was especially attacked by reformers in Reformation England, some attention should be given to its exposition.

For Thomas, man cannot reach God simply by the faculty of sense; yet through signs that can be perceived by the senses, the mind is awakened to the reality of God. [14] Hence any honor paid to an image is referred to the thing represented.

As to the Cross of Christ, the honor we pay to it is the same as that which we pay to Christ, just as the King's robe receives the same honor as the King himself . . . [15]

But since the image of a saint deserves less respect and requires a different kind of veneration from an image of Christ, Thomas distinguishes between the form of adoration in terms of the archetype represented by the object. Hence he calls *dulia* the adoration of saints through images that reflect the perfection of the gift of grace; *latria* is the adoration of God through his image. Because of the Incarnation, the Christian adores the flesh of Christ. To adore this flesh is "nothing else than to adore the incarnate Word of God"—thereby *latria*.

[W]e must say that no reverence is shown to Christ's image, as a thing—for instance, carved or painted wood: because reverence is not due save to a rational creature. It follows therefore, that reverence should be shown to it, in so far only as it is an image. Consequently the same reverence should be shown to Christ's image as to Christ Himself. Since, therefore, Christ is

13. Thomas Aquinas, *Summa Theologica* I, I q. I, art. 9.
14. *Ibid.*, Pars. II, q. 84.
15. *Ibid.*, Pars. II, ii, q. 103.

adored with adoration of latria, it follows that His image should be adored with the adoration of *latria*.[16]

If Thomas' distinction in terms of the forms of adoration are clear in theory, others might complain that such subtle differentiations cannot exist in practice. "(T)he same Person as Christ is adored with *latria* on account of His divinity, and with *dulia* on account of His perfect humanity." For the adoration of *latria* is not made to Christ's humanity for itself, but only for the Godhead to which it is united "by reason of which Christ is not less than the Father." [17]

Thomas took great pains to differentiate first between idolatry and iconolatry, then between the kinds of devotion appropriate to images (*dulia* and *latria*). Others who reflected on the problem of images during the Middle Ages as well as in the sixteenth and seventeenth centuries in England, were mostly concerned with the basic distinctions between idolatry and iconolatry; Thomas' further distinctions went mostly unheeded.

Most of the arguments defending images that were expressed during the Middle Ages, sought to clarify the various uses in which images could be employed in the Christian community. Above all, it was the educative factor that justified their employ over any taint or suspicion of idolatry. Men do not, it was argued late in the fourteenth century,

... sin in their adoration, although their mind is actually fixed on the images themselves and not on God, as simple folk are wont to do when they see a fair image artificially painted and lavishly adorned ... By a certain carnal reverence their mind is stirred to adore with bodily humiliation that image rather than any other. Yet their intention is habitually directed towards God, in whose name they do worship to such an image.[18]

16. *Ibid.*, Pars. III, q. 25. However, see *ibid.*, Pars. II, ii, q. 84.
17. *Ibid.*, Pars. III, q. 25. On St. Bonaventura and the scholastic views on images, see H. Gutman, "The Rebirth of the Fine Arts and Franciscan Thought," *Franciscan Studies* V n.s. (1945), 215–234. Though John Hus was not in agreement with Aquinas, his liturgical formulations were somewhat similar, with perhaps added caution: "It is permissable to venerate the image of the crucified Christ through a kiss, a genuflection, or bowing of the head, for through that kiss or genuflection or bowing we perform a *latria*. They become *idolatria* if we venerate the image for its own form." Quoted in Enrico C. S. Molnar, "The Liturgical Reforms of John Hus," *Speculum* XXXXI (1966), 298.
18. Hilton, *Scale of Perfection*, quoted in G. R. Owst, *Literature and Pulpit in Medieval England* (Oxford: Basil Blackwell, 1961), p. 138. Johannes Kollwitz, "Bild

Images can be the occasion of good or evil. They are good if they arouse souls to good actions; they lead men astray when idolatrously worshipped as God.

> I worship not the image of Christ, for that it is true, nor for the reason that it is the image of Christ; but I worship Christ before the image of Christ, for it is the image of Christ that leads . . . me to worship of Christ.[19]

Men require sensuous forms to sustain the foundation of their religions education; "imagining, for example, that God in his own nature has the body of a man like their own, thinking that the three persons in the Trinity are separate beings like three men. . ."[20] The argument stresses that for learned Christians, images are used "as commemorative tokens of the departed;" for the unlettered, images are concrete references to aid in devotion since men are more stirred by sight than by hearing or reading.[21]

> Take heed by his image how his head was crowned with a garland of thorns, till they wept into the brain and the blood burst out on every side, . . . So that thou kneel if thou wilt before the image, but not to the image. . . Make thy prayer before the image but not to the image. For it seeth thee not, heareth thee not, understandeth thee not . . . for if thou do it for the image or to the image thou dost idolatry.[22]

Clearly, men were urged not to worship images, but only to read them for the piety they would inspire.

The objection to images during the Middle Ages in England can perhaps be discussed in an ascending order of religious importance. Very frequently, the complaint is expressed that Christians spend too much time decorating and gilding such representations. This is not any objection to the fact of images, but to the indiscreet and unseemly attention they receive as adjuncts to Christian worship. "The

---

und Bildertheologie in Mittelalter," *Das Gottesbild im Abendland* (Witten and Berlin: Eckart-Verlag, 1959), pp. 109–10, 121.

19. Owst, *Literature and Pulpit*, pp. 141–42. An anonymous treatise on the Decalogue, here quoting the late sixth-century pope, Gregory the Great.

20. Hilton, *Scale of Perfection*, quoted in Owst, *ibid.*, p. 139. See also Joy M. Russell-Smith, "Walter Hilton and a Tract in Defence of the Veneration of Images," *Dominican Studies*, VII (1959), 180–214.

21. *Dives and Pauper* (London, 1534), chapter I. The original was written late in the 15th century. The author is not Henry Parker. See H. G. Pfander, "Dives Et Pauper," *The Library* XIV, 4th series (1934), p. 300.

22. *Dives and Pauper*, chapter II.

feet [of the image] so shod in silver show that the love and affection of priests is much set in gold and silver and earthly covetise."[23] If the Church is resplendent, the argument continues, then the poor are unclothed. Hence, the frequent objection that attention should be given to images, but in good taste and with discretion; it would be better to give one's offerings to the poor.

Christian injunctions against luxury in the liturgy and fittings of the physical fabric never proved dominant in the traditions of the Church. The Church distinguished between that poverty which was holy and voluntary and that which was squalid and involuntary. But the aspirations of medieval society did not aim at an effectual alleviation of the evils that beset the bodies of so many men. "(T)he motives of charity are likely to influence the methods of charity."[24] Consequently, men were urged to give alms with assurance that such actions would be pleasing to God who would reciprocate for them with heavenly merit. Certainly to the donor, offerings to the physical fabric of the church by way of shrines, images and ornaments rendered this assurance all the more visible.

On the other hand, there was the sentiment that images were simply unnecessary; idolatry was again not raised, but images existing as a distraction to the worshipper became the issue. It was claimed that all kinds of superstitions result in the excessive use of familiar objects of this life to illustrate the world of the next. The involved lives of saints combined with popular imagination gave rise to picturesque legends that confuse and complicate traditional symbols.[25] If the faith of simple people required tangible evidence, then it was feared their imaginations might quickly fall upon any object that could transmit God's blessings. Multiplication of these objects pressed ahead of control and those relics and images that were only to have been used as "reminders" became familiar and necessary objects of worship.

23. *Ibid.*, chapter X.
24. Brian Tierney, *Medieval Poor Law* (Berkeley: University of California Press, 1959), pp. 45–46. W. K. Jordan, *Philanthropy in England 1480–1660* (London: George Allen and Unwin, 1959), p. 146.
25. M. D. Anderson, *The Imagery of British Churches* (London: John Murray, 1955), pp. 11–12. D. J. Hall, *English Medieval Pilgrimage* (London: Routledge and Kegan Paul, 1965–6), p. 9.

One practical result was that there was no clear separation between this world and the next. If the parish church's physical fabric was holy in the eyes of the parishioners, it was also commodious and useful for secular purposes as well; wide naves were excellent for dancing and wild sport. Churchyards were filled with banquets that frequently got out of hand; fairs and markets were often held within the church proper, the merchants' booths lining the length of the nave.[26] While the use of the church for eating, playing, sleeping, and acting did not necessarily spell any conscious irreverence on the part of the users, it was feared that over-familiarity with the sacred, and clouded by the profane, can easily destroy faith and invite ridicule.[27]

> The blessed arm of sweet Saint Sunday:
> And whosoever is blessed with this right hand,
> Cannot speed amiss by sea nor by land.
> And if he offereth eke with good devotion,
> He shall not fail to come to high promotion.
> And another holy relic here may ye see:
> The great toe of the Holy Trinity;
> and whosoever once doth it in his mouth take,
> He shall never be diseased with the toothache;
> Cancer nor pox shall there none breed;
> This that I show ye is matter indeed.[28]

Then there was the objection that images appeal to the senses and arouse the lower, baser qualities in men rather than appealing to his soul. Images are spiritually dangerous in that they *can* lead to idolatry. Bernard of Clairvaux sees the basic purpose of imagery, for instance, as a source of inspiration for those who are carnally bound or simple in faith. However, to retire from the world and then to gild the liturgy of the Church and to ornament God's house with the wealth of the world seemed to him and to others, both a terrible temptation and a betrayal of monasticism. The spirituality of monks should be higher.

26. John Moorman, *Church Life in England in the Thirteenth Century* (Cambridge: University Press, 1946), pp. 145–48. J. G. Davies, *The Secular Uses of Church Buildings* (London: S.C.M., 1968), pp. 36–95.

27. J. Huizinga, *The Waning of the Middle Ages* (Harmondsworth: Penguin Books, 1955), pp. 154–57.

28. John Heywood, *The Pardoner and the Friar* (London: English Drama Society, 1906), p. 7. The play was first printed in 1533.

We [monks] who have forsaken all precious and beautiful things for Christ's sake, who have counted but dung all things fair to see, soft to the ear, sweet to the smell, pleasant to the touch, whose devotion do we intend to excite by such means?[29]

Bernard's fear over the effect of images on monks was great enough to warrant a general policy of simplicity and asceticism for the Cistercian Order. A General Chapter consisting of all the abbots of Cistercian monasteries met yearly to ensure the observance of the Rule which was to preserve the purity and simplicity of discipline. Stained glass, carvings, paintings, mosaics and elaborate inlaid work were all promptly banned from Cistercian churches. Necessary accessories to the liturgy were not to be of precious materials, but of plain wood or metal. The Cistercians vowed "to remove from their lowly chapels everything which might flatter curious eyes and charm weak souls."[30] The direct result was the appearance of an architecture that matched the simplicity of their vows with the simplicity of design.[31]

Ultimately, the deepest fear of all was that of idolatry; it was reasoned that images should be prohibited and destroyed because of the strict admonitions of Scripture and the practical misunderstanding of people who worship an artifact in place of God. Common in the sixteenth and seventeenth centuries, this argument was not much

29. A letter to the Abbot William of St. Thierry, 1124. Quoted in G. H. Cook, *English Monasteries in the Middle Ages* (London: Phoenix House, 1961), p. 145. See also G. G. Coulton, *Art and Reformation* (Cambridge University Press, 1953), chapter XVIII. G. G. Coulton, *Ten Medieval Studies* (Cambridge University Press, 1930), pp. 63–69; G. G. Coulton, *Five Centuries of Religion* (Cambridge University Press, 1923), V, 300, 321–34. Rose Graham, "An Essay on English Monasteries" in *Social Life in Early England* (ed. by Geoffrey Barraclough) (London: Routledge and Kegan Paul, 1960), p. 79.

It must be remembered that Bernard recognized the Church's role in education —thereby accepting the use of illustrations for the illiterate. See his "Apologie de la vie et moeurs des religieux," (written about 1124) in *Traitez doctrinaux de S. Bernard* (Paris, 1675, translated from Latin to French by A. de S. Gabriel), pp. 70f.

30. Cook, *Monasteries*, p. 153.

31. Yet before a century passed, the Rule came to be less rigorously observed and the elaborate and ornate Cistercian churches of Byland, Rievaulx and Tintern were built. See *Ibid.*, p. 172.

For further history of this struggle to prohibit superfluous decoration, see John Bilson, "The Architecture of the Cistercians," *Archeological Journal* LXVI (1909), 190f.

On the Franciscans, see G. G. Coulton, "The High Ancestry of Puritanism," *Ten Medieval Studies* (Boston: Beacon Press, 1959), pp. 65–66. A. H. Martin, *Franciscan Architecture in England* (Manchester: University Press, 1937), p. 11.

current in the Middle Ages. The medieval theory of knowledge—
sensibilia leading to spirituality—seemed to have prevailed over the
identification of idol with image.

The arguments against images because of luxury, superstition, the
claims of the "senses," and sometimes of idolatry, continued throughout the Middle Ages; likewise, the abuses remained which had inspired these attacks. The medieval church had always maintained
that the weakness of human nature does not invalidate that ideal
which by images man sought to express. Men could be tolerant of
human abuse; they could continually see such error in light of God's
perfection and patience. Yet before 1500, countless sermons and treatises had revealed concern with the use and misuse of images. Much
of this early criticism was made by defenders of the Church inspired
by the desire to reform rather than destroy. However, in time, there
would be those who would not be so tolerant and would hope to rid
the Church completely of images.

The history of the Middle Ages is long and complex and does not
suggest easy generalizations. However, it has been necessary to char-
acterize those factors that have immediate bearing on the problem of
future iconoclasm. This chapter has thus far raised the larger question of the devotional system and the philosophical presuppositions
that sustained religious images. The objects that will be destroyed or
mutilated in the sixteenth and seventeenth centuries must now be
described: the physical fabric of cathedrals, parish churches and monasteries and their furnishings.

The Roman Catholic Church in England around the year 1500
served the two and a half or three million Catholics with a wealthy
and imposing physical fabric of which the nineteen cathedral
churches were of particular stature and dignity.[32]

These great structures varied in plan and execution, ornament and
style. Underlying all of them, however, was an architectural organization which contained a series of parts having separate functions:

32. G. H. Cook, *The English Cathedral Through the Centuries* (London:
Phoenix House, 1957), p. 13; Philip Hughes, *The Reformation in England* (New
York: Macmillan, 1963), I. p. 33. The nineteen cathedrals were situated in seven-
teen sees. All exist today save Coventry Cathedral torn down by Henry VIII, and
St. Paul's London, which was destroyed by the Great Fire in 1666. St. Michael's,
Coventry was raised to cathedral status in 1918 and destroyed in an air raid in 1940.

the nave, aisles and transepts; the chantry chapels with their parclose screens; the chancel with altar set off from the nave by a screen, tympanum and rood-loft.[33] All of these compartments were really self-contained rooms that were extended one after another in a linear fashion to a final culmination in the high altar at the east end. A painted and ornate screen separated the chancel from the nave and deprived the lay congregation of the full sight of the altar. Atop this partition (fig. 2 affords a typical example) was the great rood or crucifix which was flanked by life-size figures of the Virgin and St. John. Frequently the chancel arch was boarded up to form a tympanum which had a Last Judgment painted on the side facing the congregation. Such a scene ensured the laity of the terrible reality of God tempered by the justice of Christ. The crucifixion thus appeared set off against this painting.[34]

Every Sunday and on the thirty-five or forty important feast days of the Church year, Christians witnessed Mass, the holy drama re-creating the bloody sacrifice on Calvary. A dramatic ceremonial, it was enriched through the graphic embroidering of ornament, symbolic movement and the repetition of details which eventually led to the consecration itself.[35]

The Mass, like images, sought to enrich the wealth and depth of man's existence by appealing to a wide range of human experience. The emotions called forth focused on both the human qualities of Christ, Mary and the saints—as well as on their relation to God. The emotional response to holy things thus brought the individual Christian to a greater comprehension of their significance. To this end, sermons, paintings, carvings, poetry and drama were all utilized by the Church.[36]

Thus many Christians took part in the ritual of medieval life that

33. G. W. O. Addleshaw and Frederick Etchells, *The Architectural Setting of Anglican Worship* (London: Phoenix House, 1954), p. 15.

34. Frederick Bligh Bond and Dom Bede Camm, *Roodscreens and Roodlofts* (New York: Charles Scribner's Sons, 1909), I, pp. 93–97.

35. "Bowing the head at end of the Memento of the dead, and striking the breast while saying *Nobis quoque* in a loud voice—these actions appear to have been introduced as a vivid presentation of our Lord's death and the impression it made on the bystanders." Joseph A. Jungmann, *The Mass of the Roman Rite* (New York: Benziger Brothers, 1951), I, p. 108.

36. V. A. Kolve, *The Play Called Corpus Christi* (Stanford: University Press, 1966), p. 4.

saw no dichotomy between this world and the signs of the next: they crept to the cross in a darkened church on Good Friday, witnessed the joyous processions of lighted candles on Easter morning, and with the pealing of bells, chanted the Resurrection anthem. On the feast of Corpus Christi, the entire parish knelt in street and field while the Host was carried in a procession amidst them.

Outside the diocesan structure, there were above 650 abbeys and priories and about 200 mendicant establishments.[37] In these places, the ideal of complete dedication of oneself to God was attempted. Some establishments were wealthy as was the monastery at Bury St. Edmunds in Suffolk with a general net income of £1659, a community of forty-four and a large and rich fabric; others were small, lowly and poor. Inevitably these buildings were the focal point of social, economic and religious life.

In general, for these men, the naturally good (objects of life) led to the supernaturally good. The remembrance of saints and the appeal for their intercession with God in the trials of this life, as well as the employ of their lives as models for imitation, was an integral part of this age.[38]

Everywhere were the signs and relics of those mortals who were believed to have overcome the temptations of this world, and, in following their Lord, had found Heaven. These men were to be venerated for they would intercede with God for those still living on earth. Giles protected the crippled; St. Katherine, little girls; St. Cecilia, musicians; while St. Blaise looked after those who suffered from sore throats. St. Bartholomew had suffered martyrdom from being flayed alive: he became the patron of tanners. St. John, having been boiled in oil, protected the candlemakers. And for women who had lost their keys, St. Osyth was looked to. Nearly every monastery owned a girdle of the Virgin or of the Magdalene to be worn by expectant mothers. Other relics protected the believer from various diseases: the bell of St. Guthlac at Repton Priory cured ailments of the head, St. Petronilla's skull at Bury St. Edmunds cured fevers while the

---

37. Cook, *Monasteries*, pp. 15, 262. "Of the 650 houses suppressed . . . about one third have disappeared without leaving a vestige of their existence, and of less than a third are there substantial remains."

38. A. G. Dickens, *The English Reformation* (London: B. T. Batsford, 1964), pp. 1–14.

image of St. Bride at Arden helped to recover lost cows or healed ill ones.[39]

Pilgrimages to the shrines of these saints resulted from a variety of motives. If God works through history and through signs, it was deemed appropriate for men to travel to those places sanctified by miracles. However curiosity was not absent from faith and the desire to benefit physically and materially as well as spiritually impelled many to make pilgrimages.[40]

At Bury St. Edmunds were the knife and boots of St. Thomas Becket and some of the coals which burnt St. Lawrence. Our Lady of Walsingham was most noted for its relic of the Virgin's milk and less noteworthy for one of St. Peter's fingers.[41] The holy thorn tree blossomed at Glastonbury and at Chertsey, fifteen miles from London, "God wrought . . . miracles . . . for those of devout hearts."[42] At Becket's tomb, cures were wrought by handkerchiefs dipped into the blood of the Martyr.

The daughter of Ralph of Bourne was cured by being wrapped in the saint's pall, a knight cured his child of a fit of terror by hanging around the boy's neck a shred of the Martyr's clothing. . . . In one instance, a knight who had brought a pretended relic of Thomas, was rewarded by the saint as though it were genuine.[43]

In terms of popular devotion, the shrines containing relics of the saints soon rivaled the high altar itself.[44] By 1500, the shrine was often a free-standing marble or stone structure (as in the shrine of St. Edmund, illustrated in a manuscript, Figure 3) whose base was adorned with images in precious metals. Pilgrims seeking favors would touch

39. Geoffrey Baskerville, *English Monks and the Suppression of the Monasteries* (London: Jonathan Cape, 1937), p. 23. Keith Thomas, *Religion and the Decline of Magic* (New York: Scribners, 1971), pp. 25–50.

40. Hall, *English Medieval Pilgrimage*, p. 2.

41. D. H. S. Cranage, *The Home of the Monk* (Cambridge: University Press, 1926), p. 70. Francis Wormald, "The Rood of Bromholm," *Journal of Warburg and Courtauld Institutes* I (1937), 31–45.

42. Percival Hunt, *Fifteenth Century England* (Pittsburgh: University Press, 1962), p. 6. Ronald Knox and Shane Leslie, *The Miracles of King Henry VI* (Cambridge University Press, 1923).

43. Paul A. Brown, *The Development of the Legend of Thomas Becket* (Philadelphia: University of Pennsylvania Doctoral Dissertation, 1930), p. 184.

44. Francis Bond, *The Chancel of English Churches* (London: Oxford University Press, 1916), pp. 29–36 on the defense and origin of relics.

or place their bodies within these niches believing that a miraculous power permeated the whole structure. On top of the base was the container of the relics of the saint, overlaid with decorative plates of gold and silver and the jewels given by generations of pilgrims. Above this was a canopy often suspended from the roof by chains.[45] Otherwise, relics were kept in small, portable caskets and could be carried in processions and pageants. All churches had some relics, the richer having more important ones. In St. Stephen's Walbrook, London, there were twenty-two relics—among them a relic of the place where God appeared to Mary Magdalen, one of the rock where God spoke to Moses, a finger of one of the Holy Innocents and a piece of the bone of one of the eleven thousand virgins.[46]

St. Cuthbert's shrine was one of the most admired:

[H]is sacred shrine was exalted with most curious workmanship of fine and costly green marble all limned and guilted with gold hauinge foure seates or places conuenient under the shrine for the pilgrims or lame men sittinge on theire knees to leane and rest on, in time of theire deuout offerings . . . it was estimated to bee one of the most sumptuous monuments in all England, so great were the offerings and Jewells that were bestowed uppon it. . .[47]

The shrine itself was protected by the high altar which was situated directly in front of it and by a large canopy that hung within the chancel.[48] During divine service, the elaborately painted cover of the shrine was raised to the tinkling of six silver bells which "did stirr all the peoples harts."

Becket's shrine at Canterbury was the most famous, the richest and most visited. The bottom part of the shrine was all of stone and supported on arches; it was here that pilgrims sat to make their petitions. A wooden canopy painted with sacred pictures concealed the

45. See Cook, *Cathedral* p. 127, wherein there is a description of the shrine of St. Hugh in London Cathedral. On the appearance, history and fate of various shrines in England see J. Charles Wall, *Shrines of British Saints* (London: Methuen and Company, 1905).
46. Charles Pendrill, *Old Parish Life in London* (London: Oxford University Press, 1937), p. 21. From an inventory of 1558.
47. J. T. Fowler (ed.), *Rites of Durham* (London: Surtees Society, 1903), pp. 3–5. (Written in 1593.) C. F. Battiscombe, *The Relics of Saint Cuthbert* (Oxford: University Press, 1956), pp. 203–307.
48. *Rites of Durham*, p. 8.

wealth of the shrine proper. When raised, it revealed sides plated with gold, damasked with gold wire, embossed with jewels.[49]

Parish churches, like the cathedral and monastic shrines, also shared in the forms of piety that gave the wealth of this world in expectation of the next. In 1500, these parishes numbered about 9,000, some of them possessing large and magnificent churches such as St. Mary Redcliffe, Bristol, while others were desperately poor and small such as the tiny Saxon village chapel of Escomb, Durham.[50] Naturally, the scale and lavishness of the parish churches depended on a variety of factors, piety included.[51] But if most counties did not share equally in wealth, their churches nevertheless partook of the general prosperity of the realm and remained the age-old repositories of the generosity of parishioners. Justly, these churches were the homes of communal life and received, retained and displayed the bequests of continuing generations.

As in the cathedrals, the chancel of parish churches was separated from the nave by the rood screen. The rood was usually fastened to the top of the screen (hence its name): sometimes it was suspended from the roof by chains. The tympanum filled the whole of the chancel arch and, as in the cathedral, held a painting of the Last Judgment.[52]

The rood screen itself varied in decoration, but in most cases was richly gilded with spiral bands of gold and black or white: frequently the web of the vaulting was colored a deep blue and set off by golden stars.[53] Behind the altar and below the east window was usually a cluster of niches or decorative panels. In more elaborate churches,

---

49. Arthur P. Stanley, *Historical Memorials of Canterbury* (London: J. M. Dent, 1906), pp. 227–28. The most valuable jewel of the shrine was probably the gift of a King of France that was described in 1446 as "a carbuncle that shines at night, half the size of a hen's egg." Wall, *Shrines*, p. 161.

50. G. H. Cook, *The English Mediaeval Parish Church* (London: Phoenix House, 1954), p. 16. *The Valor Ecclesiasticus*, a survey of the church's revenue, was made in 1534. The total number of parishes in England and Wales numbered 8,838. See Hughes, *The Reformation*, I, 32, 34 and map on 35.

51. Yet, it would appear that most were well fitted: ". . . there is not a parish church in the Kingdom so mean as not to possess crucifixes, candlesticks, censers, patens and cups of silver . . ." *A Relation . . . of the Island of England* (1500), trans. A. A. Sneyd (London: Camden Society, 1847), p. 29.

52. Cook, *Parish Church*, p. 151.

53. *Ibid.*, p. 158. E. Long, "Screen Paintings in Devon and East Anglia," *Burlington Magazine* LIX (1931), 169–176.

the retable or raised shelf above the altar was a painting that could be closed with shutters. Often on the sides were small gilded panels about a foot square, variously grouped and depicting sacred subjects.[54]

The whole interior of the parish church was a resplendence of colored glass, gilded and decorative fonts and tombs, embossed roofs and reredos. Most wall paintings had narrative rather than decorative subjects, scenes from the life of Christ and of the saints predominating.[55] God was often represented as a bearded old man with a tiny Christ on his lap and a dove representing the Holy Ghost on his breast.

Other types of paintings frequently showed Christ covered with wounds and surrounded by various tools of different trades. Such works have been interpreted either as Christ sanctifying labor or, perhaps more correctly, Christ suffering because of the sins of men in the course of their work. Everything, no matter how simple, could be a manifestation of divine presence.[56]

Crosses were everywhere—in the streets, in the court and churchyards and especially in the churches. Such a great proliferation attested not only to devotion, but confirmed the most essential sign of the Christian Church. In most churches, they stood upon altars and tombs, while others had monstrances in the form of silver crosses. These held the Host when it was displayed for veneration.[57]

The most prominent object in every church was the great crucifix or rood, placed either above the chancel arch or, if the church was tiny, over the high altar. Church lights, once by custom restricted to five (in honor of Christ's five wounds) proliferated in the face of their own popularity, as evidenced by a widespread public demand for candles.[58]

Church walls were almost hidden by the profusion of images, tab-

54. Bond, *Chancel*, pp. 51–100.
55. Cook, *Parish Church*, p. 195.
56. W. A. Pantin, *The English Church in the Fourteenth Century* (Notre Dame: University Press, 1962), p. 240. Tancred Borenius and E. W. Tristram, *English Medieval Painting* (Paris: Pegasus Press, 1927), pp. 29–37. C. Woodforde, "A medieval campaign against blasphemy," *Downside Review*, LV (1937), 357.
57. For the extent and variety of medieval plate in churches, see C. Oman, *English Church Plate 1597–1830* (London: Oxford University Press, 1957), pp. 15–30.
58. Pendrill, *Parish Life*, p. 8.

ernacles, tombs, and side altars dedicated to various saints. The number of images was multitudinous. A wealthy though not typical London church like St. Margaret Pattens dressed its statues in expensive adornments. It owned "a coat for St. Margaret of white damask edged with black velvet and lined with green buckram, fastened with a silver gilt and enameled brooch, with a kerchief of silk of Cyprus to cover the head, and two coats for the Virgin Mary, one of white damask ornamented with roses, the other of cloth of gold."[59]

Further beautification of images consisted of curtains, flowers, coloring and gilding. Mounds of trinkets and valuables were continually being left by those fortunate in their petitions. In 1368 one Thomas Morice left a "black girdle with silver buckles to the crucifix at the north door of St. Paull's, a blue girdle to the shrine of St. Erkenwald, and to the Virgin within the Cathedral [of St. Paul's] a yellow girdle with silver buckles and five gold rings."[60]

On feast days the churches were filled with the scent of fresh boughs and floral decorations. "In all the churchwardens' accounts are found payments for holly and ivy at Christmas, palm and box on Palm Sunday, roses on Ascension Day, flags and woodruff on Corpus Christi Day, and boughs of birch at midsummer."[61] Furthermore, the floor was strewn with green rushes or straw for comfort in kneeling. In season, rose petals, lavender and rosemary would be substituted.

All these external signs, ranging from the paintings and sculpture which today we call "works of art," to liturgical practices with adjuncts of altars, vestments, incense and music were understood as ordinary earthly images possessing the capacity to invoke supernatural understanding. Even the Mass itself was an earthly image whose re-enactment through certain words and movements marked the actual consecration of Christ at the Last Supper; the sacrifice of the Mass could also be understood as a lively memorial charged with its own artistic meaning as drama—the sacrifice offered on Calvary; and last, the Mass, like other images, summoned to a banquet table all who believed.

If many Englishmen depended on such external signs as hope for future salvation, still others would come to identify these very altars,

59. *Ibid.*, p. 16. 60. *Ibid.*, p. 17.
61. *Ibid.*, p. 11.

Masses, and vestments along with paintings and sculpture as idolatrous images. Indeed we have seen that an inner iconoclasm, or the theological rejection of images, was a part of medieval thinking. Outward iconoclasm, or the actual physical acts of destruction, would not emerge until the movements of Lollardy and Humanism tilled the soil and provided room for its appearance. The chapter that follows seeks to trace this cultivation.

II. LOLLARDY AND HUMANISM

> At the very least [men] can be persuaded that the bodily posi-
> tion makes no difference to their prayers; for they constantly
> forget, what you must always remember, that they are animals
> and that whatever their bodies do affects their souls.
>
> Screwtape, a devil, to Wormwood, his helper
> C. S. LEWIS, *The Screwtape Letters*

THE TWO MOVEMENTS of Lollardy in the fourteenth and fifteenth
centuries and of Humanism in the fifteenth and sixteenth centuries were different in origin, in development and in personality.
Lollards could be associated locally with various doctrinal heresies,
but when described as a sect opposed to the common faith, they were
identified with the followers of John Wyclif.[1] Humanists also could
be identified with various philosophical and cultural attitudes, but
in England in the fifteenth and sixteenth centuries, they were commonly identified with supporters of certain ethical practices based
on classical ideals.[2] Lollards were inclined to be more radical and
violent toward the issue of images; whereas Humanists were likely to
oppose the abuse of images with cynicism rather than violence. The
net effect of the two movements was to establish intellectual prece-
dents and practical acts that foreshadowed the iconoclasm of the sixteenth and seventeenth centuries. This chapter aims to describe the
peculiar course each movement followed in its relation to images.

Lollardy's assault on the medieval church focused on those elements which were most involved with its institutional aspect: excommunication, forms of penance, the adoration of saints, pilgrimages,
the cult of relics; perhaps most significantly, Lollards denied respect
to spiritual authorities whose scriptural warrant was suspect by Lollard standards. It was essential to Lollard spirituality to reject the
symbol which claimed to represent reality in favor of what they

---

1. J. F. Davis, "Lollards, Reformers and St. Thomas of Canterbury," *University
of Birmingham Historical Journal*, IX (1963–64), 1–2.
2. Roberto Weiss, *Humanism in England During the Fifteenth Century* (Oxford: Blackwell, 1941), p. 183.

claimed was reality alone.[3] In this instance, the movement can be understood as having a strong relation to future Lutheranism and, though unsuccessful, prefiguring the English Reformation.

John Wyclif, an Oxford don and one-time chaplain to Edward III, emphasized the purely spiritual functions of the clergy and advocated the role of conscience or individual judgment over the Church at large. He was impatient with the "sensible" signs that were for him a relapse into Judaism—a materiality without the substance of Christianity.[4] Spurning any ceremony which by its trappings distracted the worshipper from the truth which the ceremony had as its purpose, he saw the beauty of stained-glass windows, for instance, as a misdirection of men's admiration into self-love.[5] Like Bernard of Clairvaux, Wyclif even suspected the imagination for it works mischievously on faith—using images to produce all kinds of errors. He argued that those who seek the Trinity in the representation of an old man, a son on a cross and a dove as the Holy Spirit are simply deluded from perceiving any real spiritual significance.

Wyclif assailed the doctrine of transubstantiation and by implication the underlying reason for the parish church which held and displayed the sacrament of the Last Supper. He lay little importance on the church fabric and in time, even came to deny the need for any church edifice at all: ". . . since God is Lord of heaven and of earth, he lives not in temples made with hands, nor is he worshipped with men's hands. . . ." Churches should be free and in the open, internalized and in men's souls and not "in cold stones that must perish." [6]

Wyclif's early writings are restrained and recognize merits in

3. A. G. Dickens, *Lollards and Protestants in the Diocese of York, 1509–1558* (London: Oxford University Press, 1959), p. 9; James E. Oxley, *The Reformation in Essex* (Manchester: University Press, 1965), pp. 4–16; Ernest F. Jacob, *The Fifteenth Century 1399–1485* (Oxford: Clarendon Press, 1961), p. 282.

4. John Wyclif, *Tractatus De Ecclesia,* ed. J. Loserth (London: Wyclif Society, 1886), pp. 44f, 459. Wyclif identified Thomas Becket with his denunciation of relics, pilgrimages and images—not only because the saint had died for defending the Church's temporal powers, but had also been identified with the miracles and legends at Canterbury. Davis, "Lollards, Reformers and St. Thomas of Canterbury," 1–15.

5. John Stacey, *John Wyclif and Reform* (Philadelphia: Westminster Press, 1964), pp. 22–23, 48–49.

6. Herbert E. Winn (ed.), *Wyclif: Select English Writings* (London: Oxford University Press, 1929), III, p. 83; F. D. Matthew, *The English Works of Wyclif* (London Early English Text Society, 1880), p. 478.

images such as those in laymen's books.[7] Later he likens this attitude
to a "great blindness" spending "so much about a rotten stock, and
suffer a poor man, very image of the Holy Trinity, made of Himself,
for to lie in much mischief."[8] Fundamentally, however, Wyclif does
not equate images with idols; his argument is more a general attack
on a church which puts too much emphasis on such externals. Those
who would be suspicious of all these trappings (unscriptural in nature) would also be suspicious of images for the same reasons.

Lollardy, however, did not hold to a unified stand on all issues.
Some Lollards could claim that image worship leads to idolatry when
a man "setteth in his affection anything before God" thus giving to
another what is due to God alone. "For many believe the image to
be God and many believe God's virtue to be in the image subjec-
tively."[9] There would be others, however, who might tolerate some
simple images for purposes of instruction—but fear that too frequently, such representations are gilded at the expense of the poor.[10]

There is much discomfort for Lollards over pictorial representation. Men tend to embroider and exaggerate what really happened
thus rendering the imagination suspect in the eyes of the unlettered
who demand accurate representations. More generally, for the Lollard, images were like all external signs, unreal; and that which is
unreal is untrue. Hence that which is false is contrary to God and a
threat to men; the only exception to this is Scripture, which is di-
vinely inspired. In observing a play or contemplating a holy image,
all localizations, artifacts and analogies focus men's attention on the
finite. This view of the Lollards develops from the belief that only
reality should concern men; pictures reflect a false sense of that
which is true.[11] They held that men should take less heed of such

7. John Wyclif, *Sermones*, ed. J. Loserth, (London: Wyclif Society, 1887–98),
p. 45.
8. Quoted in Herbert S. Workman, *John Wyclif, A Study of the English Medieval Church* (Oxford: Clarendon Press, 1926), II, p. 18. See also John Wyclif,
Select English Works, ed. Thomas Arnold (Oxford: Clarendon Press, 1871), III,
pp. 462–464.
9. James R. Todd (ed.), *An Apology for Lollard Doctrines* (London: Camden
Society, 1842), pp. 85–89. (Written either by Wyclif or a follower.) See also H. S.
Cronin, "The Twelve Conclusions of the Lollards," *English Historical Review*
XXII (1907), 292–304.
10. Owst, *Literature and Pulpit*, pp. 143–45.
11. Kolve, *Corpus Christi*, pp. 21–22.

sensible signs and should redirect their attention to the inward presence of God's grace which is externalized only in good works.

The evidence of Lollard ideas on images is fragmentary and from scattered sources. The fullest and most systematic elucidation of these views exists unfortunately in the treatise of an opponent; Reginald Pecock, the soon-to-be bishop of Chichester, who is primarily concerned in presenting an *apologia* for those aspects of the Church considered tainted by the Lollards. Though some skepticism should be exercised, the Lollard view he presents has some accuracy since it was required that he describe more or less objectively those ideas which he wished to refute.[12]

Like Wyclif's presentation, the Lollard's case as presented by Pecock is not strictly the objection to idolatry, but rather one of distaste for symbols mingled with impatience over their cost, labor and bother. Man-made images can only be defended if they engender in men the memory of their archetypes. However, the reading of Scripture is held to fulfill this condition more fully. After all, "if anything is good only because it answers a certain need, it becomes unnecessary when that end is better answered by other means."[13] Words, not visual images, are the most important way for men to come to religious truths.

Since God is everywhere present, the argument of Lollards continues, no place or image is holier than any other; thus, if not for the cost, then certainly for the implicit confusion present in men's attitudes toward pictures and the possible occasion for idolatry, images should be rejected. Though the Church moves in history, it does not follow that it should adjust itself to varying contexts and diverse requirements. God's demands as contained in Scripture should take precedence over human needs that require aids damaging to true spirituality. In the long run, the Lollards argued, it would be better to spend labor on a more perfect earthly image of Christ than a mere crucifix—that is, on living men.[14]

12. Reginald Pecock, *The Repressor of Over Much Blaming of the Clergy*, ed. by Churchill Babington (London: Longman, Green, Longman and Roberts, 1860), I, p. 131–136. On Pecock's life and thought, see V. H. H. Green, *Bishop Reginald Pecock* (Cambridge: University Press, 1945). Nuttall, *The Puritan Spirit* pp. 37–42.
13. Pecock, *Repressor*, I, 191–92.
14. *Ibid.*, I, 193–94, 219–22.

Ultimately, the Lollards' case against images was related to the greater issue of reform and authority. Men who advocated the primacy of private judgment over the institutional aspects of the Church, tended to see images very much as symbol of this tangible, collective Christianity. Indeed, criticism of the Church was soon identified with heterodoxy.[15] This is evident when one William Thorpe was arrested in Shrewsbury in 1407 for preaching Wyclif's ideas. He was examined by Thomas Arundel, then Archbishop of Canterbury, and later burned for his opinions.

To Arundel's argument that with Christ becoming man, the old law against images was struck down, Thorpe answered that it is the "wonderful working of God, and the whole living and teaching of Christ" whereby we might know God. The images made from man's hand are but reflections of the "vicious living of priests" and their "covetousness."[16]

One Lollard in 1462 confessed that he would rather put his trust in good works for the poor "than to seek or worship any saint or image on earth." Another, Robert Hoke, refused to creep to the cross on Good Friday; furthermore, he allowed his parishioners to remain seated during the service.[17]

Three Lollards who had misused images were excommunicated at Leicester in 1389. When they made their submission to ecclesiastical authorities, they were forced to carry crucifixes and candles into the church, genuflect and kiss the images three times.[18] Frequently the punishment of Lollard iconoclasm centered around the "correct" use of images.

The strong Lollard dependence on scriptural authority produced

15. See Desiderius Erasmus, *The Colloquies*, trans. Craig R. Thompson (Chicago: University Press, 1965), p. 305, where a man disrespectful towards relics is called "some Wycliffite, I suppose." W. A. Pantin, *The English Church in the Fourteenth Century* (Notre Dame: University Press, 1962), pp. 238–39.

16. Thorpe's diary is reprinted in John Hale, *Select Works*, ed. Henry Christmas (Cambridge: University Press, 1849), pp. 94–98; John Foxe, *Acts and Monuments* (London: R. B. Seeley and W. Burnside, 1837–1841), III, pp. 265–66.

17. W. H. Summers, *The Lollards of the Chiltern Hills* (London: Francis Griffiths, 1906), pp. 66–67, 82. See John A. F. Thomson, *The Later Lollards* (Oxford: University Press, 1965), pp. 24–25, 28–29, 33, 35, 41, etc. for other examples.

18. Joseph Dahmus, *William Courtenay Archbishop of Canterbury, 1381–1396* (University Park: Pennsylvania State University Press, 1966), pp. 145–46.

a kind of practicality that scoffed at men's weaknesses. Where Scripture declared no explicit principle of faith, many were wont to interpret the absence as a prohibition. Their common sense attitude toward pilgrimages and other beliefs and associations led them to discard much that other men found helpful as aids to piety in this life. In the long run, however, the Lollards spent little time discussing the evils of relics, pilgrimages and images; when they did, it was more as a by-product of their general theological criticism.

The coming of Humanism to England in the fifteenth and sixteenth centuries mirrored Lollardy's impatience with the absurdity of the old order. The Humanists, however, tended to focus on those individual adjuncts to the medieval liturgy that obviously were abused and needed reforming; the criticism of these practices, such as images, relics and pilgrimages, led them quickly to criticize the Church generally—even doctrinally. Eventually such religious stands could lead individual Humanists to embrace Protestantism and possibly to a "theological" iconoclasm. Humanists like Erasmus and John Colet were as shocked as Wyclif with the superstition of the old order and were unwilling to accept the obscurantism and naïveté of the past. Humanists as such, however, were not inclined to destroy physically the trappings of the medieval church.

Erasmus, of course, was not English; but because of the force of his ideas and his own personality, he was particularly important for the development of English Humanism.[19] He more fully develops his ideas on the problems of images than any individual English Humanist; the argument here is that his ideas are not radically different from theirs.[20]

In *A Pilgrimage for Religion's Sake*, anonymously translated into

19. Fritz Caspari, *Humanism and the Social Order in Tudor England* (Chicago: University Press, 1954), pp. 28f.

20. Pearl Hogrefe, *The Sir Thomas More Circle* (Urbana: University of Illinois Press, 1959), pp. 92–93; Ernest William Hunt, *Dean Colet and His Theology* (London: S.P.C.K., 1956), pp. 56–60. The problem of the English humanists' attitude towards reform and the medieval fabric is a difficult one, not open to easy generalization. Unlike Eramus, their views on images are mostly fragmentary. Yet see, Robert Adams, *The Better Part of Valor* (Seattle: University of Washington Press, 1962); Leland Miles, *John Colet and the Platonic Tradition* (London: George Allen and Unwin, 1962), pp. 171–216; Stanford Lehmberg, *Sir Thomas Elyot Tudor Humanist* (Austin: University of Texas Press, 1960), pp. 103–05, 148–54, 180–81.

English in 1536–37, Erasmus paints the old order's dedication to pilgrimages in hot colors, showing the absurdities and exaggerations that have resulted. Petitions to images are inappropriate, he argues; indeed, the Virgin herself has spoken out in a letter wherein she complains of the "shameless entreaties of mortals."

They demanded everything from me alone, as if my Son were always a baby (because he is carved and painted as such at my bosom) . . . . Sometimes a merchant off for Spain to make a fortune, commits to me the chastity of his mistress. . . . A profane soldier, hired to butcher people, cries upon me, 'Blessed Virgin, give me booty.'[21]

In turn, the pilgrims pretend to lay offerings on the altar, but "steal with astonishing nimbleness what somebody else had placed there." But no wonder that earthly avarice prevails at the shrines, Erasmus exclaims, since they are so laden with jewels, gold and silver. The gifts and offerings of kings and princes are shown in abundance: "Everything shone and dazzled with rare and surpassingly large jewels, some bigger than a goose egg." At Canterbury and Becket's shrine, these are mixed with relics to which pilgrims are expected to kneel in adoration.[22] A sliver from the True Cross is shown but this is such a popular relic that "if the fragments were joined together, they'd seem a full load for a freighter. And yet the Lord carried his whole cross."[23]

Erasmus's point is one of practicality. He would have agreed with Candide that it is certainly preferable to stay home and cultivate one's own garden that run on pilgrimages and kiss images. Above all, he stresses acceptance of personal responsibility for one's own actions over the transfer of guilt (or punishment owing to sin) to the saints and their intercession. On the other hand, despite the fact that the colloquy preaches no outward attack on the veneration of saints,[24] Erasmus undermines this doctrine and seriously casts doubt on the purpose of religious imagery. His aim is not iconoclasm, but the return to what might be called ethical behavior or the practical following of Christ. Essentially for Erasmus, it is good works that are cen-

21. Erasmus, *Colloquies*, pp. 289–90.
22. *Ibid.*, p. 308.
23. *Ibid.*, p. 295.
24. However, see *The Shipwreck* (1523) in *Ibid.*, pp. 138–46.

tral to salvation rather than the vain rituals, disputations and false scholasticism of the medieval church.[25]

In the long run, however, Erasmus anticipates the very arguments used by Henry VIII and the English reformers to justify their own iconoclasm; indirectly, he contributes to the violence of destruction which in name he had denounced.[26] For Erasmus the whole medieval system had gradually come to mean that God could be pleased with material observances without faith, as penance reigned over penitence, and pilgrimage replaced prayer.

Humanism is an inclusive term for it covers a gamut of philosophical, cultural and educational convictions.[27] Essentially, it came to mean the mixture of Christian wisdom and classical culture or, more explicitly, an education by antique writers that is modified by Christian truth.[28] Whether Humanists were proponents of peculiar educational programs or devotees of classical Latin style, their motivation was derived from the ideal they set before them. In varying degrees, the perfection of human reality was gauged by the standards of the classical past.

Humanists such as Erasmus came to prefer St. Paul and the synoptic Gospels in place of the theological definitions of the Church. In turn, what attracted them was the primitive Church of the first three centuries wherein they believed the simple, basic Christian truths were clearer than in the "declaration of theological truths or the recognition of types and symbols and prophecies that had formed such a large part of medieval exegesis."[29] Thus Humanism produced

25. *Ibid.*, p. 312. White, *Tudor Books*, p. 77; Johan Huizinga, *Erasmus and the Age of Reformation* (New York: Harper and Row, 1957), pp. 100–16. The fullest accounts of Erasmus' views on art are contained in R. Giese, "Erasmus and the Fine Arts," *Journal of Modern History* VII (1935), 257–279. E. Panofsky, "Erasmus and the Visual Arts," *Journal of the Warburg and Courtauld Institutes* XXXII (1969), 200–227.

26. It is perhaps noteworthy that the sixteenth-century English translation of this colloquy "The Pilgrimage of Pure Devotion" was used as propaganda by Cromwell at the dissolution of the monasteries. See White, *Tudor Books*, pp. 80–82. Erasmus himself had visited Walsingham in 1512 and possibly again in 1514; Becket's shrine was probably visited sometime between 1512–14.

27. Weiss, *Humanism in England* p. 183.

28. Whether this was a true synthesis or "an artificial and unrealistic reconciliation of essentially antagonistic elements," see Douglas Bush, *Renaissance and English Humanism* (Toronto: University of Toronto Press, 1939), p. 130.

29. David Knowles, *The Religious Orders of England* (Cambridge: University Press, 1961) III, p. 143.

an emphasis on proper ethical behavior that only tolerated dogmatic theology and human abuses.[30] For just as the proper study of Christianity would mean for the Humanists the return to scriptural and patristic sources buttressed by study of the text in its original language, in practice it would or should produce the return of a faith that is at once simple and free from the incrustations of the past. In fact, one of Erasmus' dearest wishes was

. . . to extract from the most pure sources of the Gospels, the apostolic writings and their best commentators a kind of resume of the whole 'philosophy of Christ,' a resume in which simplicity would not detract from erudition, nor brevity from precision. All that is of faith should be condensed in very few articles, and the same should be done for all that concerns the Christian way of life.[31]

While the Humanists believed that the Church had substituted a false scholasticism for the *Philosophia Christi*, they also came to believe that the Church had departed from simple pious practices, by multiplying devotions, images and relics to the degree that they now distracted Christians from what was essential. Erasmus urged men to return to the Bible, to adopt the good, simple life based on the ethical writings of Greece and Rome joined to the teachings of Christ, and leave behind the formalistic doctrines overlaid with "judaic" practices.[32] Ideal religious devotion would increasingly become a spirituality devoid of formalism, legalism and external practices. Above all, for Erasmus and others, it became an ideal of a simple faith revealed by practical charity.

In fact, Erasmus and other Humanists strongly condemned all practices that they felt distracted men from proper inner attitudes. The allegorical and mysterious rites of the Church neither purify man's internal life nor justify his external action.

Now there are not a few who are given over to the veneration of the saints, with elaborate ceremonies. Some, for example, have a great devotion to St.

30. *Ibid.*, III, p. 146. Hiram Haydn, *The Counter-Renaissance* (New York: Harcourt Brace, 1950), p. 64.

31. Quoted in Joseph Lecler, *Toleration and the Reformation* (London: Longmans, Green and Company, 1960), I, p. 125. See Robert Peters, "Erasmus and the Fathers: their practical value," *Church History* XXXVI (1967), 255–56.

32. Erasmus, *Enchiridion Militis Christiani* (Notre Dame: Fides, 1962), p. 111. H. R. Trevor-Roper, *Historical Essays* (London: Macmillan, 1957), p. 40.

Christopher. Provided his statue is in sight, they pray to him almost every day. Why do they do this? It is because they wish to be preserved from a sudden and unprovided death that day. . . . What I utterly condemn is the fact that they esteem the indifferent in place of the highest, the nonessentials to the complete neglect of what is essential. What is of the smallest value spiritually they make the greatest.[33]

Erasmus's dislike of nonessentials soon led him to easy simplifications intended to keep this world tidy by separating the realm of fact from that of spirit. He wrote, "You will find that you can best maintain this piety if, turning away from visible things, which are for the most part either imperfect or of themselves indifferent, you seek the invisible." There are two worlds—the one intelligible, the other visible. In one sense man participates in both. But, like Plato, Erasmus posits physical reality as a mere shadow of true reality. Not only does the world of things have little value in itself, but can decidedly act as a snare in men's groping for salvation.

I feel that the entire spiritual life consists in this: that we gradually turn from those things whose appearance is deceptive to those things that are real . . . from the pleasures of the flesh, the honors of the world that are so transitory, to those things that are immutable and everlasting.[34]

And the world of reality can be more fully expressed in holy writ than images which remain shadows twice removed. After all, Erasmus asks, what artist could ever match the words of Christ that we read in the Gospel? "As for images, what thynges can they expresse but the fygure of hys body. If they expresse that."[35]

No relic of our Blessed Lord can possibly approach the strength and beauty of His very self. You may gaze in silent amazement at the tunic that reputedly belonged to Christ, yet you read the wonderful sayings of that same Christ half asleep . . . If these external things were the true source of holiness, then certainly there could never have been any people more religious than the Jews. They lived with Him, listened to His words, touched Him—yet most of them rejected Him.[36]

33. Erasmus, *Enchiridion Militis Christiani*, pp. 101–03.
34. *Ibid.*, p. 105.
35. *The new Testament in Englishe after the greeke translation annexed wyth the translation of Erasmus in Latin* (London, 1550), no pagination, but see "An exhortacion to the viligent studys of Scripture," See also *The Paraphrase of Erasmus upon the newe testaments* (London, 1548), I, cap. xvii, fol. lxiii (Commentary on Acts 17:22–29).
36. Erasmus, *Enchiridion Militis Christiani*, p. 110.

Unlike the Lollards, Erasmus as a Humanist valued the arts as instruments for education and as strong forces for civilizing men; he found pleasure in the practice of painting and music. But like the Lollards, he was scandalized by the profanity of much religious art; and like them, he distrusted the motives of artistic pleasure and saw the appeal to the senses as incompatible with his own views of intellectual beauty.

Although the defense of the fine arts by Humanists like Erasmus and others was hesitant and inconclusive, at least they were not iconoclasts. Their aversion to violence and their wish to transform the arts made them unlikely friends to the Lollards.[37] Yet many Humanists' inclination to regard religious images with implicit disfavor confirmed the explicit religious rejection of them by Lollardy. This was one step in the direction of reformation and iconoclasm.

37. Panofsky, "Erasmus and Visual Arts," 207–14. Giese, "Erasmus and Fine Arts," 277–279.

III. IMAGES UNDERMINED

And so believe you the Church, not because it is truth that the
Church telleth you; but ye believe the truth of the thing, because the Church telleth it.

THOMAS MORE, *Dialogue Concerning Tyndale*

The founding of monasteries argued purgatory to be; so the
putting of them down argueth it not to be.

HUGH LATIMER, on Purgatory

THE PROTESTANT BELIEF in the universal priesthood of all believers
denied the distinction between the learned who responded directly to the word of God and the unlearned, who required the media-
tion of images. The traditional justification for images, however, had
never rested solely on their use for enlightening the unlettered. Essential to the development of images in the early Church and to the theology of Thomas Aquinas, was that all men require sensible signs in
order to arrive at true spirituality. Consequently, it was only when
the control of religious images was taken from the teaching authority
of the Church and when Scripture was considered the chief medium
through which God could speak to man, that iconoclasm became
essential to the Reformation.

The character of the objections to images differed for many reformers. For some Protestants, the ubiquitous presence of these representations identified them with the church that was under attack
because of its excessive trappings and legends and/or its refusal to
heed Scripture and the Commandments.

Other reformers rejected images because as visual aids they tended
to spell out doctrinal views such as Purgatory, the intercession of the
saints, and the sacrificial character of the Mass. Those sainted beings
who had attained Heaven could be honored for their merits; indeed,
these merits reflected the gift of God's grace. Yet in the final reckon-
ing, many Protestants would insist, all acts produced through grace
redound to their inspirer, God Himself. Only Christ can be the medi-

41

ator between God and man.[1] Purgatory itself, the need for "natural" man to be purged of his weaknesses in order to obtain grace, was now denied; those images that were prayed to and which had nurtured countless devotions on behalf of the suffering souls, were now thought unnecessary if not obnoxious.

So with a marked emphasis upon God as the source and channel for all graces, as sole inspirer, and with the denial of the saints as active participants in this life, the use of images, relics, and their trappings would decline accordingly. For the flower of religious imagery could bloom only in an atmosphere that encouraged the sacred and human traditions of the medieval church. It was an atmosphere that allowed for daily miracles, for God's continual involvement (and patience) with this life. Above all, it involved an eager acceptance of nature and of this earth as worthy and good to be the vehicle of God's grace for man. If Lollards and Humanists can be said to have in any way prepared the ground for the development of English Protestantism, then it would be the latter which would bring to fruition what the former two had merely nurtured.

The reign of Henry VIII had particular importance for the role images would play in the English Church. Controversy would rage over the theological as well as practical values that such aids embodied; fundamentally different attitudes towards Salvation were inextricably involved. Though the Humanist Thomas More expressed in his own writings the ideas of many of his reformer friends (like Erasmus), he was at the same time one of the most articulate defenders of the medieval church. When More came to defend this medieval fabric which was not only under suspicion for being irrelevant, but also under attack for being offensive to God, he fell back upon the traditional defense of images.[2] Though many of these ideas have been encountered before (cf. Chapter One), More's controversy

1. George and George, *Protestant Mind and the English Reformation* (Princeton: University Press, 1961), p. 96.
2. In 1528 More received permission from Bishop Tunstal to read the writings of the English and continental reformers. His intent was refutation and this purpose inspired him to publish his *Dialogue Concerning Tyndale* in the summer of 1529. It was answered by Tyndale in 1530 (published in the spring of 1531). Thereupon More, as Lord High Chancellor, wrote a *Confutation of Tyndale's Answer*. See W. E. Campbell, *Erasmus, Tyndale and More* (London: Eyre and Spottiswoode, 1949), for a full account.

with the Protestant William Tyndale sets into focus the limits and implications of theological iconoclasm. Related to this controversy is the stand taken by others who, through a variety of political and economic reasons as well, will bring about fundamental changes in the liturgy of the English Church. Consequently this chapter includes a discussion of the great physical upheaval suffered by the medieval fabric in the wake of these different forces.

Like Bishop Pecock, More believed that reason is the means by which God's purpose is understood: that every truth known to man and every human action relating to morals is fully understood by reason working in agreement with faith. For More, the Church necessarily moves in history and thereby adjusts itself to varying contexts and needs; the use of images was one of the ways man came to know, honor and worship God.[3]

To Thomas More, visual aids such as painting and sculpture are an appropriate language for the representation of physical objects. In fact, the written word is no natural sign, but essentially an artificial means to communicate thoughts.[4] Visual aids, then, are effective in that they represent natural objects, which can reflect spiritual truths. More believed that images become not mere visual badges for natural objects, but physical means for spiritual edification. This acceptance of the natural world as a means of and a place for knowing God is carried even to the point of More's insisting that God desires man to worship Him in specific places through religious images.[5]

Consequently, according to More, men might come to know God through this earth, through the handiwork of Christians, and most especially, through the lives of his saints. The honor paid to saints redounds to God Himself for Christ chose the saints as partners in the glory that was really only His: "... he promised his apostles that at the dreadful doom, when he shall come in his high majesty, they shall

---

3. Thomas More, *The Dialogue Concerning Tyndale*, ed. W. E. Campbell and A. W. Reed (London: Eyre and Spottiswoode, 1927), p. 28. Compare Pecock, *Repressor*, I, pp. 131–36.

4. More, *Dialogue Concerning Tyndale* p. 21. Leonardo da Vinci had a similar view. See his "Painting and Poetry," *Paragone*, ed. Irma A. Richter (Oxford: University Press, 1949), pp. 49–71. Compare Pecock, *Repressor*, I, 219–22, 267–71.

5. More, *Dialogue Concerning Tyndale* pp. 29, 31, 45, 54–55.

have their honourable seats, and sit with himself upon the judgment of the world."[6]

It is right and fitting, claimed More, for men to have images in their churches. Indeed, God likes to see the commitment of the heart render devotion and love through the body. Man has ample to give to the poor; let him bring forth his riches to honor also his Creator in return splendor for what God has given man.[7]

The prohibitions requiring men not to worship any image as God do not intend the destruction of images, but only their proper use. This correct use is the worshipper's

. . . not fixing his final intent in the image, but referring it further to the honour of the person that the image representeth, since that in such reverence done unto the image there is none honour withdrawn neither from God nor good man, but both the saint honoured in his image and God in his saint.[8]

More as a Humanist could be sympathetic to the claims of reformers that images were corrupt, if not altogether tainted with the suspicion of idolatry. Certainly his friend Erasmus had made him aware of that. However, More insists that man worships God with the intent that He is God; nor is man so simple that he confounds a dead image with the living reality it represents. Should he do this, it is an abuse (like the praying for things unlawful). Images are valid in themselves, and because the Church so teaches, they are never to be judged by their abuses.[9]

More was quite aware that if graphic images of Christ and his saints were to go, other elements of the sacramental system would follow. He tended to minimize the actual abuse of images because he feared that further attacks against the Church would follow. For More, the attack of images was essentially an attack on the institution itself. Consequently, More's defense of images was essentially a de-

6. *Ibid.*, pp. 22, 150.
7. *Ibid.*, pp. 16, 19, 23. This is one answer to the perennial complaint that men should give to the poor rather than to the saints. It was directed against Erasmus, *The Godly Feast* (1522), *Colloquies*, pp. 70–71, and the arguments of the succeeding reformers.
8. More, *Dialogue Concerning Tyndale*, p. 20. Pecock, *Repressor*, I, 148–54, 248.
9. More, *Dialogue Concerning Tyndale*, pp. 60–63, 163–64, 168, 263. Again compare Pecock, *Repressor*, I, 155–60, 252.

fense of the Church's right to use such aids. He rightly understood that the question of images cannot ultimately be dealt with as an isolated problem—but one under the purview and authority of Christ's Church. The fundamental acceptance and validity of images resides in the fact that the Church of Christ cannot err in the exposition of Christ's faith; this More proves by Scripture. Thus, if the worship of images is idolatry, then the Church in its acceptance of images is in error. But this cannot be:

> ... Christ's church cannot err in any such article as God upon pain of loss of heaven will(s) that we believe. And thereupon necessarily followeth that there is no text of scripture well understanden, by which Christian people are commanded to do the thing which the church believeth that they may lawfully leave undone, nor any text whereby we be forboden any thing which the church believeth that they may lawfully do.[10]

Those who would stress interiority in the worship of God would not find these arguments convincing. Many men would urge individual conscience rather than the traditional teaching authority of the Church to decide these matters. External ceremonies, fasting, images, holy days possess little value in themselves, they might claim, save at the discretion of individual Christians.

In the spring of 1531, William Tyndale, translator of the Scriptures into English, responded to More's *Dialogue*, thus continuing the controversy. In insisting that Christians were lords over the Sabbath, Tyndale believed that images could or could not be used depending on how they aid men in coming to God. Since God is spirit, He should be worshipped in spirit. "(S)acraments, signs, ceremonies, and bodily things can be no service to God in his person; but memorials unto men, and a remembrance of the testament wherewith God is served in the spirit."[11]

Relics, ornaments, ceremonies, even the sacraments, were in times past and should be now, to do man service. Kneeling before a cross, or blessing oneself with the sign of the cross, are not evil if they inspire in man devotion and reverence. The abuse occurs when these

10. More, *Dialogue Concerning Tyndale*, pp. 79, 113. See William Clebsch, *England's Earliest Reformers* (New Haven: Yale University Press, 1964), pp. 296–97, 302.

11. William Tyndale, *An Answer to Sir Thomas More's Dialogue*, ed. Henry Walter (Parker Society; Cambridge: University Press, 1850), pp. 56–57, 64, 80, 89.

signs lead to evil and false faith. Given the weakness of men and the nature of tangible ornaments, superstition becomes inevitable when such artifacts are thought to protect the owner or render him special graces.[12] Like More, Tyndale believed that in contrast to words, pictorial representations are easier to understand; yet he feared they could be more easily misused. Since the whole purpose of representations, according to Tyndale, is to put one in the proper frame of mind, their tangibility renders them a snare to faith and leads the individual to magnification of man rather than of God. Images and relics become ends in themselves; he insists man serves them. Proof of this can be seen in the number of pilgrimages in which people believe that God is in one place rather than in another. It can also be seen in the belief that one image is more productive of grace than another. All of this is an externalization of religion to please man.[13]

The inevitable danger of images for Tyndale can be seen in the history of God's chosen people. At one time the Jews made offerings and sacrifices of animals not as satisfaction and payment for sin, "but only (as) a sign and token, that at the repentence of the heart, through an offering to come, and for that seed's sake that was promised Abraham, their sins were forgiven them."[14] Consequently the people of Israel put no justification in these externals, but let them speak for their hearts. In time, however, corruption led them to lose the meaning of their ceremonies; in reverse, they served the ritual, "saying that they were holy works commanded of God, and the offerers were thereby justified, and obtained forgiveness of sins, and thereby became good."[15]

Was it not then natural, Tyndale asked, recalling Wyclif, that with the precedent of Jewish ceremonies, Christians would also introduce false practices into the new religion? Sacraments and ceremonies are not especially dangerous if most men understand their meaning and use them as an aid. But ceremonies can easily usurp preaching and the essentials of faith. "Paul sent his napkin to heal the sick; not that

12. *Ibid.*, p. 60.

13. *Ibid.*, pp. 63–64. See also Robert Barnes, *The Whole Workes of W. Tyndall, John Frith and Doctor Barnes, Three Worthy Martyrs* . . . (London, 1573), pp. 344–45.

14. Tyndale, *An Answer*, pp. 65–66; *Expositions and Notes* (Parker Society; Cambridge: University Press, 1850), p. 214.

15. Tyndale, *An Answer*, pp. 66–67.

men should put trust in his napkin, but believe his preaching."[16]

Where More stressed the intrinsic goodness of the external act, Tyndale felt that these acts were good in themselves only if they helped develop faith and tamed the flesh. For Tyndale, it is not the intercession of saints nor their relics that are important but a faith in the promises of Christ's blood, and a prayer to the Father in Christ's name.

> Ane likewise is it of saints' bones: we may remove them whither we will, yea, and break all images thereto, and make new, or if they be abused, put them out of the way for ever, as was the brasen serpent; so that we be lords over all such things, and they our servants. For if the saints were our servants, how much more their bones! It is the heart, and not the place, that worshippeth God.[17]

Neither More nor Tyndale were concerned about the aesthetic features of images; both agreed that visual representations are not essential to the practice of true religion, yet different theologies of grace led them to place different degrees of emphasis on their use. Tyndale could accuse More of being "fleshly-minded" and his conception of God of being "beastly." More's problem, he feels, is that he is a "natural man" incapable of understanding the things of the "Spirit." This is the fundamental difference between the two. While both essentially agree that the heart is the true temple of faith, More finds certain sensuous experiences as guided by the Church an important aid to religion. Tyndale on the other hand, tries to realize the spirit directly from God without external ceremonies; an individual conscience over a corrupt Roman Church. Hence for Tyndale, the Eucharist and other sacraments were the most expressive of all images for Christians. More graphically than any painting or sculpture, such tangible signs revealed the essence of the Gospel's lesson

16. *Ibid.*, pp. 74–76, 83. Most reformers felt that the early church was untainted, owing to the fact that images had been introduced later by Rome. Thomas Bilson thought that the Schoolmen were responsible. *The True Difference Between Christian Subjection and Unchristian Rebellion* . . . (Oxford, 1585), pp. 598–99. Ussher thought the blame more extensive: ". . . partly lewd heretics, partly simple Christians never converted from paganism, the customs whereof they had not as yet so fully unlearned." *The Whole Works*, ed. Charles Erlington (Dublin: Hodges, Smith and Co., 1864), III, pp. 499, 500, 509. See also John Bridges, *The Supremacie of Christian Princes* . . . (London, 1573), pp. 490–95.

17. Tyndale, *An Answer*, p. 88, 116–117; *Expositions*, p. 217. See also Barnes, *The Whole Workes*, pp. 347, 349–351.

of redemption and love of Christ: ". . . our sacraments are bodies of stories only; and that there is none other virtue in them than to testify and exhibit to the senses and understanding of the covenants and promises made in Christ's blood."[18]

More could be a Humanist, strongly sympathetic to the need for reform, and yet protective toward many practices of the medieval church. He was cautious and fearful that reform in the hands of some men would lead to important doctrinal changes. Hence his ultimate argument in defense of images was that of the authority of the Church.

Consequently the debate between More and Tyndale was important to the reformation of images because it established early in Henry's reign the fundamental positions that would continue to be utilized in subsequent controversy. In turn, these two views would have profound practical implications for the liturgy of the English Church. Related to this controversy are the various religious debates, ecclesiastical and political legislation which sought to reshape the ceremonies and practices of the Church. Religious images would, at least, in the beginning, not be attacked, but undermined.

It might be recalled that Erasmus had wished to "purify" Christianity by separating its essential doctrines from the "additions" made to these ideas which reflected the needs of men. Likewise, Melanchthon had distinguished between the law of nature which transcends all human institutions, and the customs which merely reflect the contingencies of human life. God's law thus remains of unchangeable authority while human customs and devotions, though reflecting the other, are open to the changes of time, place, and men. Hence, for Melanchthon, Erasmus, and Tyndale (and later, for Henry VIII), images, relics, fasts and such things are by their nature indifferent, or unnecessary, to the law of nature. These traditions are allowable to men since they bring order to ceremonies and act as bridges to the other world; they are only allowable, however, if they supplement, not supplant, the essential. Should abuses occur, these accessories can

---

18. William Tyndale, *Doctrinal Treatises and Introductions to different portions of the Holy Scriptures* (Parker Society; Cambridge: University Press, 1848), p. 358.

be dispensed with for their omission would not constitute scandal.[19]

Many men came to accept such thinking, if not from Erasmus who suggested it or from Melanchthon who elaborated it, then in revulsion against the ubiquitous ceremonies that seemed blasphemous to God. Needless to say, all such distinctions of things necessary and of things indifferent were to be made specifically in a context which left out the continued authority of the Catholic Church.

Indeed, Thomas More and other Catholics felt that such distinctions between essentials and inessentials in the Christian religion were impossible to make. The Roman Church has always moved in history; various traditions such as images did not merely supplement Scripture, but made it essentially meaningful to the lives of Christians. Such an attack based on Melanchthon's dichotomies, it was argued, would tend to weaken popular devotion and worse, call the Mass, transubstantiation and other doctrines into question.

An Augustinian friar, one Thomas Topley, had recanted of heresy in 1528 and claimed that it was the reading of Erasmus's colloquies which had led his faith astray. What had been written on the abuses of pilgrimages had caused him to withdraw his commitment from the doctrine of saints.[20] If Erasmus claimed that many silly ceremonial practices were inexorably linked with true doctrine, men like Topley found it difficult to separate the two; criticism of relics and gilded images had led to disbelief in certain Christian beliefs such as the veneration of saints and in the existence of Purgatory. Furthermore, the practical implications of such distinctions as necessary doctrines and "things indifferent" had confused people since the power to decide such questions would soon be taken from the Church and granted to human agencies which more frequently than not were ruled by considerations other than that of religion.

Bishop Cuthbert Tunstal had urged Erasmus to change certain passages in the *Colloquies* that had held church ceremonies up to ridicule. For it was less what Erasmus said, but more what was im-

19. Philip Melanchthon, *On Christian Doctrine*, tr. and ed. by C. L. Manschreck (New York: Oxford University Press, 1965), pp. 306–16.
20. James McConica, *English Humanists and Reformation Politics* (Oxford: Clarendon Press, 1965), p. 146.

plied that worried conservative churchmen.[21] Erasmus himself was sensitive to these complaints; in a letter (1526) to John Longland, the Bishop of Lincoln, he sums up his defense.

If your Grace will take the time to go through the book you will find that besides instruction it has much else pertinent to the sound training of youth. Entertainment is thrown in as a bait, to entice an age sooner captivated by what is agreeable than by what is good for it. There is nothing obscene in the book, nothing irreverent, nothing to disturb the peace.[22]

Erasmus insists that he has not mocked legitimate religious practices, but has indeed ridiculed the hoaxes played on the credulous— "this charlatanism brought upon Christian devotion."

In *A Pilgrimage for Religion's Sake*, I reproach those who with much ado have thrown all images out of the churches; also those who are crazy about pilgrimages undertaken in the name of religion—something clubs, too, are now organized for. . . Attention is called also to those who exhibit doubtful relics for authentic ones, who attribute to them more than is proper, and basely make money by them.[23]

It was strange, thought Erasmus, that others did not see these distinctions. Yet was not the writer of the *Colloquies* himself unaware that, for many, an attack on superstitious devotions spelled an attack on devotions themselves? Erasmus, after all, was not intent on destroying the physical fabric of the medieval church, but only the excesses that time and human weakness had added to the Christian message. In the long run, however, many would feel that these very attacks had the net effect of horribly weakening many of the Christian practices he had defended.

Though they might weaken these practices, such views as expressed by Erasmus, Tyndale, and others could not in themselves bring down the Catholic doctrine of images or realize their actual destruction. If, however, such views worked in conjunction with the needs of the government of Henry VIII, they could effect the same end.

When Parliament met in 1529, the government faced some severely pressing problems. The story of Henry VIII's campaign for a divorce from Queen Catherine in the hope of gaining a legitimate male heir

21. Charles Sturge, *Cuthbert Tunstal* (London: Longmans, Green and Company, 1938), pp. 124–26.
22. Erasmus, *Colloquies*, pp. 626–27, 630–31, 635.
23. *Ibid.*

cannot here be recounted. Parliament, however, strengthened the support of the laity behind the King and forced the clergy to submit to royal demands by removing certain clerical prerogatives, jurisdiction and revenues. When Henry did remarry, Rome excommunicated the King and denied the validity of his divorce which Thomas Cranmer, now Archbishop of Canterbury, had pronounced. Henry's response was to sever the remaining ties with Rome, making the English Church independent of the Pope. In 1534, Henry was declared "Protector and only Supreme Head of the Church and Clergy of England." Iconoclasm under Henry would not be a policy as much as a side effect of various royal programs in the larger context of a move to subjugate the English Church to the Crown in Parliament.

In the beginning, Henry could claim that he was not interested in changing the religious doctrines of the Church; his attention reverted more on what was then considered to be the needed reform of polity and certain superstitious ceremonies of the medieval church. The government could argue that the new religious settlement reflected a serious king living up to his divine responsibilities by eliminating from the Church certain human modifications to divine commandments. And such a plan for reforming the English Church that was based on Melanchthon's distinctions between the essential and inessential practices in Christian life, could take the focus away from Henry's strengthening of Crown over Church. It could minimize the eventual depredations and spoliations and re-channel public gaze onto the King's religious reforms.[24]

Thomas Starkey, publicist for Henry's government, applied Melanchthon's ideas directly to the English scene. In *An exhortation to the people instructynge theym to unitie and obedience*, he distinguished between "things good, things ill, and things indifferent." That which is commanded by God is good; that prohibited ill; things

24. For the artistic policy of the Crown that reflected this religious role, see Roy Strong, *Holbein and Henry VIII* (London: Routledge and Kegan Paul, 1967), pp. 8f. It has been argued recently that Henry's plans also reflect a consistent sympathy with continental Lutheranism. Neelak S. Tjernagel, *Henry VIII and the Lutherans* (St. Louis: Concordia, 1965), pp. 187–88, 248. E. G. Rupp, *Studies in the Making of the English Protestant Tradition* (Cambridge University Press, 1947), pp. 89–127. It has also been suggested that Henry's program in general was broader than Melanchthon's adiaphorist notions. See J. Scarisbrick, *Henry VIII* (London: Eyre and Spottiswoode, 1968), pp. 241f.

neither prohibited nor commanded are not necessary to salvation and can be left to human agency to determine.[25] Things indifferent were all those devotional aids essential to medieval spirituality—such as images, holy days and the communion of saints. Such "indifferent" matters varied with the times, places and people in question; the arbiter for Starkey was not the universal Roman Church from which England was recently freed, but the legally constituted common authority—Henry's government. This position would find favor with the Crown as buttress for its policies, but would also seem attractive to its conciliatory stand which sought neither an outright rejection of ceremonies nor a blind obedience to them.[26]

Thus is explained perhaps the government's courting of Humanists who were sympathetic to the distinctions made by Melanchthon, Starkey and others. Already by 1531, Thomas Cromwell, Henry's minister of affairs who was to lay the legal foundations of the national church, had undertaken to sponsor in a semi-official capacity translations of the works of Erasmus that were directly relevant to the reform of the English Church.[27] English Humanists, who were suspicious of traditional theology and yet committed to what they considered were the essentials of Catholic orthodoxy, were responsive to royal policy. Was this the opportunity to help realize in England the Erasmian dream of a simple Christianity of practical charity over the formalism and legalism of the past?

Between 1534–36, however, there was very little mention of the reformation of ceremonies in the Church of England. The King was consolidating his position as Supreme Head, realizing that sudden change in ceremonies might augur reform of doctrines. This he

25. W. Gordon Zeeveld, *Foundations of Tudor Policy* (Cambridge: Harvard University Press, 1948), pp. 149–50. McConica, *English Humanists*, p. 171. Zeeveld stressed the influence of Melanchthon on Starkey while McConica suggests the latter got the doctrine of *adiaphora* from "Erasmian common property." *Ibid.*, p. 4. See also, Franklin Baumer, "Thomas Starkey and Marsilius of Padua," *Politica*, II (1936), 188–205. W. G. Zeeveld, "Thomas Starkey and the Cromwellian Polity," *Journal of Modern History*, XV (1943), 177–91.

26. Zeeveld, *Foundations of Tudor Policy*, pp. 151, 154–55.

27. The English version of Erasmus' *A Pilgrimage for Religion's Sake* in 1537 and *The Funeral* in 1534 were probably encouraged, if not subsidized by Cromwell as propaganda in aid of the government's forthcoming campaign against shrines and monasteries. See Erasmus, *Colloquies*, pp. 357–59, and Henry de Vocht *The Earliest English Translations of Erasmus' Colloquia* (Louvain: Librairie Universitaire, 1928). McConica, *English Humanists*, pp. 106f.

avoided until 1536, whereupon the government sought to assure that possible religious confusion would not produce civil discord. Religion was so bound up with the very tapestry of society that contemplated reforms had to be understood within the equipoise of politics.

The act for the Submission of the Clergy (1534) had placed the English Church through its representatives in Convocation in direct relation with the King, suggesting a comparable role to that exercised by Parliament. Henceforth, through the Royal Supremacy and through the assent of Convocation, Henry would issue articles of Christian faith and practice.

In the sermon before the Convocation of the clergy in 1536, Hugh Latimer, an old opponent of conservative churchmen and recently appointed Bishop of Worcester, complained of the abuses of images, relics and saints. "Juggling deceits" he claimed they were because ignorant people confound false miracles for true ones and thus fall into superstition.[28] This view was vigorously debated by the clergy present: after a while, the Convocation defined the place of images and relics in English churches:

[T]hat images, as well of the crucifix as of other saints, are to be put out of the church, and the reliques of saints in no wise to be reverences; and that it is against God's commandment that Christian men should make curtesy or reverence to the image of Our Saviour.[29]

Hugh Latimer had not just been persuasive; many of the clergy present already had come to fear the excesses of the medieval devotional system. Latimer, however, was most pointed in his rejection of that system. His mind focused on the old arguments of the Lollards by contrasting the excessive attention given to images with the poverty of Christ's faithful—the thirsty, the cold and the wretched.[30]

With the desire to reform apparent faults in the ceremonies of the Church, the Convocation went on to draw up the Ten Articles which were meant to be a doctrinal exposition of God's Commandments

28. Hugh Latimer, *Sermons and Remains*, ed. G. Corrie (Parker Society: Cambridge University Press, 1844–45), pp. 233, 333. *Sermons*, pp. 23, 55.

29. David Wilkins, ed. *Concilia Magnae Britanniae et Hiberniae* (London, 1737), III, p. 805. On the conflicting sides within the Convocation, see the discussion in Thomas Fuller, *The Church History of Britain* (London, Thomas Tegg, 1842), II, p. 75f.

30. Latimer, *Sermons*, pp. 36–37.

and "divers other matters touching the honest ceremonies and good and politic orders." Though ostensibly the work of Thomas Cranmer and Thomas Cromwell, these articles were perhaps influenced by Luther's Wittenberg Articles of the same year and became the first official English declaration of Protestant ideas.[31] The Articles also exhibit the Erasmian idea that religion can be understood according to the essential and nonessential. Only three sacraments (Eucharist, Penance, and Baptism) were explicitly discussed as true or "essential." Frequent distinction was made between "articles necessary to our salvation" and "certain other honest and commendable ceremonies, rates and usages now of long time used . . ."; the latter were expendable.

The sixth article in the ten prohibits the idolatrous worship of images, but advocates their use in a correct and proper way: "as laymen's books to remind us of heavenly things." Conversely, the idolatrous use of images lay in worshipping them and in imagining them instrumental in way of redemption or intercession. Article ten, on the other hand, is equivocal and vague on the doctrine of Purgatory—thus implying its continued acceptance for the time being.[32]

These articles were the legal and official representation of the government's position for the next seven years. As such, they reflect not only a doctrinal foundation that is Protestant in premise, but in end result, would be a blow to men committed to the practices and ceremonies of the medieval church.[33]

Archbishop Cranmer was encouraged by the success of the Ten Articles to pursue further a Protestant policy. Though he now tolerated images that were "reformed" and "unsuperstitious," time would show his complete rejection of them all. Religiously, images and other trappings were graphic embodiments of what Cranmer considered superstition in the Church. They were the props that supported doctrines of purgatory, devotion to saints and the impetus for relics and pilgrimage. It was important that they be abolished at the

31. Tjernagel, *Henry VIII*, pp. 165f., argues this influence.
32. C. Floyd, *Formularies of Faith Put Forth by Authority During the Reign of Henry VIII* (Oxford: University Press, 1856), pp. 13–14. Compare the Ten Articles with the Wittenberg Articles (Tjernagel, *Henry VIII and the Lutherans*, pp. 284–86, articles xvi and xvii). See Latimer, *Sermons*, pp. 93, 357.
33. On the effectiveness of the Six Articles of 1539, see below, p. 79n113.

same time the ideas they represented were anathematized. Politically, these same images, Roman Catholic in identification, were thought to be disruptive of the unity of religion which the government considered crucial to the peace of the realm.

The Ten Articles of 1536 were implemented by a series of royal injunctions carried out by commissioners or "visitors" to inquire if popular obedience was enjoyed. These injunctions were, in some instances, practical commentaries on many of the ten articles. Since it was required that images and relics were not to be superstitiously followed, but exist only to remind people of the originals they represent, their destruction would follow if "abused" or halted if "unabused." Since superstition exists in the mind of the worshipper, it was not immediately clear how this practical distinction was to be made. However, since the injunctions command that only God should be looked to "for all goodness, health and grace," then there is an explicit rejection of images and relics believed to have effacious powers associated with miracles, shrines and pilgrimages ("abused").[34]

The regulation of images, however, did not cause the uniformity and absence of strife anticipated. A rebellion in the North broke out after the publication of the Ten Articles and their implementation in the first royal injunctions. As stated before, since men live more frequently through the concrete expression of ideas than they do in the ideas themselves, the rebels upheld their traditional practices against accusations of superstition.[35]

A variety of interests had called forth the Pilgrimage of Grace, as the rebellion in Yorkshire, Lancashire and the northeastern counties was called. The "pilgrims" claimed to be marching in defense of the old religion as they knew it, but economic factors such as rising rents and land taken away from pasturage supported their fears of religious change. Though the rebellion was put down, it forced the King

34. John Strype, *Ecclesiastical Memorials* (Oxford: Clarendon Press, 1822), I, i, pp. 385, 532–34. W. H. Frere (ed.), *Visitation Articles and Injunctions* (London: Longmans, Green and Co., 1910), II, pp. 1–11. Henry Gee and William Hardy (eds.), *Documents Illustrative of English Church History* (London: Macmillan and Co., 1914), pp. 269–274. Gilbert Burnet, *The History of the Reformation of England*, ed., N. Pecock (Oxford: Clarendon Press, 1863), I, p. 345. Cyril Cobb, ed., *The Rationale of Ceremonial 1540–1543* (London: Longmans, Green and Co.), pp. 63–64.

35. *Letters and Papers, Henry VIII*, VIII, 955. Letter of Dr. Layton to Cromwell.

to see the need for a fresh attempt at conciliation in religious matters.

Conciliation spelled compromise. The publication of a new formulary was decided upon in 1537 and this took the title of *The Institution of a Christian Man*. The *Bishops' Book* (as it was popularly called) was not a theological treatise, but a handbook of faith and morals based on an elaborate exposition of the Creed, Sacraments and Commandments. Despite the fact that it was a compromise (perhaps more on the side of Protestantism), Henry was disinclined to have it published under his authority or to have it sent to Parliament or Convocation. Since the King was surveying the religious moods of the nation, it was issued under the authority of the bishops who signed it and recommended it for study by clerics.

One of the authors of the *Bishops' Book* was Archbishop Cranmer. Unlike his master, Henry, he was not ruled by considerations of political-religious compromise. He hoped that the use of images, pilgrimages, and the doctrine of the saints would be determined by his own close reading of Scripture. Melanchthon's distinction between things necessary to salvation and those unscriptured adjuncts added by human institutions was clearly appealed to; corrupt practices dating from the previous three or four hundred years might then be removed from Christian observance, he urged, resulting in an English piety based primarily on Scripture.

In the face of conservative religious and political strength, however, Cranmer would not get everything he wanted. The final text of the *Bishops' Book* typifies the extent of the Reformation thus far proposed.[36] On the second commandment, the formulary emphasized that Christians are forbidden to have "any similitude or image, to the intent to bow down to it, or to worship." Bishops and preachers are urged to teach "that God in his substance cannot by any similitude or image be represented or expressed; for not wit nor understanding can comprehend his substance. . ." But a peculiar qualification follows. The formulary goes on to re-state not Thomas Aquinas's old argument that men require sensuous aids to arrive at an understanding of spiritual truths, but the claim of the Ten Articles of the previous year that such commemorative aids remind us of the pres-

36. Thomas Cranmer, *The Miscellaneous Writings and Letters*, ed. John E. Cox (Cambridge: University Press, 1846), II, p. 351.

ence of spiritual things. The former argument involves consideration of the nature of spiritual truth and could thus justify images associated with the shrines of saints; the argument of commemoration involves only the depiction of images generally associated with spiritual things. Hence the *Bishops' Book* allows pictures of God in churches:

... not that he is any such thing as we in that image do behold (for he is no corporal bodily substance), but only to put us in remembrance that there is a Father in heaven, and that he is a distinct person from the Son and the Holy Ghost...

Cranmer was greatly disturbed with this compromise that both warned against idolatry and yet, he believed, permitted the occasion for it. He attempted to undermine this justification of images by adding to the formulary that common people ought to conceive of God without any graphic representation and thus they would not need any images of the Father. This potential occasion for iconoclasm spelled, in turn, possible political turmoil and Henry crossed out Cranmer's additions.[37]

Thus the formulary forbids bowing down to and worshipping images; but it explicitly says that they are to be allowed in churches for the purpose of instruction and provocation to faith and virtue. As has been seen, this distinction was not new, but dates from the Ten Articles, if not from medieval times.

The image of our Saviour, as an open book, hangeth on the cross in the rood, or is painted in cloths, walls or windows, to the intent that beside the examples of virtues which we may learn at Christ, we may be also many ways provoked to remember his painful and cruel passion, and also to consider ourselves, when we behold the said image, and to condemn and abhor our sin, which was the cause of his so cruel death, and thereby to profess that we will no more sin...[38]

Consequently, the *Bishops' Book* should be seen as a balance between not only what the King personally desired and felt he could have under the existing need for political and religious compromise and the hand of Cranmer who sought a reformation of ceremonies that he believed were incompatible with Scripture.[39] Though the

37. *Ibid.,* p. 101.
38. *Ibid.*
39. Melanchthon, in a letter to Cranmer, questions certain inconsistencies in

Catholic doctrine of saints and commemorative images was restated, it was not through divine sanction and authority. Such adjuncts to worship were only retained and incorporated into the articles of belief because they were thought expedient and necessary to the King for religious reasons or even for purely political needs. Consequently the implication of the theory of things "indifferent" was that there was no real permanence in religious belief; what was honored today as a politically acceptable religious practice, could be discarded tomorrow as unwise. In the beginning, at least, the medieval fabric would not be attacked, but undermined.[40]

Of course, no one would disagree with the condemnation of superstitious images; the difficulty lay in drawing the line between a valid act and its abuse. As determined by the second royal injunctions of 1538 (based on the *Bishops' Book*), this decision lay with the bishop in his diocese and with the royal visitor on authority from the King.[41] In practice, however, the bishop could be as strict as his previous commitment to reform would take him. Men like Latimer and Cranmer, for instance, could use the law as an excuse to eliminate all images.

Two parties of reform within the Church of England had developed from the very beginning. The points of disagreement naturally lay in the question as to the extent reformation should be carried out in England. Those inclined towards a Catholicism without the pope

retaining the practices of Rome after having removed the pope. *Letters and Papers of Henry VIII*, XIV, i., 631. In reality, the *Bishops' Book* of 1537 was based on Melanchthon's distinction between "immutable divine law and mutable human legislation, or between what was necessary to salvation and what was merely indifferent and politically expedient." Lacey Smith, *Tudor Prelates and Politics 1536–1558* (Princeton: University Press, 1953), p. 197.

40. *Ibid.*, p. 198.

41. The second royal injunctions of 1538 speak of images as the books of unlettered men; but the threat of misuse or idolatry existed and the king feared for his subject's souls. Henry threatened the destruction of more images if they proved to be an occasion of offense to God and a danger to Englishmen's souls. Frere, *Visitation Articles*, II, pp. 34–43 (Arts. vii, x). Gee and Hardy, *Documents illustrative of English Church History*, pp. 275–81. Burnet, *History of the Reformation in England*, I, pp. 398–99. Knowles, *Religious Orders*, III, pp. 345–49. Yet see Frere, *Visitation Articles*, II, pp. 47–48 (Archbishop Edward Lee's injunctions for York in 1538) where no adoration or veneration is permitted; implicit rejection of the communion of saints. Also *ibid.*, II, pp. 57–59 (episcopal visitation of Salisbury in 1538) and II, pp. 67–69 (episcopal visitation of Ely in 1541) where the emphasis has shifted: there is no mention of the rightful use of images.

were Gardiner (Bishop of Winchester), Lee (York), Stokesley (London) and Tunstal (Durham). The other side emerged as desiring more radical changes in doctrine and discipline: Cranmer (Canterbury), Latimer (Worcester), Goodrich (Ely), and later, Ridley (in 1547, Rochester).[42]

These two respective positions can be illustrated by way of the question over images. For Cranmer there was little if any distinction between the words *idolum* and *imago*. Both led to the denial of true worship. For Stephen Gardiner, the bishop of Winchester, the distinction was an important one and helped to point out the basic difference between what is allowed to man as an aid and what is disallowed by God.[43]

Though evidence is limited, it would appear that by 1500 the use of religious images in England was frequently associated with magic and curious devotional practices. As in the eighth and ninth centuries, many popular devotions understood the image to act much in the same way the subject of petition would itself act. Representations were not only prayed through and thought to possess magical powers, but were consequently treated as relics rather than as images.[44] Though Gardiner and others would insist on such distinctions between image and idol, there were many reformers like Cranmer and Latimer who felt that even commemorative images for the illiterate were suspect because of the possibility of their becoming objects of idolatry in the form of relics.

Changes in attitude that reflect an evolution in thinking from a grudging toleration of images to their out-and-out rejection can be seen in the example of Hugh Latimer. Born in 1492, Latimer studied

42. Clifford Dugmore, *The Mass and the English Reformers* (London: Macmillan, 1958), pp. 105–06.

43. Smith, *Tudor Prelates*, p. 176. George Tavard, *Quest for Catholicity* (London: Burnes and Oates, 1963), p. 9. On the disruption of family life due to these new distinctions, see the "Narrative of William Maldon of Newington," Alfred W. Pollard (ed.), *Records of the English Bible* (London: Oxford University Press, 1911), pp. 268–71.

44. Mathew, *Byzantine Aesthetics*, p. 97. On the miraculous image which would call forth feelings and emotion, impel pilgrimages and acts of piety, see J. Kollwitz, "Bild und Bildtheologie im Mittelalter," *Das Gottesbild im Abendland*, p. 130. Stephan Beissel, *Geschichte der verehrung Marias in Deutschland waehrend des mittelalters* (Freiburg im Breisgau: Herder, 1909). Stephan Beissel, *Wallfahrten zu Unserer Lieben Frau in Legende und Geschichte* (Freiburg in Breisgau: Herder, 1913).

at Cambridge and became interested in the New Testament studies of Erasmus and in Luther's interpretations of the Pauline doctrine of justification by faith. He had rejected many of these ideas and, instead, had urged for the internal reform of the Church by ecclesiastical authorities. But after 1524, Latimer became more convinced by the doctrine of justification by faith alone and its corollary that pilgrimages, images and ceremonies would not bring men to salvation. In fact, time would show that it would be these very practices that would be denounced loudly by the future reformer.

In 1529, Latimer had urged on his listeners that the honoring of gilded saints and the Church fabric will count nothing if "works of mercy and commandments" are left undone.[45] Two years later, writing to Sir Edward Buynton with some disillusionment, Latimer regretted his past devotion to images of saints since he thought they could do him "good."

It were too long to tell you what blindness I have been in, and how long it were ere I could forsake such folly, it was so corporate in me: but by continual prayer, continual study of scripture, and oft communing with men of more right judgment, God hath delivered me, etc.[46]

In 1532, Latimer was suspected of heresy probably because, like many men, he was not certain as to what was or was not essential in religion. To his accusers, he claimed never to have preached anything contrary to truth, the decrees of the Fathers or the Catholic faith. What he does seek, he writes to the Archbishop of Canterbury, is "a reformation in the judgment of the vulgar." He notes that it is lawful to use images, to go on pilgrimages, to pray to saints, and to pray for the souls in purgatory. But these things are voluntary, he claims, and should be so tempered that the Commandments and other obligations to God which bring eternal life to those who observe them, are not neglected.[47]

And like Cranmer's sought-for reformation, Latimer looked to a necessary setting of God's house in order. He believed some aspects of religion are essential to salvation and must be retained; there are other matters that are of human origin which are not hurtful in

45. Latimer, *Sermons*, p. 23.
46. *Sermons and Remains*, p. 333.
47. *Ibid.*, p. 353.

themselves, with the reservation that these man-made trappings may actually have obstructed God's work. In fact, Latimer implies that most abuses, including abuses of images, can readily be disposed of if godly preachers would trumpet their excesses. Should this happen, their use would diminish accordingly. A year later, Latimer became more explicit.

> Saints are not to be honoured . . . dead images are not to be prayed unto; for they have neither ears to hear withal, nor tongue to speak withal, nor heart to think withal, etc. They can neither help me nor mine ox; neither my head nor my tooth . . . and yet I shewed the good use of them to be laymen's books, as they be called; reverently to look upon them, to remember the things that are signified by them, & c. And yet I would not have them so costly . . . that the image of God for whom Christ shed his blood) . . . lack necessaries, and be unprovided for. . .[48]

Latimer could argue that all false ideas about images must be eliminated before they could again be used effectively; he urged the removal of images fundamentally not on the basis of idolatry but, that being "indifferent," they can be dispensed with without loss to piety.

The claims of piety, however, did not prevail. If Henry's government encouraged Melanchthon's distinctions and tolerated Latimer's outcries for reform, its overriding concern was that changes in the English Church must be accompanied by civil harmony; the government also saw that such theological distinctions could be useful in its own search for revenue. Faced with the heavy burdens of foreign alliances at a time when the treasury was depleted, Henry frankly needed money. Consequently, the fate of English monasteries, their devotions and way of life and the images and shrines of saints they preserved would not be destroyed for reasons of Melanchthon's distinctions (or Erasmus's)—or even for Latimer's vehement accusations against them. In fact, the dissolution of the monasteries and their images would have only an indirect connection with the development of Protestantism in England.

The monasteries seemed to be the richest, if not safest, victim around. The expenses of government were multiplying, the risk of foreign invasion demanded more expenditures for the military and the uprisings against the Crown (like the Pilgrimage of Grace) cost

48. *Ibid.*, p. 233. Harold S. Darby, *Hugh Latimer* (London: Epworth Press, 1953), p. 75.

sums of money that the King did not have and which he could not extract from Parliament.[49]

If Cromwell's aim was to make the Crown financially independent by endowing it with monastic wealth, he could scarcely declare this as reason for dissolution. Consequently, when the approximately 300 smaller monasteries (incomes of less than 200 £ per annum) were dissolved in 1536, it was done in the name of the breakdown of monastic morality and efficiency. The rest of the monasteries were taken over by various methods during the following four years; their confiscation was then ratified by statute in 1539.

The suppressions could be publicly defended on good moral grounds. Wealth resulting from endowments, lands and movables was granted to the King who promised vaguely to "do and use therewith . . . to the pleasure of almighty God and to the honour and profit of this realm." Such a dissolution, it was claimed, was but a legal act of Parliament, a result of the "vice, mischief and abomination of living" of the monks themselves.[50]

Iconoclasm had been witnessed before in England but the long period of immunity from greedy kings which the plate and furnishings of English churches enjoyed during the latter Middle Ages makes the destruction under Henry VIII seem unique. Where the Norman, Angevin and early Plantagenets "primed the plate of English churches, the Tudors went far towards eliminating it."[51]

Henry's previous dissolutions (under Wolsey in 1524 and 1528)

49. G. Baskerville, *English Monks and the Suppression of the Monasteries* (London: Jonathan Cape, 1937), pp. 120f. On the political and economic situation surrounding the Dissolution, see R. B. Wernham, *Before the Armada: the Growth of English Foreign Policy 1485–1588* (London: Jonathan Cape, 1966), pp. 132–33. On the wealth of the abbeys as seen by inventories, see Mackenzie E. C. Walcott, "Inventories and Valuation of Religious Houses at the time of the Dissolution, from the Public Record Office," *Archaeologia* XLIII (1871), 201–49.

50. G. W. O. Woodward, *The Dissolution of the Monasteries* (London: Blandford Press, 1966), p. 66. Dodds, *Pilgrimage of Grace*, I, 136–37. The monastic visitors of 1535–36 emphasized in their findings (*Compendium Compertorum*) both sexual misconduct and the superstitious veneration of relics. (While the language of the surrender deeds of 1538–40 speaks of idleness, superstition and "dumb ceremonies.") Woodward, *Dissolution*, pp. 33, 51–53, 108, 118–20.

51. Oman, *Church Plate*, p. 111. Baskerville, *English Monks*, pp. 96–97, 103, 107; Woodward, *Dissolution*, p. 49. James Gairdner, *The English Church in the Sixteenth Century* (London: Macmillan, 1902), pp. 51–52, 56–57. Knowles, *Religious Orders*, III, 157–64, 470. On pre-Reformation iconoclasm, see Gairdner, *English Church*, pp. 51–57.

were really the transfer of assets from one religious body to another, without any real embezzlement of church goods. The dissolution of monasteries and movements towards suppression of the abbeys in the fourteenth and fifteenth centuries were political and economic in motivation, but differed from Henry's final suppressions in two important respects. These latest suppressions were ultimately more comprehensive in scope in that they sought to destroy the institution of monasticism.[52] But they also differed from previous suppressions in that they took place in a larger context of a struggle over basic changes in religion.

Since Henry acted as Supreme Head of the English Church, he could claim to reform Christian discipline by eliminating the monasteries as chief supporters of pilgrimages, images and superstitious cults—using here Erasmus' and Melanchthon's distinctions between the essential and inessential beliefs necessary to salvation.

Buildings being images, they could also fit into the categories of "abused and unabused" as would paintings and statues.[53] Monastic buildings were not only havens for the "superstitious" accoutrements of the medieval fabric, but were in themselves directly related to the experiences of men who saw monastic life as instrumental for salvation. When such a life proved obnoxious, it could be argued that the buildings which were constructed to maintain such lives, were also obnoxious. They could be used as quarries, transformed into a parish churches, but they could not be left to remind Englishmen of their former purpose.

An examination of the actual destruction undertaken by Henry would show that the monasteries were also discredited in the eyes of the law and of popular estimation through the discovery of superstitious images. Thus Henry's campaign would not only sweep up the

52. Roger Merriman, *Life and Letters of Thomas Cromwell* (Oxford: Clarendon Press, 1902), I, 97–98. Out of the total number of English monasteries suppressed in England, about one-third have left no trace, another one-third remain as ruins. Hamilton Thompson, *English Monasteries* (London: Cambridge University Press, 1913), p. 36. Cook, *Monasteries*, pp. 15, 262.

53. In Hampshire, a distinction was made between those buildings "assigned to remain," and those "deemed to be superfluous"—with the former being the barns, stables and other structures of practical value; the latter consisting of the church and cloister buildings. Joseph Kennedy, *The Dissolution of the Monasteries in Hampshire and the Isle of Wight* (University of London, Master's Thesis, 1953, unpublished), p. 150.

shrines of saints in abbeys and cathedral priories, but might well include those in secular cathedrals such as St. Erkenwald in St. Paul's, St. Richard at Chichester and St. Hugh at Lincoln. Royal visitation committees were sent by Cromwell to assess the church goods of the monasteries, sell some and bring others to London.[54] All buildings and ornaments were included in this assessment. In practice, it will be seen that the royal commissioners were eager and ready to pack up anything that caught their greed or fancy.

When four commissioners struck at the Abbey of St. Edmund's in Suffolk in 1536, the shrine of St. Edmund itself afforded them not merely the elimination of idolatry but the possession of bright gold as well.[55] Religious reform could be an exceptionally useful guise for lucrative depredations.

The altar will be worth taking down, but it is such a piece of work that they cannot finish it before Monday night or Tuesday morning; "which done we intend both at Hyde and St. Mary's to sweep away all the rotten bones that be called relics; which we may not omit lest it should be thought we came more for the treasure than for avoiding of the abomination of idolatry."[56]

Yet the charge given to the royal visitors was also to destroy the relics of the saints themselves. This was accomplished together with the theft of the saints' treasures. However, Cromwell's agents sometimes came too late. Many times, movable treasures had been taken or hidden by the dispossessed monks who had shrewdly read the times and had acted to save what they could. At Glastonbury Abbey, three commissioners spent a week searching for lost treasure hidden in the walling and vaults.[57]

54. As it is to be expected, very little church plate escaped either of these men, the monks' uncertain efforts, or the laity's greed. The result: "It would seem that practically none of the monastic church plate which was in use at the time of the Dissolution has survived to our time." Oman, *Church Plate*, pp. 113–19.

55. G. H. Cook (ed.), *Letters to Cromwell and Others on the Suppression of the Monasteries* (London: *John Baker*, 1965), p. 114. Knowles, *Religious Orders*, III, pp. 203–05, 268–90. G. W. O. Woodward, *Reformation and Resurgence, England in the Sixteenth Century* (London: Blandford Press, 1963), pp. 74–77. See Wilkins, *Concilia*, III, pp. 799–802, "The King's instructions to send in the true value of all the possessions of the church and churchmen." (1535)

56. *Letters and Papers, Henry VIII*, XIII, i. 401 (1538). Pollard, Wriothesley and Williams to Cromwell (St. Swithin's, Winchester).

57. H. H. Brown, *The Church in Cornwall* (Truro: Oscar Blackford, n.d.), p. 45. Cook, *Letters*, p. 243. *Letters and Papers, Henry VIII*, XIII, i, 1287.

In other instances, the inmates of monasteries tried to save what they had by denying they had it; this denial, of course, undermined the very reasons for monasteries.

Never have cause to the contrary; for your lordship shall be well assured that there is neither Pope nor purgatory, Image nor Pilgrimage, nor praying to dead Saints, used or regarded amongst us; but all superstitious ceremonies set apart, the very honour of God and the truth of his holy words, as far as the frail nature of women may attain unto, is most tenderly followed and regarded with us.[58]

Frequently neighbors took matters into their own hands when they saw their abbeys threatened. When the royal commissioners arrived in Exeter, they ordered the rood loft of the priory of St. Nicholas to be torn down. Women of the city, however, broke the door down and interrupted the destruction. Hurling stones, they pursued one man to the tower from which he was forced to leap out of a window, thus breaking a rib.[59]

More frequently, however, the people of the neighborhood made off with building materials, livestock and plate. As one who had benefited from the suppression at Hayles remarked, "[it was] there now catch that may catch."[60] The church contained so much treasure that the eager found much that was neglected by the commissioners. First the church itself was spoiled, then the abbot's lodging, dortor and frater, with the cloister and all the buildings with the abbey walls. By night and day, the greedy tore up the lead from the roof and extracted any door, window or ornament left. Even the tombs of the dead were broken and carted away.[61] The need for building materials in the area often determined whether the building was to be levelled.

This present month . . . I advertised your lordship of the length and greatness of this church, and how we had begun to pull the whole down to the ground, and what manner and fashion they used in pulling it down. I told your lordship of a vault on the right side of the high altar, that was borne up with four great pillars, having about it five chapels, which be compassed in with the walls 70 steps of length, that is 200 feet. All this is down on

58. Cook, *Letters*, pp. 215–16.
59. Baskerville, *English Monks*, pp. 156–57.
60. *Letters and Papers, Henry VIII*, XVII, 8. Cook, *Letters*, pp. 211–12.
61. Michael Sherbrook, "The Fall of Religious Houses," in A. G. Dickens (ed.), *Tudor Treatises* (Yorkshire Archaeological Society CXXV, 1959), p. 124.

Thursday and Friday last. Now we are plucking down an higher vault, borne up by four thick and gross pillars 13 feet from side to side, about in circumference 45 feet. This shall (go) down . . .[62]

At the dissolution, Sir Richard Gresham bought Fountains Abbey from the King; lead was stripped from the roof but the walls were not touched until Sir Stephen Proctor purchased the property in 1597. In building a fine house for himself (now Fountains Hall), he used the stone from the infirmary and other conventual buildings lying south and east of the cloister. What stained glass remained was also utilized. Elsewhere, parts of monastic buildings were used for the sake of economy: an arch here, a wall there, an undercroft converted into a cellar.[63]

Cromwell used the stone from the Crutched Friars for repairs to the Tower of London; the porch of St. John's was used to adorn the church of All Hallows the Great.[64] Henry granted and sold monastic houses to courtiers: Holy Trinity Aldgate went to Lord Audley, the Charterhouse to Lord North, the leper hospital of St. Giles to Lord Dudley while Lord Cobham opted for Blackfriars. Soranzo, the Venetian ambassador, wrote in 1551 of the "many large palaces making a very fine show, but disfigured by the ruins of a multitude of churches and monasteries." Those monasteries which were not converted into homes for the rich were used for the poor as tenements (St. Edmund Bury and Egglestone Abbey, figures 4, 5),[65] or as homes for Flemish weavers as with Glastonbury Abbey.

Sometimes the cost of destruction was so prohibitive that Crom-

---

62. Cook, *Letters*, pp. 138–39. John Portinari to Cromwell. This accounts for the dearth of monastic ruins in south and eastern England where there was a relatively large population and small amounts of stone. See Dickinson, *Monastic Life*, p. 138. The Benedictine cathedral of Coventry itself was dismantled and became a quarry for buildings in Coventry. Cook, *Cathedrals*, p. 313. For the building of Sandgate Castle, Henry used materials from abbeys and churches. *Letters and Papers, Henry VIII*, XIV, ii, 645.

63. Egglestone Abbey in York was also converted into a residence through the conversion of the domestic buildings. (Fig. 5)

64. Eliza J. Davis, "The Transformation of London" in R. W. Seton-Watson (ed.), *Tudor Studies* (London: Longmans, Green and Co., 1924), p. 306.

65. Nikolaus Pevsner, *London: the Cities of London and Westminster* (Baltimore, Penguin, 1957), pp. 47–48. Some of this activity should be seen in relation to the "changing pattern of English social aspirations," Jordan, *Philanthropy in England*, pp. 253f.

well was advised that it would be more profitable to leave the walls to remain as a quarry while the masonry could be sold later at a more convenient time. John Freman estimated that it would cost at least £1000 to tear down all the monasteries of Lincolnshire. His proposal was easier, if not profitable: making the church uninhabitable by destroying stairs and roofs and leaving the stones for quarry.[66]

Sometimes when the church and surrounding buildings were sold as a quarry, there was a clause requiring the owner or lessee to destroy the buildings within a certain amount of time. Cromwell probably wanted to insure that there would be no place for the monks to return should the religious climate change. "The nest had been destroyed lest the birds should build there again."[67] Then, of course, many of the agents were suitors for the townspeople who could use the monastic buildings for secular purposes. It was after stripping the church of the Grey Friars at Reading, that the people were given that building for a town hall.[68]

Church goods and domestic articles were sold at auction. Everything of value was put up for sale and it is unlikely that much remained unnoticed. The sales themselves were frequently conducted in a haphazard and disorderly way. Richard Burgoyne, auditor at the Sales at Stafford, complained that much that had been confiscated was spoiled by the manner of removal.[69]

Sometimes the commissioners superintending the sales appropriated articles for themselves; as frequently, church wardens in the vicinity of the suppressed houses would purchase fittings for their own parish churches.[70] Then there were the great dealers and speculators, like James Luson from Wolverhampton who seems to have travelled about following the sales. At the sale of the Grey Friars in Stafford, he

66. Cook, *Letters*, p. 181. *Letters and Papers, Henry VIII*, XI, 242.

67. Knowles, *Religious Orders*, III, p. 386.

68. Cook, *Letters*, pp. 200–01.

69. Francis Hibbert, *Monasticism in Staffordshire* (Stafford: J. C. Mort, 1909), p. 132.

70. C. R. Councer, "The Dissolution of the Kentish Monasteries," *Archaeologia Cantiana* XLVII (1935), p. 142. In some of the transactions, images were defaced and sold to individuals; in other instances, it is not indicated if the image was defaced. See *Life and Letters in Tudor and Stuart England*, ed., Louis B. Wright (Ithaca: Cornell University Press, 1962), pp. 266–67, 269–72.

bought the entire church and ornaments except for the lead and bells and one stone wall for £29/1/8. At Austin Friars, he purchased decorated vestments, tiles, shingles, timber, stone, glass and iron and the rood loft and statues of John and Mary.[71]

What was not taken at the moment was, at a later time, returned to; vacated buildings still possessed iron hooks, service books and building materials. If the church was levelled, attention centered on the abbot's lodging, the cloister and all the other buildings within the abbey walls. The lead was eagerly sought after at up to £4 a fodder, and the bronze abbey bells proved to be valuable prizes, eagerly sought for melting to make siege weapons. Lead was plentiful in the gutters which edged the roofs of the abbey buildings. Frequently the process of removing the roofing lead caused further destruction to the building because the roof timbers were then used as fuel for melting the lead,[72] although the more expeditious way was to burn the wood of the choir seats and rood screens that had not been sold.[73] If, as in most instances, the royal commissioners got there first, they transported the cast lead to the royal storehouses to be assessed and then sent it to the coast for export. But with the roofs gone, the churches and other buildings became victims to the eroding effects of the weather.

The most valuable treasure was carted away in wagons to the royal treasury in London. The plate and images in precious metals were melted down, some images of untoward veneration exported, and much broken up. Given the fact that very few precious objects taken at the Dissolution have remained in the royal treasury, it can be surmised that most valuable works of art were destroyed for their metal or stones. The French ambassador Marillac reported to his king that men were employed in the Tower to "coin money days and night of the silver plate obtained from the spoil of the abbeys."[74] The vestments, altar cloths, and hangings were often sold or appropriated by the royal commissioners. "Many private men's parlours were hung

71. Hibbert, *Monasticism in Staffordshire*, p. 133.
72. Woodward, *Dissolution of the Monasteries*, pp. 126–27.
73. Cook, *Monasteries*, pp. 254, 257.
74. *Letters and Papers, Henry VIII*, XVII, 415 (June 1542). A. J. Collins, *Jewels and Plate of Queen Elizabeth I. The Inventory of 1574* (London: British Museum, 1955), p. 84f.

with altar-cloths, their tables and beds covered with copes, and many made carousing cups of sacred chalices."

The stripped buildings themselves were either sold as private houses, left as churches or sanctioned as new cathedrals and colleges.[75] The large priory church of Holy Trinity, Aldgate which had been given by the King to Sir Thomas Audley, Lord Chancellor of England, was offered in trade by the new owner to the parishioners of St. Katherine Christ Church in exchange for their small church. Audley had plans to utilize this land, but upon the refusal of his offer, he offered the priory church to anyone who would tear it down and cart it away. Upon getting no takers, Audley pulled the fabric down himself. "At that time any man in the city might have a cart-load of hard stone brought to his door for six pence or seven pence, with the carriage."[76]

Many of the monastic buildings were well built of stone and thus proved convenient and safe storehouses for certain businesses. At Austin Friars, Sir William Paulet used the steeple and choir for the storage of corn, coal and other things. His son, the Marquis of Winchester, sold the tombs and monuments of the nobility, the paving stones, and whatever was left for £100; the place became a stable for horses. The King's hunting nets, tents and other equipment were stored in the churches at the Charterhouse and at St. John's, London. Under Elizabeth, this transformation quickened: Blackfriars became the home of the Revels, the Minories became an armoury and St. Mary Graces was changed into a depot for naval stores.[77]

In many instances the royal visitors came face to face with the prescriptive rights of the laity to worship in the nave or in one of the aisles of the dissolved monastic church. The laity's appeals rarely saved the whole fabric and they were often left only with what they had rights to. At Leominister, Thorney, Binham and Wymondham, only the parochial nave remains because the people in those towns already had parish churches and could not afford the upkeep of the

75. Cook, *Monasteries*, pp. 255–56 259. Many hangings reverted to the king. See W. G. Thomson, *A History of Tapestry* (London: Hodder and Stoughton, 1930), pp. 243–44.

76. John Stow, *Survey of London* (London: J. M. Dent and Sons, 1956), pp. 112, 128–29.

77. Davis, "The Transformation of London," pp. 305–06.

larger fabric. Thus the abbey churches of Bury St. Edmunds, Ciren-
cester, Abingdon and Glastonbury were destroyed.[78]

On the other hand, many churches such as at Bolton (figure 13),
Malmesbury and Tewkesbury survived because they were purchased
as parish churches.[79] At Croyland Abbey, the choir, transepts and
central tower were demolished; the western arch was left to form,
with the nave and the two aisles, a church for the town. An east wall
was made by filling in the space between the screen and the arch. At
Bolton, there had been an altar in the nave at which the tenants of
the convent had worshipped. Thus, it alone was left after the suppression.[80] The cathedral priory of Bath and Wells, on the other hand,
was offered to the city, but was declined. The fabric was stripped and
left vacant. By 1560, another owner again presented the remains to
the citizens for use as a parish church, but it was described as a
"carcase."[81]

Political reasons also motivated the government to destroy certain
shrines and relics. Henry's royal proclamation of November, 1538
had specifically removed the twelfth-century St. Thomas Becket from
the Church calendar. Once Chancellor of England under Henry II,
Becket had become Archbishop of Canterbury and had clashed with
the king over the powers of Church and State. Henry's proclamation
claimed that Becket was both rebel and traitor and that his canoniza-
tion had taken place because Becket "had been a champion to maintain [the pope's] usurped authority." Accordingly, the saint's images
were ordered removed throughout the realm.[82]

Since the shrine of Becket was included in the monastic property
of Canterbury, it was legally forfeit to the crown; since the images of
Becket had been worshipped and regarded as possessing sanctity in
themselves (hence the pilgrimages), they were all to be destroyed,
with the shrine's wealth reverting to the King. Henry could have it

78. Rose Graham, "An Essay on English Monasteries," in Geoffrey Barraclough,
Social Life in Early England (London: Routledge and Kegan Paul, 1960), p. 91.
79. Knowles, *Religious Orders*, III, p. 387.
80. A. Hamilton Thompson, "Priory of S. Mary, Bolton-in-Wharfedale,"
Thoresby Society XXX (1928–31), 1–180.
81. Cook, *Cathedrals*, pp. 312–13.
82. Paul Hughes and James Larkin (eds.), *Tudor Royal Proclamations* (New
Haven: Yale University Press, 1964), pp. 270–76 (no. 186).

both ways. The King (or Thomas Cromwell) wouldn't have to look far for a justification for the destruction of the images of a man long acclaimed for his identification with Rome and equally long declared by Lollards to be the source of superstition.[83]

Henry himself would have personally disliked any saint venerated who had called his monarch into dispute. Since St. Thomas had come to represent the autonomy of the Church threatened by the Crown, Becket's very name called up opposition to royal tyranny and could stimulate popular reaction against Henry's acts of sacrilege. The identification of Becket and Henry II in the twelfth century with that of St. Thomas of Canterbury and Henry VIII in the sixteenth century would not be missed.

Throughout the realm, Becket's name was erased from all books, his images and pictures pulled down, defaced and destroyed, his shrine looted and levelled, his relics scattered.[84] One reaction to Henry's pronouncement came from Ireland where the communicants of a parish, bearing the name of the dishonored saint, asked their bishop to tell them which of the saints should replace Becket as their patron. He replied that they should take someone like St. Paul or St. Peter. "But," asked one of them, "what if the king should banish him too out of heaven?" When another said, "Then let us dedicate our church to the Most Holy Trinity, for if anyone can keep his place, it is the Most Holy Trinity." And so they did.[85]

Erasmus had complained about the wealth of Becket's tomb, but he feared that the poor probably would not get its riches. When the shrine was raided, it was reported that so much gold was discovered that eight strong men were required to carry it out of the church.[86]

83. Davis, "Lollards, Reformers and St. Thomas of Canterbury," pp. 1–15.

84. Forty-five paintings of Becket remain today, probably one-sixteenth of the original number before the royal proclamation. See C. E. Keyser, *A List of Buildings in Great Britain and Ireland Having Mural and Other Painted Decorations* (London: Eyre and Spottiswoode, 1883). See also Wilkins, *Concilia*, III, pp. 847–48. In the church of East Stoneham, an image of Becket was made into a female saint in obedience to Henry's decree. Tancred Borenius, "Some Further Aspects of St. Thomas of Canterbury," *Archaelogia* 83 (1933), 182.

85. Nicolas Sander(s), *The Rise and Growth of the Anglican Schism* (1585) (London: Burns and Oates, 1877), p. 143.

86. Erasmus, *Colloquies*, p. 70. ("The Godly Feast"), 1522. Burnet, *History of the Reformation*, I, pp. 387–88. C. E. Woodruff, "The Financial Aspects of the Cult of St. Thomas of Canterbury," *Archaeologia Cantiana* XLIV (1932), 21–25.

A more graphic description of what awaited the despoilers is taken from an anonymous Italian's account during the reign of Henry VIII:

But the magnificence of the tomb of St. Thomas . . . is that which surpasses all belief. This, notwithstanding its great size, is entirely covered over with plates of pure gold; but the gold is scarcely visible from the variety of precious stones with which it is studded, such as sapphires, diamonds, rubies, balas-rubies, and emeralds; and on every side that the eye turns, something more beautiful than the other appears. And these beauties of nature are enhanced by human skill, for the fold is carved and engraved in beautiful designs, both large and small, and agates, jaspers and cornelians set in relieve, some of the cameos being of such a size that I do not dare to mention it. . .[87]

Erasmus's fears about Becket's tomb were realized. The rich shrine of Walsingham which he had ridiculed in *A Pilgrimage for Religion's Sake*, was also despoiled of its wealth along with other shrines like Ipswich and Islington, their images sent to London to be burned and the shrines themselves desecrated and levelled.[88]

The shrine of Edward the Confessor at Westminster Abbey posed different problems for the royal government. Commissioned by Henry III in 1241, it was a larger coffer with saddleback roof and of "purest gold, precious stones," and decorated with images. Because Edward was a symbol of royal power, Henry was loathe to move against it. Though still a saint's image, it remained also a royal one and its destruction could not be tolerated. A compromise was established: its ornament was stripped off, its relics scattered, but the shrine was kept.[89]

87. C. A. Sneyd (ed.), *A Relation of the Island of England about the year 1500*, p. 30. A. P. Stanley, *Historical Memorials of Canterbury* (London: J. M. Dent, 1906), pp. 250–51.

88. John Williams, *Account of the Monastic Treasure Confiscated at the Dissolution of the Various Houses in England* (Edinburgh: Abbotsford Club, 1836). This is an account book and inventory compiled by one Williams, "master-treasurer of the Jewels" to Henry VIII. It lists the loot from each house. Charles Wriothesley, *A Chronicle of England During the Reigns of the Tudors (1485–1559)*, ed. W. W. Hamilton (London: Camden Society, 1875), I, pp. 83–84. Strype, *Ecclesiastical Memorials*, I, i, p. 389 (surrender of the Abbey of Grey Friars at Reading, 1536); Wilkins, *Concilia* III, p. 840 (Commission for taking down St. Richard's shrine at Chichester). Fowler (ed.), *Rites of Durham* (1593), p. 102. Battiscombe, *The Relics of Saint Cuthbert*, pp. 80–90 (on the destruction of St. Cuthbert's shrine at Durham).

89. Hall, *Mediaeval Pilgrimage*, pp. 181–82. On the gain from the shrine, see

If much destruction was the result of economic and political factors in the guise of religious reform, honest attempts at ferreting out superstition were also factors in English iconoclasm. Thus it was that the humble image of St. Anne at Buxton in Derbyshire, long revered for its claim of possessing healing powers, was taken down and destroyed along with the valueless crutches, sheets and shirts that had been left behind as offerings.[90]

Frequently the royal commissioners ran into images that were so tainted with popular superstition that their confiscations would seem to be justified. These poor relics of bone, cloth and hair journeyed with both silver and gold; the former were destroyed and the latter melted down. So Dr. Layton, a visitor, could write to Cromwell that Mary Magdalen's girdle "wrapped and covered with white" was being sent with "drosses of silver and gold." He even promised that Our Lady's girdle of Bruton, all done in red silk, which was an aid to women traveling, "shall not miscarry en route."[91]

The Cistercian Abbey of Boxley in Kent had long been noted for its famous Rood of Grace. This was a remarkable crucifix that had inspired pilgrimages and devotions because of its miraculous power of movement: "For he was able, most cunningly, to nod with his head, to scowl with his eyes, to wag his beard, to curve his body, to reject and to receive the prayers of pilgrims."[92] In 1510, the young Henry VIII had visited the rood and had made his offering.

During the dissolution of the Abbey, Geoffrey Chamber, a royal visitor, wrote Cromwell that in pulling down the monastery and its images, he discovered that the venerable Rood of Grace contained "certain engines and old wire" that caused the eyes and lips of the corpus to move.[93] When the Rood was brought to London, John Hilsey, the Bishop of Rochester, preached against it at Paul's Cross

---

the inventory of 1520. J. Perkins, *Westminster Abbey* (London: Oxford University Press, 1938–52), III, 203–04.

90. Cook, *Letters*, pp. 113.

91. Cook, *Letters*, pp. 39–40. *Letters and Papers, Henry VIII*, XIII, ii. 719.

92. Letter of John Hoker, minister of Maidstone to Bullinger, May, 1538, in G. C. Gorham's *Gleanings of a few Scattered Ears* (London: Bell and Daddy, 1857), p. 17. On the Rood's history, see William Lambarde, *A Perambulation of Kent* (London: Baldwin, Cradoch and Joy, 1826), pp. 205–08. M. Maclure, *The Paul's Cross Sermons* (Toronto: University Press, 1958), p. 30.

93. Cook, *Letters*, p. 144. *Letters and Papers, Henry VIII*, XIII, i, 231.

in 1538. The crucifix was made of wood and paste, but had concealed wires which, in manipulation from the rear, could move its parts.

> Then when the Preacher began to wax warm, and the Word of God to work secretly in the hearts of his hearers, the wooden trunk was hurled neckover heels among the most crowded of the audience. And now was heard a tremendous clamour of all sorts of people;—he is snatched, torn, broken in pieces bit by bit, split up into a thousand fragments, and at last thrown into the fire; and there was an end of him.[94]

It was reported that the King hardly knew whether to "rejoice at the exposure or to grieve at the long deception."[95] Nevertheless, Henry's zeal against superstition did not lead him to punish the abettors of such deception. No one was punished: the abbot and monks of Boxley were merely pensioned off.[96]

Henry even seems to have felt a particular devotion to Our Lady of Walsingham. In the early years of his reign, perhaps in the hope of a son and heir, Henry had walked barefoot from Barsham Manor to the shrine (a distance of two miles) and had made his offerings. At the same time, records indicate that he ordered a candle be burned there continually. After the birth of a prince in 1511, he paid another visit; his offerings were renewed after the infant's death. But Henry was only doing as so many English monarchs had done by paying their respects to the shrine, making gifts and extending rights for favors received and expected. Nobles and commons had emulated their example and soon the road to Walsingham had been filled with pilgrims who quickly made it the most famous shrine of Our Lady in England.[97]

Erasmus has described how the shrine appeared early in the six-

94. Gorham, *Gleanings*, pp. 17–19. C. Hopper (ed.), *London Chronicle During the Reigns of Henry the Seventh and Henry the Eighth* (Westminster: Camden Society, 1859), p. 11.

95. *Letters and Papers, Henry VIII*, XIII, 348 (1538). John Hoker to Bullinger.

96. See Aymer Vallance, *Greater English Church Screens* (London: B. T. Batsford, 1947), pp. 10–12, for a full account of the Rood of Grace with the suggestion that the royal visitors might have exaggerated the contrivances to produce a more damaging case against the monks.

97. Hall, *Mediaeval Pilgrimage*, p. 122. J. C. Dickinson, *The Shrine of Our Lady of Walsingham* (Cambridge: University Press, 1956), p. 42. Philibert H. Feasey and Henry Curties, *Our Ladye of Walsingham* (Weston-Super-Marne: Walters, Clatworthy and Co., 1901), pp. 24–25.

teenth century. It was a small chapel with narrow door, only illuminated by candles and, of course, by the glitter of jewels, gold and silver. The shrine of the Holy Virgin stood somewhat in the dark to the right side of the altar: "a small image . . . of no extraordinary size, material or workmanship, but in virtue most efficacious."

But what had taken centuries to build could quickly be destroyed (figure 14). In 1535, before the royal injunctions of August, 1536, an inquiry was made into the shrine and its holdings. This was probably in preparation for the confiscation that was soon to take place. The questions were detailed as to the value of the offerings, the relics there, what miracles had taken place, the history of the house and statue, whether Our Lady's Milk (a relic) was liquid or not.

By July 25, 1536, a letter to Cromwell from one of his agents reported that the shrine's money, jewels and movables had been confiscated.[98] The claims of economic gain were intimately tied to the campaign against superstition. Only a little later, Hugh Latimer could write to Cromwell that the great shrines and images of Worcester, Penriee, Ipswich, Doncaster and Walsingham "would make a jolly muster" burning in Smithfield.[99]

Latimer was a man who, as has been seen, was not content merely to speak out against images. In August of 1537, he ordered the statue of Our Lady of Worcester in the priory of St. Mary to be stripped of its garments. When the lady was naked, she proved not to be a madonna at all, but an unidentified bishop of Worcester. To one Thomas Emans, this made no difference at all, "Though Our Lady's coat and jewels be taken away from her, the similitude of this is no worse to pray unto . . . than it was before." Witnesses claimed, however, that he also said, "Ye that be disposed to offer, the figure is no worse than it was before, and the lucre and profit of this town is decayed through this . . . Lady art thou stripped now? I trust to see the day that they shall be stripped as naked that stripped her."[100]

Emans was committed; Our Lady along with some of the most venerated pictures and statues of England journeyed the road of hu-

---

98. *Letters and Papers, Henry VIII*, XI, 165; III, i, 1376. Hall, *Mediaeval Pilgrimage*, pp. 124–25.

99. Latimer, *Sermons and Remains*, p. 345.

100. *Letters and Papers, Henry VIII*, XII, ii, 587.

miliation and despair to arrive in London to be destroyed as superstitious and idolatrous.[101]

In 1538, the abbot of Hayles in Gloucestershire wrote to Cromwell
for permission to destroy the shrine purporting to hold a relic of
Christ's blood. It was known throughout England as the Holy Blood
of Hayles and had been presented to the house in 1270. Despite the
fact that there was little monetary value in question, Cromwell sent
the Bishop of Worcester, Hugh Latimer, to look into the matter.
This prelate found the relic to be an "unctuous gum, and a com-
pound of many things"—doubting that it was even blood.[102]

The whole investigation is interesting in that it shows Cromwell's
zeal did not always vary in proportion to the value of the image.
Though he desired his share of loot, reform of the church still clothed
his purpose and certainly, if not always, justified his actions.[103] By
Cromwell's order, the relic was sent to London to be exposed by
Bishop Hilsey, "to be no blood, but honey clarified and colored with
saffron."[104]

In the long run, however, there was no lack of willing destroyers
of the medieval fabric. Everything of value was "either spoiled, carted
away or defaced." Popular iconoclasm could take many forms, for
most of the destruction sprang from a wide variety of motivations—
profiteering, political associations, religious reform, even caprice.
Stated intentions and convictions frequently vanished to reveal the
coalescence of divergent purposes.[105] Iconoclasm is as complex as the
making of the Reformation of which it is a product.

Thirty years after the Suppression, one Michael Sherbrook asked

101. *Chronicle of the Grey Friars of London*, ed. J. G. Nichols (London: Camden
Society, 1852), pp. 54–55. Wriothesley, *Chronicle*, I, pp. 80–81. Allan G. Chester,
Hugh Latimer, Apostle to the English (Philadelphia: University of Pennsylvania
Press, 1954), p. 131. Hopper, *London Chronicle During the Reigns of Henry VII
and Henry VIII*, p. 13. St. Uncumber, nevertheless, survived and can be seen at
Westminster Abbey.

102. Cook, *Letters*, p. 207.

103. *Letters and Papers, Henry VIII*, XIII, ii, 707–710; Latimer, *Sermons and
Remains*, p. 407. Yet see Merriman, *Life and Letters of Thomas Cromwell*, I, pp.
174–75. And *Letters and Papers, Henry VIII*, XIII, ii, 401–02, where the agents did
away with relics to allay suspicion of greed.

104. Wriothesley, *Chronicle*, I, p. 90. See *Ibid.*, I, pp. 75–76, where twenty years
previously, the abbot of Hayles was reported to have said about the holy relic,
"Tush, thou art a fool, it is but a duckes bloode."

105. See below, p. 3f.

of his father (who had bought various materials from the Abbey at Roche) if he thought well of the religious orders and the religion then practiced.

> And he told me Yea: For said He, I did see no Cause to the contrary: Well, said I, then how came it to pass you was so ready to distroy and spoil the thing that you thought well of? What should I do, said He: might I not as well as others have some Profit of the Spoil of the Abbey? For I did see all would away; and therefore I did as others did.

In the final assessment whether the abbeys taught superstition or true religion, "all was one: for all was Fish that came to the Nett."[106]

The reformation that Henry VIII set into motion came about through secular and dynastic motives; it appeared also, however, as a manifestation of religious change and reform. Sympathetic to projected Erasmian reforms in religion, Henry created a concrete situation wherein the medieval church, its images and devotions, were undermined.[107] Thus the net effect of his settlement lies less in his specific programs of reform, than in the implications of these programs. For the Henrician settlement was an Erasmian one which could attract both Protestant and Humanist for a variety of different reasons. One result of Henry's program was to allow the pragmatic affairs of the state to determine church policy; self-interest to pursue policies that undermined both the theology and the ceremonies of the medieval church. This was to be a legacy that would outlive both Cromwell and Henry.

For instance, images were classified according to whether they were worshipped ("abused") or merely taken as a sign of remembrance ("unabused"). Did the king insist on this dichotomy because of a special favor for those elements of his father's faith? Or did the king read the realities of political-religious life and wish to leave behind some of the medieval ceremonies of the Church? If the second possibility is true, then perhaps Henry recognized the wisdom of a patient reformation and made such distinctions to allay both those who wished to retain images and those who prayed for their destruction.

---

106. Dickens, *Tudor Treatises*, p. 127. On the authorship of this treatise, see *ibid.*, pp. 28–29.

107. The latest biography of Henry calls his desire for reform, "Erasmian." Scarisbrick, *Henry VIII*, pp. 246–50.

Foxe reports an event in 1546 that suggests the latter design. Cranmer, as Archbishop of Canterbury, sought further reformation of what he felt were corrupt practices still within the Church. Apparently the King was amenable for, among other things, both decided to allay superstition through the suppression of vain ceremonies such as covering images and creeping to the cross on Good Friday.

But Henry soon changed his mind. Stephen Gardiner, Bishop of Winchester, had been sent to France to try to arrange a league between the Catholic monarch, Charles V, Francis I, and his master, Henry. The King feared that the success of his diplomatic plans might be jeopardized by further religious innovations. For this reason, he instructed the primate to wait for a "more apt and convenient time."[108]

The alliance never came to be; Henry died soon after and the paper printed by Foxe suggests what might have happened had Henry's plans come to fruition.

And thus much touching the end of king Henry, who is he had continued a few months longer ... Most certain it is, and to be signified to all posterity, that his full purpose was to have repurged the estate of the church, and to have gone through with the same, so that he would not have left one mass in all England.[109]

We shall never know Henry's true intentions on the matter of ceremonies, saints and images. At times the King seemed willing to trade religious doctrine for diplomatic security; in other instances, he insisted upon technical theological distinctions that showed keen regard for the religious issues at stake. Yet a possible key to his character was his allegiance to the old faith that was spelled out in terms of the formal, external practices he had known as a child.[110] Perhaps as in the dissolution of the monasteries, the king's own feelings were not clear and his program was worked out piecemeal by others. Yet his was not the desire to punish those who had duped others through images, nor were he and his agents so scrupulous that they sought to

108. Foxe, V, pp. 561–64. See also Cranmer, II, pp. 415–16, and Lacey B. Smith, "Henry VIII and the Protestant Triumph," *American Historical Review* LXXI (1966), 1257–58, 1264, and Scarisbrick's treatment, *Henry VIII*, pp. 467–468.

109. Foxe, V., pp. 561–64.

110. Scarisbrick, *Henry VIII*, pp. 248–49, 403–20, 473–75. L. B. Smith, *Henry VIII* (Boston: Houghton Mifflin, 1971), pp. 100–101.

destroy a shrine before taking the money. In Lincoln Cathedral there were the three shrines of St. Hugh, St. John of Dalderby and Little St. Hugh. In 1540, the first two shrines were destroyed and 6,906 ounces of silver (along with various jewels) journeyed to the royal treasury. The shrine of Little St. Hugh was without wealth and allowed to remain until the Civil War.[111]

Likewise, Henry VIII did not permit the destruction of St. Winefrede's Wall, a shrine near Chester to which pilgrimage was frequent. Perhaps because his grandmother, Margaret Beaufort, had built its chapel, he decided not to destroy it, but merely to farm out the right to collect its revenue from pilgrims.[112]

Nevertheless, whatever Henry's personal feelings were, their net effect was to thwart the influence of the conservatism of Gardiner and the Catholics and to lay a ground work of Protestantism that was to endure.[113] The last nine years of his life showed Henry retaining Cranmer as "the bulwark of his claim of religious supremacy" and Gardiner "to serve the purpose of his concerns in international diplomacy."[114]

What was left of the medieval fabric by the early sixteenth century continued to have its rare champions in men like Thomas More and others. Yet their defensive, traditional arguments were in the wake of a profound theological onslaught by men like Tyndale and Erasmus. These reformers spoke out against the human incrustations to divine commandments and ridiculed the folly and excess of the universal church. Reformers like Hugh Latimer could justify their icono-

111. Wall, *Shrines of British Saints*, pp. 137–39.
112. Hall, *Mediaeval Pilgrimage*, pp. 34–35, 39, 41. Archbishop Laud will later convince the Privy Council to destroy the devotional articles at the shrine; the image of St. Winifrede was not disfigured until 1637.
113. The Six Articles proved ineffective. The so-called Catholic reaction of 1539–49 has been greatly over-emphasized by historians and points more to diplomatic needs than to religious change. Tjernagel, *Henry VIII*, pp. 194–204, 211–27, 234. Haller has commented, "Towards the end of his reign, Henry made as though to arrest the revolutionary process he had started, and better men than he in his entourage tried to maintain the old stabilizing doctrines and practices; but it was too late . . ." William Haller, *Foxe's Book of Martyrs and the Elect Nation* (London: Jonathan Cape, 1963), p. 21.
114. Tjernagel, *Henry VIII*, p. 213. Whether this was due to a temporary diplomatic manoeuvre or reflects a dalliance with Protestantism, see Dickens, *English Reformation*, p. 194. Smith, "Henry VIII and the Protestant Triumph," pp. 1237–64.

clasm by way of the grievous effects imagery had on public morality. Men became idle through devotion to the madonna and the saints; with their removal, it was hoped, men would turn to good works, or as Latimer writes, "from ladyness to godliness."[115]

In turn, Melanchthon's distinctions between things indifferent (contingency in religious matters) and things eternal (immutability of God's law) became the mask which veiled the political and economic encroachments of the government. Both Henry and Thomas Cromwell could legally redistribute the wealth of the monasteries and supervise the destruction of the physical fabric of the Church. Their religious policies were frequently determined by the exigencies of the moment, by the changes in Parliament and popular sentiment aggravated by the needs of the royal treasury. One consequence of the collision as well as collusion of these divergent forces was the beginning of the destruction of the physical fabric of the medieval church in England.

The heirs of Lollardy also saw that with these new attacks on the medieval fabric, a new martyrology would become necessary—one that would consistently reflect new needs for new men. In 1536, John Bale wrote a play against Thomas Becket who was seen as the chief agent of papal power in the England of Henry II. Bale aimed at not just an attack, but by "taking over enemy territory and using enemy ammunition" to create new saints in place of the ones about to fall. In 1544, Bale published a history of John Oldcastle, one of the leading Lollards, wherein he contrasted the "false myracles, erronyouse writtynges, shrynes, relyques," of the papists, with those "godlye and valeaunt warryours" who had given their lives fighting for the cause of Christ against Anti-Christ.[116] It was in the same context that the royal arms of Henry replaced the holy rood; the legal government of England not the Church would be arbiter between old and new, abused and unabused religious practices.

The growing iconoclasm witnessed under Henry also suggests the

---

115. Latimer, *Sermons and Remains*, p. 403.
116. Margaret Aston, "Lollardy and the Reformation: Survival or Revival," *History* XLIX (1964), pp. 149–70. On Bale and a discussion of his plays, see David Bevington, *Tudor Drama and Politics* (Cambridge: Harvard University Press, 1968), pp. 97–105; S. Anglo, *Spectacle, Pageantry and Early Tudor Policy* (Oxford: Clarendon Press, 1969), pp. 267–69.

emergence of a profoundly new attitude towards salvation. Thomas More and other Catholics had clearly seen that the Church's traditional teaching on justification by faith with predispositions of contrition and charity was threatened by Protestant beliefs that salvation had been "won by Christ; it had only to be accepted in faith, it had no longer to be achieved."[117] This doctrine of justification by faith alone would come to shake the whole theological, ethical, liturgical and aesthetic foundations of Rome's sacramental system with its ideas of Heaven, Hell and Purgatory, its elaborately developed doctrines on works and indulgences, its support of monastic spirituality and pilgrimages.

With growing emphasis on Christ as sole mediator between God and man, English piety would in time cease to be expressed through the Virgin Mary and the saints, in tangible signs and ceremonies. Sacraments would be reduced from seven to two; the pulpit would supplant the altar. The Roman liturgy would be radically changed so that nothing forbidden by Scripture would be allowed in worship.

Concomitantly, biblical stories would replace the legends of saints and their images. No longer would the English Church conceive of itself in terms of tangible continuity strengthened in unity and achieved by charity as sign of its authenticity. Under Henry, but especially during the reign of Edward, the Church will come to be defined as a congregation of those with faith in Christ; the ideals of simplicity, order and fidelity to Scripture will replace the significant and yet tangible signs and images of the Roman rite.

In perspective, much of the iconoclasm that did prevail was of the sort which reflected no sustained plan, no general religious reform— but the very human motivation that could be gentle as well as fierce, grasping as well as religious. In the long run, then, the King's personal sympathies are unimportant. Even if Henry retained his belief in the Mass as sacrifice, priestly celibacy, images and ceremonies, the substance of Catholic doctrine to sustain them was gone. English reformers were looking to Edward VI and further reformation.

117. Horton Davies, *Worship and Theology in England, 1534–1603* (Princeton: University Press, 1970), pp. 17f.

IV. IMAGES ATTACKED

In the face of such shape and weight of present misfortune, the
voice of the individual artist may seem perhaps of no consequence than the whirring of a cricket in the grass; but the arts
do live continuously, and they live literally by faith; their names
and their shapes and their uses and their basic meanings survive
unchanged in all that matters through times of interruption,
diminishment, neglect; they outlive governments and creeds
and the societies, even the very civilizations that produced them.
They represent the substance of faith and the only reality, they
are what we find again when the ruins are cleared.

KATHERINE ANNE PORTER, *Flowering Judas and Other Stories*

H ENRY VIII had profoundly disturbed the traditional workings of
the English Church and in so doing, as we have seen, had undermined the uses of religious images. He had not left a strong new
religious settlement in its place; the tendency toward Protestantism
was clear to many, but the sympathies and religious hopes of the king
had proven confusing.

With the new reign of his son, Edward VI, who was only a boy,
there would be various continuities and discontinuities to the religious program which had been sketched out before Henry's death.
Amidst the shifting politics that followed, some points of differentia-
tion over images can be seen.

The Henricians like Bonner and Gardiner still favored the late
king's distinction between abused and unabused images. These categories had stemmed, of course, from Melanchthon's further dichotomy between scriptural commandments necessary to our salvation
and human additions that could be dispensed with at any time.
Since it had been argued that images, pilgrimages and relics all partook of the latter category, then Henry's government might allow
them or do away with them depending whether they were superstitiously employed (abused) or simply "reminders" (unabused).
Though the Henricians recognized that many images were misunder-

stood by their users, they felt that the correct teaching of the value of religious representations was to be preferred to their wholesale elimination.

Others, however, like John Hooper, soon to be Bishop of Gloucester, were not so tolerant; they favored abolishing everything Roman or "unscriptural" in the worship of God. Guided by the influence of Calvin, these reformers sought the complete destruction of images in England. Their attitudes towards religious images, like Calvin's, were based on a conception of God as incorporeal and invisible—thus unpredictable. When God chose to act, according to Calvin, His presence was revealed through signs such as clouds, smoke or flame. All these "afforded clear intimations of his incomprehensible essence . . . and operated as a restraint on the minds of all, to prevent their attempting to penetrate any further."[1] Corporeal representations of God were always unworthy, they argued, for they tended to reduce the fear of Him while increasing error about His attributes. Calvin and Hooper refused to accept images as one way for the spirit to reach God. Even if they were utilized as just a remembrance, images would evoke too much interest on the part of the worshipper. "Nor is it of any importance, whether they worship simply the idol, or God in the idol, it is always idolatry, when Divine honours are paid to an idol, under any pretense whatsoever."[2]

In the center (at least in the beginning) were those close to the new King, Lord Protector Somerset and the Archbishop of Canterbury, Thomas Cranmer. Both men were obligated to respect the legal Henrician settlement that accepted unabused images. Though there was much that they felt was distasteful about images, they aimed to follow a religious program that would steer a middle course: one less likely to alienate too many people.[3]

It was better to attempt such reformation in king Henry the VIII his days, than at this time, the king being in his infancy. For if the king's father had

1. John Calvin, *Tracts and Treatises* (Grand Rapids: B. Eerdmans Company, 1958), I, 97. *Institutes of the Christian Religion* (Philadelphia: Presbyterian Board of Christian Education, 1930), I, 98.

2. *Ibid.*, I, 106; *Tracts*, I, 148–49. Hence Calvin rejects the concepts of *dulia*, *latria*, etc. See *Institutes*, I, 107–08, 113–114, 131; III, 333–34.

3. Dugdale, *Mass and English Reformers*, p. 112.

set forth any thing for the reformation of abuses, who was he that durst gainsay it? Mary, we are now in doubt how men will take the change or alteration of abuses in the church. . .[4]

Somerset and Cranmer, however, were unwilling to leave these abuses for very long within the established church; though both men felt the need for caution, both (for different reasons) would soon introduce changes to the Henrician settlement.

Somerset and many of the Humanists who surrounded him had sought, in the Erasmian manner, to make of religion a purified, vital force in the state at large. These Humanists saw their true roles in applying Christian examples and classical traditions to a society whose values had undergone change. This new ideal represented an attitude emphasizing active moral qualities over the more intellectual or theological virtues. It resulted in a preference for moral philosophy and the study of rhetoric rather than theology and the study of logic. Such an affirmation would carry one, as it did Erasmus, to the struggle against religious folly and superstition in the lives of men.

In comparison with the ends of medieval society, this change in values was secular in effect rather than intent. Important questions of human activity were understood in an ethical framework (rather than metaphysical) and applied to this life (rather than the next) and gauged by reason and civil government (rather than faith and church).[5] It was a Humanism that showed little patience with images and other adjuncts of medieval worship. Images were rejected not because they were idols, but because they appealed to a "grosser" side of man—ultimately with a human folly grown rampant.

As has been seen, Cranmer also was chary of changing the legal Henrician settlement that still tolerated images of a commemorative nature. Yet it was clear to the archbishop that these same images had proved a formidable obstacle for many who sought true faith. The Jews, he believed, had preserved their faith by rejecting images and false ceremonies; so, too, the primitive Christians, for four or five hundred years, had refused to condone images in their churches.

4. Cranmer, *Miscellaneous Writings*, II, p. 416.
5. Arthur B. Ferguson, *The Articulate Citizen and the English Renaissance* (Durham: Duke University Press, 1965), pp. 140, 165–67, 271–72. H. Baron, "Secularization of Wisdom and Political Humanism in the Renaissance," *Journal of the History of Ideas*, XXI (1960), 131–50.

Cranmer believed it was Antichrist himself, the Bishop of Rome, who wrought a rupture with the past and introduced idolatry. First it was pretended that images were only to be used as a remembrance —as laymen's books; then they were worshipped.[6]

Throughout the Reformation, Cranmer had placed his trust in Scripture as the ultimate criterion for Christian belief. In matters of ceremony and the public worship of the Church, however, such things as images were variable and contingent on changing customs and needs—"the Church had the power to alter, replace, or suppress."[7] Since the early church fathers and the primitive church had apparently remained faithful to the demands of Scripture, both could be used as standards or as practical guidelines for present policy. Primitive Christianity, as Cranmer saw it, was really Christianity freed from the accretions of Rome; oral traditions, added ceremonies and practices like the use of painting and sculpture had evolved as the church evolved.[8]

Despite his legal reservations, it was clear to Cranmer that images were so tainted with idolatry that they ought to be eliminated in England. He said as much when he addressed Edward at his coronation.

Your Majesty is God's Vice-regent and Christ's Vicar within your own dominions, and to see, with your predecessor Josias, God truly worshipped and idolatry destroyed, the tyranny of the Bishops of Rome banished from your subjects, and images removed.[9]

Such words were taken as an invitation to destruction which, in turn, encouraged further arguments in favor of iconoclasm.

Like Cranmer's, these arguments inevitably included the contrast between God's Commandments which all Christians are obligated to obey and man's willful ways which would seduce him from truth. Many agreed with Catholics that the authority of God's will for-

6. Cranmer, op. cit., II, 176–79 (to the rebels of Devon who sought the return of the old religion in 1549). See Dr. Nicholas Udall's answer to the same article in Nicholas Pecock (ed.), Troubles connected with the Prayer Book of 1549 (Westminster: Camden Society, 1884), pp. 165–68.

7. Cranmer, op. cit., II, p. 55. G. M. Bromiley, Thomas Cranmer, Theologian (New York: Oxford University Press, 1956), p. 25.

8. George Tavard, Holy Writ or Holy Church (London: Burns and Oates, 1959), pp. 219–20. George Tavard, The Quest of Catholicity, a Study in Anglicanism (London: Burns and Oates, 1963), pp. 15–16.

9. Cranmer, op. cit., II, 126–27.

bids all worship of images, but English reformers refused to accept Thomas Aquinas' distinctions between veneration and worship.

Essentially, Scripture remained the criterion by which most images were condemned. The second commandment was mulled over, enlarged upon and finally dissected into three parts. The first demands that one should in no way represent God in any graphic or sensuous way. The second forbids the honoring of such representations; while the third shows that there is no need to portray God by images, man's worship being essentially spiritual.[10] If the reformers did not always use Scripture in their attack, they could as well draw upon a vast body of ancient literature of the Fathers (particular favorites being St. Augustine and Origen) or the proceedings of the Councils—especially the Council of Constantinople.[11]

In so many of these tracts, which were frequently pastiches of such authorities, there is a clear feeling of disgust about man-made objects of beauty. Bishop John Hooper of Gloucester was particularly offended with the prospect that art contrived by man could teach anyone anything about God.

Oh! blasphemous and devilish doctrine, to appoint the most noble creature of God, man endued with wit and reason, resembling the image of the everlasting God, to be instructed and taught of a mute, dumb, blind and dead idol![12]

God is the supreme artist and we should contemplate his handiwork in the things of this earth; Hooper objects not to the materiality of man-made objects, but to the fact they were created by man. It was

10. Henry Bullinger, *The Decades*, ed. Thomas Harding (Parker Society; Cambridge: University Press, 1849–1852), I, 222–37 (dated 1587). John Bradford, *Writings*, ed. Aubrey Townsend (Parker Society; Cambridge: University Press, 1848), I, 152 (1562). Thomas Rogers, *The Catholic Doctrine of the Church of England*, "An Exposition of the Thirty-Nine Articles," ed. J. J. S. Perowne (Parker Society; Cambridge: University Press, 1854), pp. 221–23 (1579).

11. Nicholas Ridley, "A Treatise on the Worship of Images," *Works*, ed. Henry Christmas (Parker Society: Cambridge: University Press, 1854), pp. 81–96. Origen, Clement of Alexandria, Tertullian and, in fact, most writers up to the middle of the fourth century decried the use of art in the Church. Origen, *Contra Celsum* (Edinburgh: T and T Clark, 1911), pp. 480–87; Edward James Martin, *A History of the Iconoclastic Controversy* (London: SPCK, n.d.), pp. 18–24. The so-called Council of Constantinople of 754 A.D. was really only a synod; it condemned all images as idols; it, in turn, was condemned by the Council of Nicaea II in 787 A.D.

12. John Hooper, *Early Writings*, ed. Samuel Carr (Parker Society; Cambridge: University Press, 1843), p. 39. "A Declaration of Christ and his Office, 1547."

argued that these contrivances could not be comparable either to God's beauty or that of the natural world. Hooper would allow preachers to teach "unto the senses" but this could be done by illustrating the Resurrection not through man-made images, but "by the grain of the field that is risen out of the earth and cometh of the dead corn that he sowed in the winter."[13]

Since living man is greater than his picture, God is greater than his image. What is particularly objectionable for most of the reformers is the lack of veracity which the artist puts into the holy image:

The forme is nothing but the skill and draught of the craftsman, proportioning a shape not like unto Christ whom he never sawe, but his owne fancie leadeth him . . . and in that case you worshippe not the similitude of our saviour, but the conceite of this maker. The workeman is ever better than the worke; for so much as there is no grace in the image which came not from the carver. And since no man boweth to the workman why should you kneele to the work of his handes?[14]

Despite the urgency of these arguments, the government thought it more politic to move slowly. Henry had left the established religion in a period of transition; it did not at all follow, however, that the government needed to define church doctrine at this time. It was in the reforming party's interest to tolerate the initial religious confusion over what was "essential" in religious matters that prevailed at Henry's death so that in time, it could be correctly directed. Obedience rather than definition was required.[15]

Whatever the new order was to be, however, was not only up to Cranmer and Somerset. Religious forces had been unleashed that could not be contained because of the efforts of men who desired to push beyond the point that England's present leaders were willing to go. Though monasteries had been eliminated, the Henrician Church had still retained many of the trappings of the old order. Things had changed so fast that most people did not know what they

13. *Ibid.*, p. 46 (1547). See also Roger Hutchinson, *Works*, ed. John Bruce (Parker Society; Cambridge: University Press, 1852), pp. 11–12 (1550).

14. Thomas Bilson, *The True Difference between Christian Subjection and Unchristian Rebellion* . . . (Oxford, 1585), p. 557. See also Joseph Hall, *The Works*, ed. D. A. Talboys (Oxford: University Press, 1837–1839), IX, p. 349 for a seventeenth-century version.

15. A. F. Pollard, *England under Protector Somerset* (London: Kegan Paul, Trench, Truebner and Co., 1900), pp. 91, 95, 97, 102.

were required to believe and which ceremonies they were to participate in. Little wonder that many did not wait for the government to
define the new religious establishment; they took it upon themselves
to instigate changes which often resulted in plunder and desecration
(fig. 15).[16]

Soon after Henry's death, the vicar and churchwardens of St. Martin's Church in London tore down all the statues in the church and
replaced them with the royal arms and texts of Scripture. The excuse
was that the crucifix and other images were so decayed that they fell
apart at a touch. The churchwardens confessed, however, that they
might have taken down the images through excessive zeal, for the
parishioners had complained of idolatry.[17] The government had no
choice but to reprimand the parties involved and insist on reinstate-
ment of some of the images. For despite the encouragement from
many sides for their destruction,[18] commemorative images were still
legal, as they had been under Henry. Since both Cranmer and the
Privy Council had chosen to bide their time and to retreat from overt
definition of religious doctrine, they left the reformation of abuses
to be carried out by committees of visitation. Consequently, the Edwardian government's first position on images was a redefinition of
the injunctions of Henry and Cromwell. Distinction was again made
between religious images that are sacrificed to (idolatrous) and
images that are commemorative ("whereby men may be admonished
of the holy lives and conversation of them that the said Images do
represent.")[19]

This warning was, in turn, qualified by the royal proclamation of

16. C. Sydney Carter, *The English Church and the Reformation* (New York:
Longmans, Green and Co., 1925), pp. 120–21. For this early iconoclasm in the reign
both in London and in the provinces, see W. K. Jordan, *Edward VI The Young
King* (Cambridge: Harvard University Press, 1968), pp. 145–51.

17. *Acts of the Privy Council*, n.s. II, pp. 25–27 (1547–50).

18. Helen C. White, *Social Criticism in Popular Religious Literature of the
Sixteenth Century* (New York: Macmillan, 1944), pp. 106–07.

19. Edward Cardwell, *Documentary Annals of the Reformed Church of England, 1546–1716* (Oxford: University Press, 1844), I, pp. 4–31 (articles 3, 28). See
especially "Articles to be inquired of in the King Majesty's visit," at the end of
the articles. Strype, *Ecclesiastical Memorials*, II, i, pp. 56, 72–83. A. Sparrow, *A
Collection of Articles, Injunctions, Cannons* (London, 1675), p. 2. Peter Heylyn,
Ecclesia Restaurata (Cambridge: University Press, 1849), I, p. 71. Wilkins, *Concilia*,
IV, pp. 3–8. G. Constant, *The Reformation in England* (New York: Sheed and
Ward, 1942), II, pp. 48–49.

July, 1547 which placed considerable emphasis on the possible abuses concomitant with use of images, and made some allowance for their proper use as "a remembrance." The emphasis, in the proclamation, however, lay considerably more on the inherent danger of images than on any possible benefit they might provide; in fact, continued observance of many still legal ceremonies was required though they "as yet (were) not abrogated."[20]

Royal visitations were inaugurated in 1547–48 in order to insure adherence to the king's proclamation.[21] Though the royal injunctions inevitably made distinction between images abused and images properly used, in practice it was difficult to keep these qualities separate. Not only were images, relics and maypoles forsaken and destroyed, but the pulpits were filled with men calling on their parishioners to destroy what had formerly been among the godly articles of the church.[22] In other instances, the prankster joined forces with the reformers:

There was many golden images in Wykam's colleage by Wynton. The churche dor was directly over agaynste the usher's chamber. Mr. Forde tyed a longe coorde to the images, lynkyng them all in one coorde, and, being in his chamber after midnight, he plucked the cordes ende, and at one pulle all the golden godes came downe with *heyho Rombelo*. Yt wakened all men with the rushe.[23]

The images in St. Paul's and in most London churches were pulled down and broken; many of these churches were then whitewashed. Much of the latent iconoclastic feeling of the populace bore down now on the images associated with Rome.[24] Yet the real reaction of the public towards images is difficult to determine.[25] Much icono-

20. Hughes and Larkin (eds.), *Tudor Royal Proclamations*, I, 394, 396–97, 400–01 (#287).

21. Frere, *Visitation Articles*, I, pp. 135–36; the Edwardine visitation articles of 1547 "carried out changes, which, whether they were advisable or not, were at any rate based on an arbitrary extension of visitatorial power, and made at a time when episcopal authority was inhibited." See also *ibid.*, II, pp. 103–13 (articles 18, 34); 114–30 (articles 3, 28).

22. Gairdner, *English Church*, p. 242.

23. Quoted in Maclure, *The Paul's Cross Sermon 1534–1642*, p. 42, from *Narratives of the Days of the Reformation*, ed. J. G. Nichols (London: Camden Society, 1859), p. 29.

24. On iconoclasm in Essex, see Oxley, *Essex*, pp. 150–52.

25. Jordan claims, however, that popular opinion was far in advance of the policy of the government. *Edward VI, the young King*, pp. 148–50.

clasm received tacit support owing to the passivity of the government and active support from the sermons of Bishop Nicholas Ridley at court. This eager prelate preached against pictures and seemed to encourage those who would destroy.[26]

The authorities seemed to wink at individual acts of iconoclasm. One such incident that inflamed Bishop Gardiner took place in his own diocese in the city of Portsmouth. A crowd had pulled down some images and had abused them roughly: ". . . an image of Christ crucified so contemptuously handled as was in my heart terrible—to have the one eye bored out and the side pierced!"[27] Neither the city fathers nor the military had interfered even though this clearly violated the laws of both Edward and Henry ("unabused" images still being lawful).

Gardiner was clearly upset and protested to the military authority, Captain Edward Vaughan. What circumstances in the city had produced such an unhappy event? Did the good captain think the people of Portsmouth should be instructed on the proper use of images? The question was serious, thought Gardiner since Germany had witnessed a destruction of religious images that soon had led to civil upheaval and an attack on legitimate authority.

For the destruction of images, containeth an enterprise to subvert religion, and the state of the world with it, and especially the nobility, who, by images, set forth and spread abroad, to be red of all people, their lineage and parentage, with remembrance of their state and acts. . .[28]

Gardiner argued that just as the Church provides religious instruction to the illiterate by means of images, so the state and the nobility impress upon men's minds their authority through seals and blazonry. This can be seen in the royal seal itself with St. George on one side and the king on the other.

26. Maclure, *Paul's Cross Sermons*, pp. 40–41; Jasper Ridley, *Nicholas Ridley* (London: Longmans, Green and Co., 1957), pp. 118–22. On Ridley, see his *A treatise on the Worship of Images*, supposed to have been presented to Edward VI. However, since Elizabeth was also presented with the same work, its authorship might not be his. *Ibid.*, p. 119; Foxe, VIII, pp. 701–07; Ridley, *Works*, ed. H. Christmas (Cambridge: University Press, 1841), pp. 81–95.

27. J. A. Muller, *Stephen Gardiner and the Tudor Reaction* (New York: Macmillan, 1926), p. 151.

28. Foxe, VI, p. 27. See also, Stephen Gardiner, *Letters*, ed. J. Muller (Cambridge: University Press, 1933), pp. 272–76.

Gardiner went on to claim the disrespect towards religious images produces disrespect in the attitude of lower classes towards higher authorities. Since both are attitudes of the mind, Gardiner was convinced that if the liturgical worship of the Church were to disappear, there would be a profound repercussion in political order.[29] This had been the concern of Henry (and in time to come, of Elizabeth and Charles I): religious disorders can easily merge into the political and social arena; images and their destruction therefore could come to have profound social implications.

Captain Vaughan sent Gardiner's letter on to the Lord Protector who was pointed, but polite, in his reply. Somerset claimed that the government did indeed distinguish between superstitious images and those which were not. Fundamentally, the Protector understood three kinds of images: First, the King's arms and ensigns which are honored and worshipped "after the decent order and invention of human laws and ceremonies"; second, idolatrous images which are sacrificed to superstitiously; third, images of a commemorative nature—that are used as a "remembrance."

Though Somerset fundamentally agreed with Gardiner as to images' true purpose, he ultimately judged them all adversely because of their abuses.

We cannot but see that images may be counted marvellous books, to whom we have kneeled, whom we have kissed, upon whom we have rubbed our beads and handkerchiefs, unto whom we have lighted candles, of whom we have asked pardon and help: which thing hath seldom been seen done to the gospel of God or the very true Bible. . . Indeed images be great letters: yet as big as they be, we have seen many which have read them amiss.[30]

And that is the whole problem as Somerset saw it: the difficulty of distinguishing true images from false, because false images are not merely representations of objects that do not exist. He pointed out that false images can be representations of something that actually

29. Smith, *Tudor Prelates*, pp. 230–31.
30. Foxe, VI, pp. 28–29. Gairdner, *English Church*, pp. 243–44. Strype, *Ecclesiastical Memorials*, II, i, pp. 52–55. At this time, the royal collection housed paintings of Christ and the saints. Was Somerset responsible for this collection? See W. A. Shaw (ed.), *Three Inventories of the years 1542, 1547, 1549, of Pictures in the Collections of Henry VIII and Edward VI.* (London: G. Allen and Unwin, 1937), pp. 22–23.

did exist (such as a crucifix for the Crucifixion). These religious representations have produced profound confusion in the simple through their use as devotional objects rather than as simple religious reminders; in fact, Somerset claimed, people make what they want or need out of images; far from being instructed by visual aids, they tend to idolize them and set them up as ends. An example of this confusion, he declared, lay in Gardiner's own reference to St. George on the royal seal; like many confused people, the Bishop of Winchester thought what was actually the king to be St. George.[31]

Thus it is what we make of images—their implications and their abuses that makes them idols or not. If a disturbance had taken place in Portsmouth, Somerset insisted that the bishop should have removed the cause of disturbance. Fundamentally, however, since the whole business of images has caused such dissension, Somerset declared it would be better to abolish all such religious representations and have the matter done with.[32]

Somerset's desire to abolish all images because of possible political and social dissension did support Gardiner's insistence that images had come to mean much more than the commemoration of religious events. However, the Protector's Erasmian background had not prepared him for much tolerance towards Gardiner's distinctions of abused and unabused images in the dangerous context of controversy and strife.

There be some so ticklish, and so fearful one way, and so tender stomached, that they can abide no old abuses to be reformed, but think every reformation to be a capital enterprise against all religion and good order. . .[33]

Somerset interpreted the magistrate's duty as walking the center line —not rushing into new error or doting conservativism, but a reformation of abuses without contention and strife.

31. Gardiner, however, replied to this so-called error of confusing the King for St. George. Speaking of the King's seal, he used "common language . . . after the olde sorte, when, as I conject, of a good will the people, taking Saynt George for a patron of the realme under God and having some confidence of succor by Gods strength derived by him, to encrease the estimatyon of there prince and soveraign lord, caled there king on horsebake in the feat of armes, S. George on horsbake." Muller, *Letters*, p. 289.
32. Foxe, VI, p. 28.
33. *Ibid.*, VI, p. 30.

Gardiner, obviously, was not pleased with this answer. His feelings were against an over-emphasis on preaching and he felt that all the senses should be appealed to in the act of worship.

These men [referring to the reformers] speak much of preaching; but note well this, they would we should see nothing in remembrance of Christ, and therefore can they not abide images... They would we should taste nothing in memory of Christ, and therefore they cannot away with salt and holy bread. . . . Finally they would have all in talking they speak so much of preaching, so as all the gates of our senses and ways to man's understanding should be shut up saving the ear alone.[34]

Images serve man, argued Gardiner; if correctly used, they can be kneeled before, bowed to, and censed. In his view, the image communicates to the understanding, which stirs up the mind "to consent in outward gesture of worshipful regard. . ." This is not to mean that such adoration is done to images, but to what they signify.[35] Gardiner believed that man must worship something; better it should be a respect toward religious images which engender respect towards God and king, than that disrespect which aims to destroy by refusing to give allegiance to anything but Scripture.

Feeling this way, Gardiner went himself to Portsmouth and after an inquiry could find no evidence of idolatry. Destruction of images he did find and was surprised that Cranmer did not heed the Henrician religious establishment that legally could not be changed during King Edward's minority.[36]

The situation was soon intolerable. What reason was there to issue laws that attempted to make important, but theoretical distinctions on images, when in reality, all images bore the brunt of attacks of vandalism? The feeling of Somerset was not that images were a waste of time, a distraction, or were necessarily idolatrous. He came to oppose even what Henry had allowed (unabused images) essentially because there was too much controversy over their use. Since the

---

34. Muller, *Gardiner*, pp. 126–27 (the fragment of *The Examination of the Hunter*, ca. 1544). See also, Gardiner, *Letters*, pp. 480–92.

35. Foxe, VI, p. 60 (in a letter to Ridley). Se ealso, Muller, *Gardiner*, p. 149, and Gardiner, *Letters*, pp. 255–63 (letter dated February, 1547).

36. Foxe, VI, pp. 36–37 (Gardiner's answer to Somerset). See also Muller, *Gardiner*, p. 151 and Gardiner, *Letters*, pp. 286–95. Pollard, *Somerset*, p. 112.

disputes were so venomous, the net effect was that the Privy Council, acting at a time when episcopal authority was inhibited, issued an order commanding all images to be "removed and taken away."

Writing to Archbishop Cranmer in February of 1548, the Council claimed that the royal injunctions had in some places been carried out, but in others, "strife and contention" ruled the day. "Wilful men" kept images or restored them at their pleasure whether they were "abused" or not; "further inconvenience is very likely to ensue, if Remedy be not provided in time." Peace would only exist when all images "be clean taken away and pulled down."[37]

Cranmer personally endorsed the Order of Council of February, 1548 and sent the substance of the command to his suffragan bishops.[38] The Henrician position on many matters of faith was clearly threatened. Not only had this conservative stand taken a traditional view of religious doctrine and practices, but it had centered its opposition to current religious innovations on the ground that neither the Council nor Parliament had authority to make religious changes during Edward's minority.

In June of 1548, Gardiner preached before the King and, among other things, his stand on images reveals some attempted accommodation with Cranmer and the government. He referred to images as things "indifferent," acceptable as long as they are used for their proper function. When abused, they should (if essential to salvation, like Baptism) be reformed. If they are not essential (like the veneration of images), they can either be reformed or abolished. "We had palms and candles taken away . . . but the religion of Christ is not in these exercises. . . Men must in such things be conformable."[39] The very next day Gardiner was arrested and sent to the Tower, where he remained for five years. With the chief spokesman for the Henrician position on images temporarily put to public rest, the removal of images by order of the Privy Council gained strength.

---

37. Cardwell, *Documentary Annals,* I, pp. 47–49. Strype, *Ecclesiastical Memorials,* II, i, pp. 124–25. Foxe, V, pp. 717–18. On the importance of this event, see R. Strong, "Edward VI and the Pope," *Journal of the Warburg and Courtauld Institutes,* XXIII (1960), pp. 311–12.
38. Wilkins, *Concilia,* IV, 22 (February 24, 1547).
39. Muller, *Gardiner,* p. 180.

There had been a variety of practical responses to the order of the Council. This order had not demanded destruction (though this was frequent), but simple removal of images. The vagueness of what constituted images (even given their legal removal) led to a certain vagueness in their disposition. Many compromises were evident because the thrust of the order was that images should be removed because of dissension; thus systematic removal was not demanded (for this might cause altercation), but many of the decisions were left to individual discretion and flexibility.[40]

Two kinds of response were evident: some images were simply destroyed, others were saved by parishioners and went "underground" until Mary's reign. It was believed by many that the illegality of images would last only for the life of Edward VI. His sister Mary's Catholicism augured for their future return. Then again, religious reasons did not always prevail, for practical necessities such as cost and availability of the materials saved many a monument. Most painted windows would have been destroyed or removed, but for the expense of ordering new ones of white glass to keep the wind out.[41]

Whiche ben the most profytable sayntes in the chyrche?—They that stonde in the glasse windowes, for they kepe out the wynds for wastynge of the Lyghte."[42]

Stained glass that was deemed excessively idolatrous was either destroyed or taken down and put in storage (for future patching or in readiness for a religious reaction?).[43] Then again, an examination of many parish churches shows that the so-called idolatrous parts of the windows were simply cut away and replaced with plain glass (figure 16); frequently this entailed the removal of heads or symbols of saints.

40. Frere, *Visitation Articles*, II, pp. 230–40 (art. 59), 244–45 (art. 1, 10), 266, 276, 277, 293, 296, 320. Strype, *Ecclesiastical Memorials*, II, i, pp. 355–56, 400–02. Jordan, *Edward VI, the young King*, pp. 184–87.
41. Frere, *Visitation Articles*, II, 126. J. C. Cox, *The Parish Churches of England* (New York: Scribners, 1935), p. 18.
42. Quoted in Christopher Woodforde, *The Norwich School of Glass-Painting* (Oxford: University Press, 1950), pp. 202f.
43. At the end of one churchwarden's accounts for 1549, there is the note, "It. to remember what was done wt all the old glasse of the wyndowe in the church." C. Kerry, *History of the Municipal Church of St. Lawrence, Reading* (Reading, 1883), p. 76.

Saints had been beheaded before in loyalty to their God; this was a new beheading.

Destruction, however, was frequently carried to brutal excess. Not only was the sculpture of St. Cuthbert, Wells, mutilated but projecting parts of niches were levelled and plastered over (figures 17, 18). Even small individual figures of saints, hidden on fonts and hard to find in dark places, were systematically decapitated. Doom paintings were taken from tympanic arches and destroyed—most frequently by removing the offending crucifix. The painted rood screen of Binham Priory, Norfolk was cut down and painted over with white and then covered with texts from Tyndale's translation of the New Testament (figures 24a, 24b). Since then, the older images have reappeared through both white paint and the letters.

In 1549–50, some of the bishops started to direct the removal of the high altars of stone that in many instances, contained carvings. These were replaced with wooden communion tables (figure 25). Soon the Privy Council ordered this practice to be observed throughout England.[44]

Men's needs had changed and the furniture of their churches changed accordingly. Altars for the sacrifice of the Mass were no longer to be; now the table became the Lord's board whereon men "feed upon him, that was once only crucified and offered up for us. . ."[45]

The Lord Protector Somerset was removed from power in 1550 and was replaced by John Dudley, Earl of Warwick who refused the title of protector, and claimed to be only a trusted royal councilor to Edward. This new leader also had a political attitude towards religion and saw even more that his success and advancement would lie in furthering the forces of radical Protestantism. Reform was to continue in England for all that it would owe less to popular feelings or theological convictions; instead, personal ambitions would direct religious changes that would control the fate of religious images. Warwick would eradicate the influence of the Henrician Catholics,

44. Wriothesley, *Chronicle*, II, p. 41.
45. Foxe, VI, pp. 5–6. G. W. O. Addleshaw and Frederick Etchells, *The Architectural Setting of Anglican Worship* (London: Faber and Faber, 1938), p. 28. Wilkins, *Concilia*, IV, pp. 60–61 (Ridley's visitation article for London, 1550). IV, pp. 65–66 (Council Order to Ridley to take down altars).

appoint bishops sympathetic to radical Protestantism and, in the process, secure financial advancement for himself and his friends.[46]

The order of the Council that had condemned all images was given greater effectiveness. There was passed through Parliament a bill which in its general establishment of the Book of Common Prayer, again ordered all images in churches to be removed or destroyed. Though this decree made no distinctions among types of religious imagery (all were condemned), distinction was made with respect to images as a whole.

Provided always that this act or any thing therein conteyned shall not estend to any Image or Picture sett or graven upon any tomb in any Church—only for a Monument of any King, Prince, or Nobleman or other dead person which hath not been commonly reputed and taken for a Saint. . .[47]

Iconoclasm was now law by statute. If the law did not make any distinction between acceptable and unacceptable religious images, it did emphasize a difference between religious and secular images. Church wealth would help to pay the King's debts. The issue was no longer reform, but profit and public order.[48]

Vicars and churchwardens were naturally watchful for future plunder; many hastened to sell their vestments and plate not only for fear of further confiscation, but also for general expenses to the church fabric.[49] Then, in December of 1547, Somerset ordered inventories to be made of all remaining church ornaments. The express purpose was to save them "from the greed of certain wealthy men and prevent their alienation and sale."[50] Much church wealth was sold off by

46. Dugdale, *The Mass and English Reformers*, pp. 141–44.

47. *3–4 Edward VI, c. 10.* Strype, *Ecclesiastical Memorials*, II, i, 288–90.

48. John Hooper, *Later Writings* (ed. Charles Nevinson) (Parker Society; Cambridge: University Press, 1852), pp. 129, 143.

49. *1 Edward VI, c. 14*; all along, countless images were secretly exported to France for sale. This explains perhaps the reason why so many English carvings are known on the continent. Yet there is no real evidence that they were sent either before or after the Reformation. *Calendar of State Papers, Foreign* (1547–53), 237. Letter from Sir John Mason to Council, 10 Sept. 1550. *Proceedings of the Society of Antiquaries* XXXI (1918) 57–62; XXXIX (1917) 1–27 (for English carvings in Spain). *Archaeological Journal* XXVII (1920) 192–206 (in Denmark and Iceland). *The Antiquaries Journal* XII (1932) 302–03 (in Holland). *Ibid.*, V (1925) 55–62 (in Germany). *Journal of British Archaeological Association* (1948) 1–12 (in France).

50. Constant, *Reformation in England*, II, 154. Even the royal treasury was tapped. Before 10 February 1549, general stock was taken of ornaments from the

churchwardens before the arrival of the King's agents. The profits were used for various purposes—with the remodelling of church buildings to meet the requirements of the new communion service and the purchase of new accessories receiving some attention.[51]

It was after Somerset's fall that confiscation became general. To meet the government's pressing debts and to build up a needed reserve, Warwick (Duke of Northumberland after October, 1551) could look to neither monastic lands nor chantries; bishops' lands, however, were plundered and the coinage was debased. Then, in March of 1551, the fears of many vicars were realized. The government decreed that all the remaining wealth of the churches in the form of gold and silver plate, jewels, vestments and church furniture were legitimate resources to pay off royal liabilities. Neither religious reform nor the wickedness of the clergy was referred to, but merely, the king "had need presently of a masse of money." Accordingly, on that date, commissions were appointed "to take into the King's hands such church plate as remaineth to be employed unto his Highness' use."[52]

These commissioners traveled up and down England taking inventory and seizing what was left in the much-abused churches. Their work was interrupted by the young King's death in 1553, but their inventories still exist. Though these records cannot be considered an exhaustive survey, they do reveal what little remained officially in the churches.[53]

---

royal chapels that were considered unseemly. By 3 March, crosses, chalices, cruets, and other church furniture left by Henry (more than 16,000 oz. of plate) were removed from the Jewel House. Collins, *Jewels and Plate*, pp. 90–91.

51. For a discussion of Warwick's assault on ecclesiastical property, see W. K. Jordan, *Edward VI: the threshold of power* (London: George Allen and Unwin, 1970), pp. 386–401.

52. *Acts of the Privy Council* III, N. S. (1550–52), 228. Gairdner, *English Church*, p. 305. Pollard, *Somerset*, p. 270.

53. *The Edwardian Inventories for Bedfordshire*, eds. F. C. Eeles and J. E. Brown (London: Longmans, Green and Co., 1905), pp. xviii–xxi. *The Edwardian Inventories for Huntingdonshire*, eds. S. C. Lomas, T. Craib (London: Longmans, Green and Co., 1906). *Edwardian Inventories for the City and County of Exeter* Beatrix F. Cresswell (ed.), (London: Longmans, Green and Co., 1909). *Edwardian Inventories for Buckinghamshire*, eds. F. C. Eeles and J. E. Brown (London: Longmans, Green and Co., 1908). Cardwell, *Documentary Annals*, I, pp. 110–13. *Acts of the Privy Council*, III, (1550–1552), pp. 104, 109, 148, 154, 228, 263, 467. See Constant, *Reformation*, II, pp. 144–56 for the plunder and distribution of church goods. *English Church Furniture, Ornaments and Decoration*, ed. Edward Peacock (London: John Camden Hotten, 1866), pp. 212–23 for manuscripts relating to the

Since the dissolution of the monasteries, many of these parish churches had experienced penury and distress. Throughout the 1540's, they were falling into ruin not only because there was little money to repair them, but because the physical fabric of the church was now a fair object for plunder. The government had demanded plate to pay its debts, royal commissioners had stolen what they could and parishioners were tempted to sell privately whatever they might filch or annex.[54] The bishops were ignored and the Church treated much like a bureau of the state: to serve and be plundered at will. Perhaps it is no wonder that destruction was so virulent at this time; iconoclasm had by now lost much of its religious significance and had come to include considerable confiscation and blatant greed.

Consequently, the underlying motives for Edwardian iconoclasm were different in kind from Henry's position of reform; while it is true that Henry recognized that unlawful iconoclasm spelled a danger to the political settlement, it was perhaps more important that his distinctions over images were based on some genuine need for religious reform.

In the beginning, Somerset and Cranmer had respected Henry's distinctions and were committed to defending the religious settlement bequeathed by the late king. However, situations had changed with the growth of Protestantism under Edward. Certain political necessities revolving around the question of order, and the changing opinions of powerful people close to the king, resulted in greater incidents of iconoclasm which eventually led to government plunder. Somerset's motives are less clear than Cranmer's, but it can be seriously questioned whether the Protector would have wished to keep even so-called commemorative images.

The reign of Edward VI saw a more systematic destruction of images than hitherto had been seen in England. This could happen because, on one hand, Henry VIII's tidy distinctions between abused and unabused images were proven misleading, untenable and were, in practice, swept away; on the other hand, much Edwardian iconoclasm

---

confiscation of church goods in Lincolnshire (in the Public Record Office). Strype, *Ecclesiastical Memorials*, II, ii, pp. 15–16, 208, 210–11; H. B. Walters, *London Churches at Reformation* (London: SPCK, 1939), pp. 11, 19.

54. Walters, *London Churches*, pp. 7–8.

resulted from the fact that the control of the government had fallen to men who, through a variety of practical reasons, were sympathetic to Protestantism and further reformation.[55]

By the time Edward died, in 1553, the churches of England were no longer the receptacles of medieval splendor they once had been. Though in the next reign they were to gain respite from depredation, their earlier condition would never be seen again.[56]

55. Jordan argues that the great majority of confiscated church wealth was "transmitted into social ends and uses which made of England a more fitting dwelling place for Christian men." Jordan, *Edward VI, the threshold of power*, p. 401.

56. See *Churchwardens' Accounts of the Town of Ludlow in Shropshire* (Westminster: Camden Society, 1869), pp. 33-52, for one example.

V. IMAGES RETURNED

The question is not between God's house and His poor: it is not between God's house and His Gospel. It is between God's house and ours.

JOHN RUSKIN, *The Seven Lamps of Architecture*

AT EDWARD'S DEATH, England was neither ardently Protestant nor Catholic. Mary, the new Queen, came to power not because of a great Catholic revival but because she was Henry's legitimate daughter. When Parliament met in October of 1553, it repealed the laws and injunctions of Edward and Henry and restored, in name, the liturgy and ornaments of the Roman Catholic Church. But Parliament would not repeal the royal supremacy established by Henry and enjoyed by Edward nor would it allow for the restoration of church lands and property.[1]

Mary herself was in a dilemma. To officially recognize the plunder of church wealth under Henry and Edward would be tantamount, in her eyes, to giving implicit approval to a wrong done to God Himself. Yet Mary wished for such a restoration of ecclesiastical wealth in order to insure, as well as to hasten, the return of the physical fabric necessary for the Catholic liturgy. Shrines, images and relics were not, in Catholic eyes, merely a collection of adjuncts to God's service, but were important manifestations of religious doctrine and practice. At the same time, however, the new Queen recognized the economic and political implications in this desired restoration that would conceivably endanger the order of the realm. Those who had gained from the plunder of churches in previous reigns were not about to release their profits.[2]

Though Mary could not undo the past, she moved to improve a situation made desperate by the actions of Warwick late in Edward's

1. Conyers Read, *The Tudors* (London: Oxford University Press, 1936), p. 128.
2. Knowles, *Religious Orders*, III, p. 422. There was some attempt to return church goods by court action, but it was completely unsuccessful. A. G. Dickens, *The Marian Reaction in the Diocese of York* (London: St. Anthony's Hall Publications, 1957), Part II, pp. 19–21.

reign. The statute of 1553 that repealed the general Edwardian settlement also forbade the defacing and spoiling of altars, crosses and
crucifixes.[3]

The Queen issued royal articles respecting the uniformity of religion, but she had no royal visitation. This power was returned to the
bishops who undertook inspections of their own dioceses.[4] Scripture
lessons, which had been painted on church walls to replace religious
imagery during the reign of Edward, were now washed off; the royal
arms which had been substituted for the holy rood by the Edwardian
commissioners were taken down. This last ornament of Protestant
ascendancy had especially irritated Catholic reformers who claimed
that Protestants had thrown down the arms of Christ (the cross) and
had substituted the arms of the king (three leopards and three lilies,
a serpent and a dog). Some insisted that this was a declaration that
Protestants worshipped not the Lord God, but the Lord King.[5]

The Marian bishops, in their articles of visitation, required the
setting up of a "decente roode of five fote in length at the lefte with
Marie and John, and the patroon or 'hedde' sainte of the church,
proportionate to the same." In order to insure permanency, it was
added that such images were not to be painted on cloth, but made of
timber or stone.[6] Accordingly, rood lofts, screens, crucifixes, images,
vestments and images were all to be returned and set up in their
former places. Church furniture and ornaments that had been condemned under Edward, were taken from hiding.[7]

3. *1 Mary c. 2* (1553). (The Queen's first proclamation on religion is reprinted
in Cardwell, *Documentary Annals*, I, pp. 114–17.) See also, *1 Mary c. 3.* and Strype,
Ecclesiastical Memorials, III, i, p. 83.

4. Frere, *Visitation Articles*, I, 143; II, 322–29.

5. Nicholas Sander(s), *Rise and Growth of the Anglican Schism* (1585) (London:
Burns and Oates, 1877), p. 172.

6. Wilkins, *Concilia*, IV, pp. 145–48. See the visitation articles of Cardinal Pole
in his inspection of Canterbury diocese in 1557. *Ibid.*, IV, p. 170 (art. x). We have
no record of the administration of these injunctions. We may, however, discern
their operation in Archdeacon Harpsfield's visitation of 1557. Here the standard
questions about ornaments and furniture, rood with Mary and John are asked.
The church fabric and accessories are frequently described as "ruinous," *Catholic
Record Society*, XXXXV (1950).

7. Bond and Camm, *Roodscreens*, I, p. 103. Wilkins, *Concilia*, IV, p. 108. Frere,
Visitation Articles, II, p. 320, 354–55. Strype, *Ecclesiastical Memorials*, III, i, pp.
333, 477–87. Commissions of inquiry were also established to investigate the embezzlement of church goods during the late Edwardine inventories. See *Edwardian
Inventories for Bedfordshire*, pp. 17–39.

Many of the Marian preachers took to contrasting the return of the Catholic Church to the disorders of the previous reigns. The chaos and ruin of the churches' physical fabric was matched, it was claimed, only by the indifference of Englishmen.[8] These preachers were not inclined to examine the theological justification of iconoclasm. They publicized the malice and mischief that they believed had been crucial to the success of Protestant attacks. Hugh Glasier, chaplain to Queen Mary, for instance, made no distinction between vandalism and religious iconoclasm; like others, he proved completely unsympathetic to the Erasmian arguments of things "indifferent" and to Cranmar's arguments based on Scripture, both of which, in part, underlay iconoclastic attacks. In ignoring the religious impetus to iconoclasm, Glasier could quite rightly claim to be focusing on some of the real reasons for iconoclasm: the greed and mischief of men. In a sermon preached at Paul's Cross in August of 1555, he thought it "a great shame for so many [Englishmen] to lie in bed, and sit upon cushions, made of the church stuff, for the which ye have payed, either little or nothing at all," while the churches of England stood naked and bare.[9]

The response of Marian preachers like Glasier to the attack on the role of images in the life of the Church did not result in a re-examination of these adjuncts, but simply in a demand for the return to the familiar trappings of the Catholic Church. Though images might spell popery to Protestants, to Catholics they suggested proper and decent respect in worship. Accommodation was out of the question and images soon began to reappear in churches.[10]

The medieval need for sensuous aids in worship was predicated on the assumption that images were essential to the understanding of divine mysteries. Bishop Bonner, in his visitation of London in 1554, claimed that the purpose of holy water was to remind individual Christians of their own baptism and the shedding of Christ's blood

8. Henry Pendleton, "Homily of the Authority of the Church," quoted in J. W. Blench, *Preaching in England in the Late Fifteenth and Sixteenth Centuries* (Oxford: Basil Blackwell, 1964), p. 280.

9. Sparrow Simpson, *St. Paul's Cathedral and Old City Life* (London: Elliot Stock, 1894), pp. 178–79.

10. Cardwell, *Documentary Annals*, I, 168–70. *Churchwardens' Accounts of Ludlow*, pp. 52–88. What happened in Essex was particularly noteworthy. See Oxley, *Essex*, pp. 188–91.

upon the Cross "and also to put him in remembrance, that as he washed his body, so he should not forget to wash and cleanse his soul, and make it fair with virtuous and godly living."[11]

Bonner also repeated the arguments of Thomas More that such images are only signs or memorials of Christ and his saints and that all reverence made is not done to the materiality of the image, but to its prototype, the purpose of all adjuncts in worship being their ability to stir up love and devotion in the communicant. When a Christian kisses the Bible, Bonner insisted, it is not for love of the ink and paper, but for its thoughts which kindle the heart.[12] The Marian clergy agreed with Thomas More that natural and man-made objects of this world exist to buttress the faith of Christians; abuses associated with these things do not invalidate their power for good.

And who so will be saved, there must he begin his work; not that those [ceremonies] do give salvation, but that the contempt of those bringeth damnation; not that those give us that light, whereby we seek for to see Christ and his benefits in his churche, but the same do rather blind those eyes, wherewith Eve saw the apple to her damnation: which were her eyes corporall, and the eyes of her natural discourse and understanding.[13]

Bonner and other prelates were also prepared to reiterate the old distinctions between idol and image. Basically, this difference lay in the prototype represented; in the case of the idol, its original is false, i.e., religiously untrue. The true evaluation of the second commandment, they claimed, results not in God forbidding us to make images, but in a prohibition against transferring God's honor to objects as such. Ultimately, images possess a greater power than Scripture for convincing individual Christians of the mysteries of faith: "they are

11. Quoted in Francis Bond, *Chancel of English Churches* (London: Oxford University Press, 1916), p. 255. On the visitations of Bonner, see Cardwell, *Documentary Annals*, I, p. 152; Frere, *Visitation Articles*, II, pp. 330–59 (articles 54, 57, 61, 105); 360–72 (articles 18), 424. On Pole's metropolitan visitation of Lincoln, see Strype, *Ecclesiastical Memorials*, III, ii, pp. 389–413. William Schenk, *Reginald Pole, Cardinal of England* (London: Longmans, Green and Co., 1950), pp. 142–58.

12. Edmund Bonner, *A profitable and necessarye doctrine, with certayne homelyes adoiyned thereunto* (London, 1555), no pagination. An answer to this treatise is found in John Bale, *A Declaration of Edmonde Bonners Articles, Concerning the cleargye of London Dyocese* (London, 1561).

13. Strype, *Ecclesiastical Memorials*, III, ii, 503. (Pole's sermon to the citizens of London in behalf of religious houses).

most apt to receive light that are more obedient to follow ceremonies, than to read."[14]

In addition to these religious reasons, images were also defended by the Queen and her bishops, because they had become identified with the Catholic Church now restored in England. Protestants had attacked images as being unscriptural and confusing to men; religious iconoclasm had brought about public disorder. No wonder that the Marian clergy had come to believe that a clear understanding of the kinds of worship practiced by Christians was an important factor in preserving the very same public order now threatened. If Thomas Aquinas' discussion of *dulia* and *latria* was again appealed to, it was not only to clarify the proper reverence shown to relics and images. Tied up with such distinctions was Gardiner's argument of iconolatry as one support for the basic harmony of society: "Also with this honour of Dulia we honour our Parents, Superiors, and all revered persons."[15]

Consequently, it was Mary's policy to bring back the ceremonies and adjuncts of the medieval church, and to initiate a policy of reconstruction of the churches that had suffered during the reformation of England's religion. The despoiled churches themselves were reminders of the victory of Protestantism over Roman Catholicism in the reign of her half-brother, Edward.

Even given this royal desire, there were practical as well as theological obstacles to the return of images. Many churches had seen too much neglect or destruction in the past two reigns. The priory church of St. John of Jerusalem, for instance, had been used under Henry as a storehouse for the King's "toils and tents, for hunting, and for the wars, etc." Under Edward VI, the main part of the church with the bell tower had been blown up; some of the stone remaining was then used as building material for the Lord Protector's house in the Strand. Under Mary, part of the choir and some side chapels were salvaged.

14. *Ibid.* Bonner, *A profitable and necessarye doctrine*, section on the second commandment.
15. Laurence Vaux, *A Catechisme of Christian Doctrine*, 1583 (Manchester: Chetham Society, 1885), ed. by Thomas Grave, p. 26. Under Mary, Vaux was warden of Manchester; under Elizabeth, he would go to Louvain and write his catechism.

It was patchwork, but the project was carried through and even some of the priory's lands were returned.[16]

Shrines had long ago disappeared in England and the queen was resolved to rebuild at least some of them. Especially extensive were her plans to restore the abbey at Westminster and in particular, the shrine of St. Edward "to some measure of its original comeliness." In 1556 Mary appointed her own confessor, John Howman of Fecken- ham to be in charge of reestablishing the Abbey. The new abbot got to work almost immediately so that the shrine of St. Edward was re- stored several months later. Such work took a considerable amount of money, time and patience: what resulted reflected the uncertain times of Mary's reign. Since the golden feretory in which formerly the saint's remains had resided was missing, the substructure of the old monument was adapted for this purpose. But since the base had been so very badly hacked away, Feckenham built a new cornice, fixed as best he could the frieze and filled many of the holes with plaster painted to imitate marble. St. Edward's remains were reinterred in a special cavity made into the substructure inself. In place of the lost feretory, he built a wooden structure with gabled roof and wain- scoted oak (figure 26).[17]

Naturally, to complete the shrine, many other alterations were necessary so that the general effect and final product of restoration was something patched and plastered, hasty and clumsy. But the intent of both Feckenham and the Queen was to bring back the devo- tions of the old religion through restoring the accoutrements of the past. The goal, as seen at least in the reconstruction of the shrine of St. Edward, was to be realized through the power and sympathy of the Crown.[18]

Furtive iconoclasm continued throughout the reign. In March 1555, the image of a bishop which had just been set up over the door of the church of Thomas of Acars, London, was "shamefully man-

16. Stow, *Survey of London*, p. 387. For some indication of how thoroughly the reformers had done their work and the projects of restoration faced by the new Catholic bishops, see Hughes, *Reformation in England*, II, 236–43.

17. W. R. Lethaby, *Westminster Abbey and the Kings' Craftsmen* (New York: E. P. Dutton and Co., 1906), p. 322. Edward Carpenter (ed.) *House of Kings, The Official History of Westminster Abbey* (New York: The John Day Company, 1966), p. 125.

18. Perkins, *Westminster Abbey*, II, pp. 78–87.

gled, the head and the right arm being clean smitten off: the which Image once before this time had the head likewise stricken off, and was afterwards newly set up"[19] and then again its stones were broken.

During one Easter service, when the priest with crucifix had proceeded from the choir to the font, a parishioner asked his companion "whether will he go with that in his arms to christen it." He was answered, "No, he will drown it." Even such seeming humor was prohibited: both men were punished in ways similar to that meted out to Lollards. They were forced to appear at the parish church without shoes and hat and with a candle to march in procession to the cross and there kneel before the altar.[20]

There were also theological problems to the return of Catholic images. The previous reigns' rejection of images and their drawing up of impossible distinctions such as "abused" and "unabused," had rendered their return most difficult. Too much had happened not to expect confusion in the people. Were idols in Edward's reign now to be called images under Mary? When Bonner questioned one young man on the subject, he received the answer: "God hath taught us what they be: for whatsoever is made, graven, or devised by man's hands, contrary to God's word, the same is an idol."[21] The reformation of an abuse had destroyed the very thing abused.

One of Marian Catholicism's greatest enemies, however, was not the confusion of the populace over the need for religious images. Confused people might well be educated, if not coerced, to accept orthodox practices. More to be feared was the influence of English reformers, who continued to give shape to a liturgy based overwhelmingly on Scripture and a theology suspicious of the arts. These Protestants who had supported iconoclasm under Edward continued to write and speak out against images as exiles in such places as Frankfort, Strassbourg and Zurich.[22] It was in particular the liturgical writings of Huldrych Zwingli that gave strength and configuration to their arguments against Mary's revival of images.

19. *London Chronicle 1523–1555* in *Camden Miscellany XIII* (London: Camden Society), p. 42. See also *Acts of the Privy Council* V (N.S. 1554–56), p. 97.
20. Dickens, *Marian Reaction in the Diocese of York*, Part II, pp. 9–10.
21. Foxe, VII, p. 108.
22. Knappen, *Tudor Puritanism*, pp. 118f. Clebsch, *England's Earliest Protestants*, p. 313.

As a follower of Erasmus, Zwingli had sought for a revival of Christianity by way of a return to an examination of Scripture, the early Fathers and the world of *bonae litterae*. Like Erasmus, Zwingli came to attack the external forms of Catholic Christianity that appeared so much at odds with the early church as he knew it.

Luther originally had sought only a spiritual reformation within the context of the then-prevailing ecclesiastical tradition. He believed that liturgies and devotions could be retained as long as they were correctly understood. Zwingli, by contrast, attacked this ecclesiastical tradition completely, and in the long run was as incapable of accepting the form of the medieval fabric as he was its substance. Because of his commitment to the humanist ideal of a *Christianismus renascens*, Zwingli could not imagine a spiritual reformation without a concomitant institutional and liturgical reformation as well.[23]

It was Erasmian Humanism to which Zwingli looked to carry out the program of spiritual renewal. And like Erasmus, Zwingli reflected upon the fundamental chasm and antipathy between flesh and spirit, this world and the next. External manifestations of religion he considered valueless because they are corporeal while the true Christianity posited itself almost wholly on the inner experience.

If ceremonies are to be retained for a time, they are to be abolished sometime. What prevents their abolition now, especially since the world is looking to this, and all the pious and learned are moving toward this. . . what evil, now, is going to befall us if the rubble of ceremonies is cleared away in its entirety, in as much as God declares that He is worshipped in vain by these things?[24]

But Zwingli's desire for reform was carried into action to a degree and with a break not foreseen by Erasmus.[25] Though recognizing the Erasmian tension between body and soul, Zwingli transferred this to a dichotomy between form and content in religion and sought what would become the absolute purity of worship. This would center on

23. Charles Garside, *Zwingli, and the Arts* (New Haven: Yale University Press, 1966), p. 36.
24. *Ibid.*, p. 39. Quoting from the *Archeteles* of 1522.
25. As evidence of his conservatism, Erasmus wrote in 1525, "The reformers turn the images out of the churches, which originally were useful and ornamental. They might have been content to forbid the worship of images and to have removed only the superfluous." J. A. Froude, *Life and Letters of Erasmus* (New York: Charles Scribner's Sons, 1844), pp. 335–36.

private prayer—the individual alone before God: What resulted as far as communal worship is concerned, would be an attempt to mirror this perfection: a liturgy exclusively scriptural in form and content.[26]

English Humanists had long shared this suspicion and contempt for the devotions and images of the medieval church. Most of these reformers had been as demonstrative as Erasmus in their repudiation of images; more were willing now to be guided by Zwingli's practical program of iconoclasm which had resulted in the Town Council of Zurich prohibiting Christians from making, setting up and revering religious images.[27] From exiles in Strassburg, Geneva, Zurich and Frankfort, these English reformers became more zealously Protestant than before. They would, in great part because of their Continental experiences, help to mould the eventual role of images in the forthcoming Elizabethan religious settlement.

Under Henry VIII, images had become identified with Roman Catholicism in the minds of Englishmen. The inevitable result of Mary's program of church renewal and the continued Protestant attack was that images were identified with a government now Roman Catholic in character. Just as heresy had become synonymous with treason, images were indelibly branded by a Roman Catholic government that could not inspire loyalty. The Marian defenders of images could not counteract the force of religious iconoclasm of the previous two reigns and its continuance in the influence of Zwingli.

The moods of Englishmen changed slowly. It is doubtful that parishioners and church wardens were willing to purchase expensive refurbishing for their churches. The religious situation had drastically changed so quickly that it is no wonder the art of Mary's reign had a temporary or makeshift appearance. Many parishes showed this skepticism as to the stability of the revived regime and the unwanted expense of providing images that later might be declared illegal by erecting painted canvas to take the place of carved figures on the rood screens.[28] At Ludlow, in Norfolk, the great rood was replaced by a makeshift painting of the Crucifixion on boards. The London church

26. Garside, *Zwingli*, pp. 35, 38, 42, 52.

27. H. Zwingli, *Hauptschriften* (Zurich: Zwingli Verlag, 1940), I 245–93; B. J. Kidd, *Documents Illustrative of the Continental Reformation* (Oxford: Clarendon Press, 1911), pp. 408–09, 427–441.

28. Brown, *Church in Cornwall*, p. 49.

of Michael Cornhill paid £8/10. for a rood with Mary and John, and 17/- for a large beam to support it. This created some problems in its erection—rollers and a crane being required to hoist it into place. When Queen Mary died, the parish was eager to sell the whole lot for 8/.[29]

The religious situation under Mary was confusing and shifting, and her reign brought not stability but additional bewilderment to most Englishmen. The Queen found that it is harder to restore than to destroy—even harder when the men one depended on to direct this restoration had neither the zeal of the iconoclast nor the direct agency of the crown. The demands of Catholic orthodoxy required Mary to return ecclesiastical powers to her bishops; the campaign to return images to English life was simply part of a larger scheme that had as its end the restoration of the medieval church and its ceremonies. The actions of Cranmer and his party in their years of ascendancy had not converted the majority of Englishmen to Protestantism. Nevertheless, they had done their job well in preparing the ground for the eventual growth and fruition of new ideas on salvation, grace and the sacraments—ideas which did not seek embodiment in painting, sculpture and architecture.

Perhaps the symbol of Marian Catholicism and the reign itself could be seen in the shrine of Edward the Confessor—patched up and supported by glass in place of mosaic, plaster in place of marble and all held together by the good intentions of the Crown. But this was not enough to create an acceptance for either Roman Catholicism or those "laudable and honest ceremonies that were wont to be used." Nor were the employment of the traditional defenses of images, the old arguments based on Aquinas and More, but voiced by Bonner, Pole and Gardiner, sufficient to create enthusiasm for the return of religious images in England.

29. J. Charles Cox and Charles B. Ford, *The Parish Churches of England* (New York: Charles Scribner's Sons, 1935), p. 17. Pendrill, *Parish Life*, p. 29.

VI. COMPROMISE

... although images should not be broken, yet the people should be carefully taught and admonished not to worship them; as indeed, many churches to this day retain images, but worship them not. However, it is much more prudent and safe to remove them altogether.

WILLIAM WHITAKER, *A Disputation on Holy Scripture*, 1588.

IN HER SHORT REIGN of 5 years, Mary had been unsuccessful in convincing Englishmen to return to the Catholic faith. Her Government's policies had clearly failed in this regard, but further estrangement that did occur was due in great part to what had preceded Mary's rule. The English Church had become so politicized and had changed so substantively since Henry VIII that a confusion bred of controversy had settled over religious practices. By 1558, many Englishmen could count as many as three changes, corresponding to the previous three reigns, in the religion of the established Church. These changes were not only of an external nature, but included basic conceptions of Christian doctrine.

During Mary's reign, some two hundred or so English divines had fled England and had come into contact with the reformed churches of Switzerland and Germany. In Zurich, Strassburg, and Frankfort, these exiled men had adopted a prayer book of utmost simplicity: versions of the 1552 Prayer Book which in the name of public order had eliminated many traditional practices as "indifferent." Further contact with continental practices and doctrines had led many of these English exiles to conclude that the second Edwardian Prayer Book still remained popish and in need of reforming.[1] It would be

1. Patrick Collinson, *The Elizabethan Puritan Movement* (Berkeley: University of California Press, 1967), pp. 45f. J. E. Neale accepts Christian Garrett's thesis that the exiles formed a "deliberate migration and then in the 1560s, a cabal." J. E. Neale, *Elizabeth I and her Parliaments 1559–81* (New York: St. Martin's Press, 1958), pp. 51f. Christina Garrett, *The Marian Exiles* (Cambridge: University Press, 1938), p. 1. As far as the effectiveness of these exiles, Michael Walzer argues that "modern politics begins in England with the return of the Genevan exiles." *The Revolution of the Saints* (Cambridge: Harvard University Press, 1966), p. 113.

upon these Marian exiles who had come into direct contact with the iconoclasm of Calvin and Zwingli that Elizabeth would depend for the realization of her religious settlement.[2] Likewise, many of these exiles looked to the new Queen to be the appropriate instrument in reforming and disciplining the Church.

When the zealous anticipated events at Mary's death, and burned and destroyed the rare objects of the past together with the somewhat more tawdry ones of recent date, they revealed feelings toward religion that Mary had not been able to erase. Even the Lord Mayor of London did nothing (though he was later rebuked) about the destruction of images, vestments and books at St. Mary-le-Bow. Public processions were attacked and frequently the cross was seized and broken.[3]

When Mary's half-sister, Elizabeth, acceded to power, she inherited a past which forced her to act in certain prescribed directions. Images had been called indifferent things, but they had come to signify much that was both political and religious in England. Elizabeth had inherited both these associations as well as a general confusion as to what constituted an unabused image. The future role of religious images in the Church, if not their actual fate, would be determined by the Queen's response to the present context tempered by her own thinking on the matter. But what was her view of religious images?

When Elizabeth returned to Westminster Abbey for the opening of Parliament after her coronation, she was greeted by the abbot and the chapter who were clad in full canonicals bearing torches, incense and holy water. Elizabeth's reaction was significant for it spelled to many the impending doom of the Marian liturgical order. "Away with those torches, for we see very well."

As has been clearly indicated in previous reigns, any religious settlement contemplated by the Queen could not be considered outside a discussion of the political needs of the state. Like Somerset before her, Elizabeth sought reformation less than peace and uniformity. Her preference might have been for some form of Henrician

2. Of the eight communities of exiles, there were about 800 exiles of whom 67 were clergymen and 117 theological students. Two exiles became privy councillors of Elizabeth, 16 became bishops (among whom were Cox, Grindal, Horne, Jewel Sandys).

3. *Calendar of State Papers, Venetian* (1558–80), p. 84.

Fig. 2. Eye, Suffolk. Church of Sts. Peter and Paul. A reconstructed Gothic church, showing rood screen [ca. 1480]; loft and rood were erected in 1925.

Fig. 3. *Above.* Shrine of St. Edmund (British Museum, Harley 2278, fol. 4v).

Fig. 5. *Opposite.* Yorkshire. Egglestone Abbey. Houses to north of altar, looking south. In 1548 the site was granted to Robert Strelly, who probably converted the domestic buildings into a residence.

Fig. 4. *Below.* Bury St. Edmunds, Suffolk. The abbey church; ruins of the western front. After dissolution in 1539, the monastic buildings were quarried; later the ruins were adapted for dwellings. (Engraving: I. Kendall, 1787. From the copy in the Map Room of the British Museum.)

Fig. 6. *Above.* Monmouthshire. Tintern Abbey. Interior of church, looking east.

Fig. 7. *Opposite.* Monmouthshire. Tintern Abbey. Exterior of church, looking west.

Fig. 8. *Above.* Yorkshire. Rievaulx Abbey. North transept.

Fig. 9. *Opposite.* Yorkshire. Fountains Abbey. General view from the southwest.

ig. 11. *Above.*   Yorkshire. Fountains Abbey. Aerial view.

g. 10. *Opposite.*   Yorkshire. Fountains Abbey. Nave looking west.

Fig. 12. *Above.*　Somerset. Glastonbury Abbey, looking west.

Fig. 13. *Opposite.*　Yorkshire.　Bolton Abbey, looking south from the chancel.

Fig. 15. *Above*. National Portrait Gallery, London. *Edward VI and the Pope* (painted after February, 1548). Detail shows early acts of iconoclasm.

Fig. 14. *Opposite*. Norfolk. Ruins of Walsingham Priory. Once among the most famous of English shrines, it was built to commemorate the apparition in 1061 of the Blessed Virgin to the lady of the manor.

Fig. 16. *Below*. Great Massingham, Norfolk. Parish church; mutilated glass from the chancel showing defaced saints and the Lamb of God.

Fig. 18. *Opposite*. Wells, Somerset. St. Cuthbert's Church. Mutilated niches and recumbent figure [ca. 1470] from the south transept. The reclining figure of Jesse was surmounted by 21 niches containing figures of his descendants. All were destroyed and the projection of the niches levelled and plastered over.

Fig. 17a, *above*; Fig. 17b, *right*. Wells, Somerset. St. Cuthbert's Church. Mutilated sculpture [ca. 1450] once in the reredos, north and south transepts.

Fig. 19. Cambridgeshire. Ely Cathedral. Mutilated sculpture [ca. 1340] from the Lady Chapel showing the Life of the Virgin. The destruction was probably ordered under Edward VI.

Fig. 20. *Left.* Binham, Norfolk. St. Mary's Priory. Detail showing mutilation of octagonal font. Upper panels originally represented the Trinity, the Sacraments, and angels holding emblems.

Fig. 21. *Below.* South Cerney, Gloucestershire. Parish church. Head of Christ and stigmatized foot, all that remains of a 12th-century rood screen.

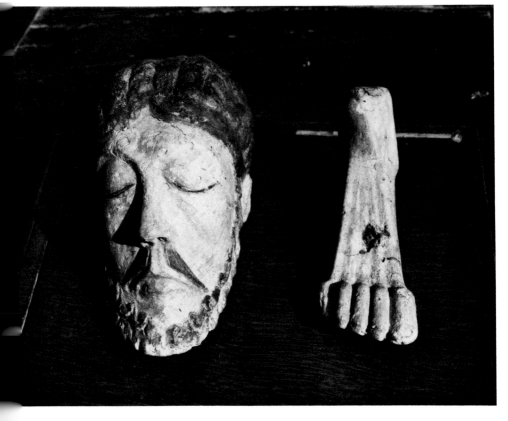

Fig. 22. Attleborough, Norfolk. Mural painting [ca. 1500] portrays Moses, David, Jeremiah, and angels holding attributes of the Passion. A large cross, taken down in 1844, was located where windows are now constructed.

Fig. 23. Wenhaston, Suffolk. Church of St. Peter. Doom Painting [c. 1500] showing the Last Judgement, once located in the tympanic arch. Unpainted areas and peg holes for attachment of carved figures show clear evidence of the rood that was removed and destroyed.

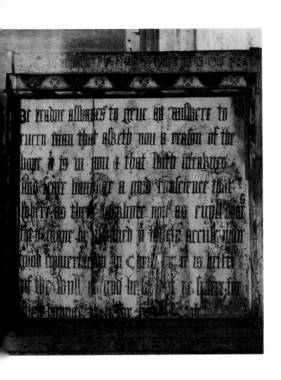

Fig. 24a. Detail of rood screen, below, in St. Mary's Priory. The original figures are reappearing beneath the lettering through the fugitive wash.

Fig. 24b. Binham, Norfolk. St. Mary's Priory. Base of medieval rood screen cut down, whitewashed, and painted over with texts from Tyndale's translation of the New Testament. The screen is now incorporated in the choir stalls.

Fig. 25. Edwardian holy table. Great Massingham, Norfolk.

Fig. 26. British Museum. Engraving [1625] by Thomas Cecill, was inspired by the cult of the Virgin Queen, and shows Elizabeth I as St. George liberating Truth from her cave by defeating the hydra of Rome.

Fig. 27. London. Westminster Abbey. Shrine of Edward the Confessor. The wooden structure atop the shrine replaced the monument that was destroyed. It is the work of John Feckenham, last abbot of Westminster, and is dated 1557.

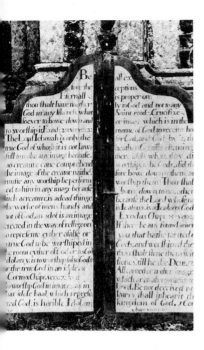

Fig. 29a. *Below.* Preston, Suffolk. The royal arms, possibly painted over a medieval triptych.

Fig. 29b. *Left.* The triptych closed, its wings painted over with the text of the Ten Commandments.

ELIZABETHA MAGNA   REGINA ANGLIA

28. *Opposite.* Tivetshall, Norfolk. St. Margaret's Church. Painting of arms of Elizabeth I replacing the tympanum Doom Painting.

Fig. 30. *Right*. Chediston, Suffolk. St. Mary's Church, showing the rails before the altar, early 17th century.

Fig. 31. *Below*. Croscombe, Somerset. Church of St. Mary the Virgin with a screen of 1612 and royal arms replacing the rood.

Fig. 32. Oxford, Oxon. St. Mary's Church. South porch added in 1637 by Nicholas Stone.

Fig. 33. London, St. Paul's Cathedral. Reconstruction of St. Paul's by Inigo Jones. (From Wenceslaus Hollar, view of St. Paul's, north prospect; from William Dugdale, *The History of St. Paul's*, London, 1718.)

Fig. 34. *Above*. Blythburgh, Suffolk. Mortices in the stone floor once contained ornamental tomb brasses.

Fig. 35. *Right*. Lincolnshire. Lincoln Cathedral. Mutilated sculpture [ca. 1280] from the Judgement Porch (south porch).

Fig. 36. Hampshire. Winchester Cathedral. Two mutilated sculptures—a headless deacon holding a book, and the head of a bishop —of the late 14th century, now in the triforium gallery of the cathedral.

Fig. 37. *Left.* Tivetshall, Norfolk. St. Margaret's Church
Mutilated bench ear.

Fig. 38. *Below.* Southwold, Suffolk. Church of St. Edmun
King & Martyr. Details of mutilated screen [ca. 1500].

Catholicism, but political instability inherited from religious controversy forced upon her a program of religious comprehensiveness: the inclusion of as many Englishmen as possible in the state church. Elizabethan Anglicanism was to become a compromise solution that insisted on outward conformity without rigorous definition of church doctrine. Insisting on a common liturgy was itself dangerous for such practices connoted specific theological positions; however, such practice was felt to be a far lesser danger in contrast to the forced acceptance of theological definition.

Given the variety and contradictions of prevailing religious views, it was hoped that common religious practices would become the bulwark of a peaceful and harmonious state. If the Roman Catholic Church had been identified with the Marian government, the Elizabethan government would be identified with an English Church that would walk a middle ground between Catholic and Protestant. The duty of outward religious conformity would become as binding as that of civil obedience.

We hold that seeing there is not any man of the Church of England but the same man is also a member of the common-wealth; nor any man a member of the common-wealth, which is not also of the Church of England; therefore as in a figure triangular the base both differ from the sides thereof, and yet one and the self-same line is both a base and also a side; a side simply, a base if it chance to be the bottom and underlie the rest. . .[4]

At the same time, Elizabeth inherited the same internal struggle between Protestants who wished to continue reform and those Protestants who wished to consolidate previous gains. The latter feared further reformation would carry England into the arms of Calvinism with the resultant abolition of traditional forms of worship, episcopacy and the Book of Common Prayer.

Elizabeth responded to this context of controversy by issuing a proclamation forbidding all innovations;[5] then in February of 1559,

4. Richard Hooker, *Works* (ed. John Keble, Oxford: Clarendon Press, 1874), III, p. 330.
5. Carl S. Meyer, *Elizabeth I and the Religious Settlement of 1559* (Saint Louis: Concordia Publishing House, 1959), p. 13. W. H. Frere, *The English Church in the Reign of Elizabeth and James* (London: Macmillan, 1904), pp. 9–10. Powell Mills Dawley, *John Whitgift and the English Reformation* (New York: Charles Scribner's Sons, 1954), pp. 46, 50, 53. John Strype, *Annals of the Reformation* (Oxford: Clarendon Press, 1824), II, i, 69–71.

Parliament revived the religious structure that existed at the death of Edward VI. The ornaments of church worship were to be those of the first Book of Common Prayer.[6]

On the matter of religious images, the Elizabethan settlement of 1559 was somewhat of a compromise between that of Henry and that of Edward. Elizabeth's injunctions were drawn up by William Cecil and his advisers, but were based on Edward VI's injunctions of 1547. The early Edwardian articles had reflected a Henrician view of images: rejection of images associated with devotion or adoration and acceptance of images only in their commemorative aspects.

Except for minor phrases and wordings, Article II of 1559 was the same as Article I of 1547.

... to the intent that all superstition and hypocrisy crept into divers men's hearts, may vanish away, they shall not set forth or extol the dignity of any images, relics or miracles; but declaring the abuse of the same, they shall teach that all goodness and health ought to be both asked and looked for only of God, as of the very Author of the same, and none other.[7]

In another article retained, Elizabeth required the destruction of all "monuments of feigned miracles, pilgrimages, idolatry, and suspicion," but added a demand that walls and glass windows be preserved and repaired (articles 23). The Edwardian article III of 1547 that had defined the "proper" use of images in terms of instruction and remembrance of Christian events, was dropped in 1559. The Elizabethan injunctions never condemned all images; only "abused images, tables, pictures, paintings..." were criticized.[8] Her government did not contribute any new insight into the problem of distinguishing, in practice or in theory, abused from unabused images.

Elizabeth's retention and exclusion of certain Edwardian views on images was consistent with her general attitude toward religious re-

6. *I Elizabeth, c.* 2 (1558–59). Heylyn, *Ecclesia Restaurata*, II, p. 302. Meyer, *Elizabeth I*, pp. 31–32, 46, 65. While clearly a compromise, the settlement was not completely to the liking of the Queen, for it forced more significant concessions from the crown than from Parliament. G. R. Elton, *England Under the Tudors* (London: Methuen, 1955), p. 247.

7. Cardwell, *Documentary Annals*, I, pp. 210–42. Frere, *Visitation Articles*, III, pp. 1–7 (articles 2, 9, 45); pp. 8–29 (articles 2, 23, 25, 35). Henry Gee, *The Elizabethan Clergy and the Settlement of Religion* (Oxford: Clarendon Press, 1898), pp. 46–65.

8. As in article 35, Cardwell, *Documentary Annals*, I, p. 226.

form. Like her brother and father before her, the Queen did not confront the thorny questions other reigns had not been able to solve. Clearly, this was the case in the distinction between "abused and unabused" images; while she allowed for the destruction of the former, she made no mention of the latter. Elizabeth desired a return to order and control of church affairs by the legally appointed officers; is it possible she feared to include any distinction between abused and unabused (as had the injunctions of 1547) because they created the very occasions of so much contention as to justify the drastic action of the Privy Council?[9]

To supplement the injunctions of 1559, Parker and other bishops issued "A Declaration of Certain Principal Articles of Religion" in 1559. These articles were intended as doctrinal and were binding until Convocation could replace or supplement them. Again, Article X of the Declaration made no mention of the proper use of images:

> Last of all, as I do utterly disallow the extolling of images, relics and feigned miracles, and also all kind of expressing God invisible in the form of an old man, or the Holy Ghost in the form of a dove, and all other vain worshipping of God, devised by men's fantasies. . .[10]

A series of royal visitations were inaugurated in the summer and autumn of 1559.[11] If the Queen had wished restraint and the cessation of illegal iconoclasm by eliminating all reference to "unabused" images, then she would learn that too much had already happened to

9. Haugaard claims that Elizabeth left out the important article three of 1547 (which explained that images could be properly used as a "remembrance") because that same article had also ordered the removal of any image which had caused idolatry in any way, thus providing the legal precedent for the Privy Council's destruction of all images. However, it should be pointed out that article 23 of 1559 required their destruction if "abused." William Haugaard, *Elizabeth and the English Reformation* (Cambridge: University Press, 1968), pp. 140–41.

10. Cardwell, *Documentary Annals*, I, pp. 263–67. This declaration continued to be used as authoritative even after 1564. The Convocation of 1563 also did not clarify the articles of faith. Yet article XXII of the 39 articles of 1563 linked images with the concept of purgatory and so rejected them along with the invocation of saints as "Romish." Edmund Gibson, *Codex Juris Ecclesiastici Anglicani* (Oxford: Clarendon Press, 1761), p. 321. E. Cardwell, *Synodalia* (Oxford: University Press, 1842), I, pp. 34–72. The wording is almost the same as Edward VI's article 23 in the 42 articles of 1553. (*Ibid.*, I, p. 11.) See also Strype, *Annals*, I, i, p. 508.

11. Cardwell, *Documentary Annals*, I, pp. 242–43, 247. Frere, *Visitation Articles*, III, pp. 76, 79, 82, 100, 104, 106. Strype, *Annals*, I, i, pp. 248, 251, 254. Frere, *English Church*, pp. 35–41. C. G. Bayne, "The Visitation of the Province of Canterbury, 1559," *English Historical Review*, XXVIII (1913), 652–53, 676.

call a halt to destruction simply through a subtle phrasing in her injunctions. The old question of what is an unabused image created an ambiguity that would give license to the populace to do more than the articles had intended.

At Bartholomew's Fair in Smithfield, at St. Paul's Churchyard and at other places, great bonfires consumed the roods and images whose presence in churches previously had been mandatory.[12] This was done by great popular support "with such shouting, and applause of the vulgar sort, as if it had been the sacking of some hostile city."[13] The government was not prepared to stop this destruction, but to temper and direct the popular movement that had inspired it. Whatever was politically desirable became the end of governmental action; tolerance of iconoclasm was one such policy. The popular mood of compliance to the royal visitations was illustrated when frequently the royal visitors commanded assistance in the burning of images in the churchyards. Many churchwardens and ecclesiastical officials, who in Queen Mary's days were responsible for the restoration of images, were now most determined to scatter and burn them.[14]

Marian sympathizers now spoke out against this new iconoclasm that clearly would result in the destruction of Catholic worship. Abbot Feckenham, who had supervised the restoration of the Confessor's shrine in Westminster Abbey, compared the current crisis with that of the previous reign. In Mary's time, law was respected for there was "no spoiling of churches, pulling down of altars, and most blasphemous treading down of the sacrament . . . there [was] no scrinching and cutting off the face and legs of the crucifix. . ." But with the coming of the new Queen, Feckenham insisted, everything is changed and "turned upside down."[15]

There was at least one reaction to current iconoclasm through an attempt to bring back the old Catholic ways. A marble figure of

12. Machyn, *Diary*, pp. 207–8. W. P. M. Kennedy, *Parish Life Under Queen Elizabeth* (London: The Manresa Press, 1914), p. 46. Wriothesley, *Chronicle*, II, pp. 143, 146. Haugaard, *Elizabeth and the English Reformation*, p. 185.

13. John Hayward, *Annals of the First Four Years of the Reign of Queen Elizabeth* (ed. John Bruce) (London: Camden Society, 1840), p. 28. Aymer Vallance, *The Old Colleges of Oxford* (London: B. T. Batsford, 1911), pp. xiv–xv.

14. MacCaffrey, *Exeter*, p. 193.

15. Abbot Feckenham in the House of Lords, *The Rambler*, VII, n.s. (1854–59), pp. 185–86.

Christ, standing in the Cathedral in Dublin, was observed to bleed through its crown of thorns; it created quite a disturbance.[16] The image was later examined and it was discovered that a sponge filled with blood had been placed inside the head that very morning. The culprit, a former monk of the Cathedral, had sought the return of images through this "miracle;" the net effect, however, was the very opposite and images continued to be associated with superstition.

Though the injunctions of 1559 did not authorize the destruction of copes, vestments, altar cloths and books, popular zeal came to give wide interpretation to the phrase of the injunctions—"monuments of superstition." They were destroyed in the general conflagration.[17] Likewise, since a workable distinction between abused and unabused images had never been published, the visitation committees also over-stepped the bounds of the injunctions by destroying tombs and images of noblemen.[18] These objects had for centuries occupied parish churches, and though they had a certain religious content, until now they had been relatively safe from destruction. Once the suspicion of idolatry filled the air and controversy dictated what was legal in art, even these largely secular images began to look suspect. Long ago, Stephen Gardiner had predicted such a turn of events; if religious images were to be destroyed, he had argued, the political order of society would be disrupted and men would come to attack even the badges and symbols of government and nobility.

While the Queen, backed by much public opinion, countenanced the destruction of monasteries, she demanded respect for the memory of the dead—even of those who had founded monasteries. In September of 1560, Elizabeth issued a proclamation against not only those who broke or defaced windows, but also against the destruction of tombs and monuments by people "partly ignorant, partly malicious or covetous." While the government could countenance the spolia-tion of religious images if popularly motivated, it felt it could not wink at acts of destruction which undermined the primary structure

16. Jeremy Collier, *An Ecclesiastical History of Great Britain* (London: William Straker, 1852), VI, pp. 250–51.
17. Wriothesley, *Chronicle*, II, p. 146. V. Brook, *A Life of Archbishop Parker* (Oxford: Clarendon Press, 1962), pp. 77–78. Strype, *Annals*, I, 254–255.
18. W. P. N. Kennedy, *Elizabethan Episcopal Administration* (London: A. R. Mowbray and Co., 1924), I, pp. lxii-lxiii.

of society. The images of the nobility, like the badges of government were guarantees of that order. Yet, as Gardiner had pointed out, the attack against religious images would indeed lead to a similar response directed against political order.

When the Queen marshalled her defense of these tombs, curiously she fell back on the traditional argument upholding commemorative religious images which, it was claimed, intend "only to show a memory to the posterity of the persons there buried . . . and not to nourish any kind of superstition." Clearly at stake was the "honourable and good memory of sundry vertuous and noble persons deceased" whose images were set up for their posterity and not for any religious honor.[19] Elizabeth, however, was unwilling to apply this argument to religious images.

The past history of ambiguity over what constituted acceptable images, coupled with the indiscriminate popular destruction of them, had its effect on the development of English tomb sculpture. Religious feelings of the wealthy no longer could be expressed in the adorning and erecting of churches, nor could even their tombs reflect their devotion through images of the Blessed Virgin or of the saints. The new tombs erected during the late sixteenth century were magnificent and sumptuous revelations of the deceased's rank and station and were adorned with the personified, abstract virtues of the departed: faith, wisdom, charity, hope. All sorts of symbolic ornaments came to be carved on tombs: Indians, skulls and crossbones, scythes, urns, weeping cherubs holding doused torches were substituted in place of the traditional Christian symbols that were every day being destroyed.[20] These changes of a conceptual nature suggest not a prog-

19. Hughes and Larkin, *Tudor Royal Proclamations*, II, 146–48 (#469). Robert Steele, *Tudor and Stuart Proclamations* (Oxford: Clarendon Press, 1924), 526. Strype, *Annals*, I, i, 279–80. For a full commentary on this proclamation, see John Weever, *Ancient Funerall Monuments* (London, 1631), pp. 54ff. For an interesting discussion on tombs, see Buxton, *Elizabethan Taste*, pp. 135–67.

Some powerful country families had tombs with religious subjects; such as that of John Lews and his wife, Agas, in Old Selsey which portrayed St. George and the Dragon and the martyrdom of St. Agatha. These tombs were not threatened if the secular power was there to protect them. K. A. Esdaile, *English Church Monuments 1510–1840* (New York: Oxford University Press, 1946), p. 25. On the other hand, Stow lists a considerable number of churches in London where the tombs and monuments of noblemen were defaced. Stow, *Survey of London*, pp. 122, 123, 205, 233–34, 286–87, etc.

20. Fred H. Crossley, *English Church Craftsmanship* (London: B. T. Batsford,

ress from religious to secular representation; rather, the character of traditional Catholic imagery gave way to a new religious imagery devoid of traditional identifications and hence safe.

The destruction of the sacred image of Christ and his saints was paralleled by the curious rise of the "sacred" image of Elizabeth the Queen. The cult of the Virgin Queen as God-ordained ruler stemmed from the continuation of the medieval ruler image with the actual religious power enjoyed by the Tudors. In place of the holy rood and other religious images now tainted and hunted down, the royal coat of arms was placed on the chancel arch. Honor toward this royal emblem, if not a kind of civic veneration, was now demanded from Englishmen, who had long been taught that respect paid to an image redounds to its prototype.[21] Again, many of the arguments justifying Catholic imagery found parallel support in the employ of royal images.

In fact, when Paolo Lomazzo's theories of art were translated into English in 1598, his translator, Richard Haydock, found it convenient, if not politic, to omit any discussion of images of God and the saints. Yet, the arguments justifying such images were not dropped but were simply transferred to a defense of the image of the ruler and the seals of the commonwealth. When Haydock omitted these references, he explained,

Here the author entreth into a large discourse of the rise of Images, which because it crosseth the doctrine of the reformed Churches, and his greatest warrent thereof is his bare assertion, I have thought good to omitte.[22]

Even if John Jewel, Bishop of Salisbury, compared the Tudor monarchs with the Byzantine emperors who officially adopted a policy of

---

1941), p. 107. Eric Mercer, *English Art, 1553–1625* (Oxford: Clarendon Press, 1962), pp. 217f. It must be pointed out, however, that funeral monuments constructed as family records predate the Reformation. Iconoclasm hastened the process. *Ibid.*, p. 221.

21. Roy C. Strong, *Portraits of Queen Elizabeth I* (Oxford: Clarendon Press, 1963), p. 39. Edward Smith, "The Doctrine of the Prince and the Elizabethan Episcopal Sermon: 1559–1603," *Anglican Theological Review*, XLV (1963), 83–92. The practice of setting up the royal arms continued from the reign of Henry VIII until the nineteenth century.

22. Giovanni Paolo Lomazzo, *A Tracte contining the Arts of curious painting, carving and building*, tr. Richard Haydock (London, 1598), p. vii, introduction.

iconoclasm as a protection against idolatry,[23] official apology for the royal image had to keep separate the differences between images of the prince and images of God: the first could not justify the second.

> Earthly similitudes of your making may not control the heavenly precepts of God's own giving. The images of Princes may not well be despited or abused, least it be taken as a sign of a malicious heart against the Prince, but bowing the knee or lifting up the hand to the image of a Prince is flat and inevitable idolatry.[24]

In the long run, however, it would seem that the Church of England successfully filled the void left by the Catholic image cult now discredited, by maintaining this sacred cult of the monarch. And since men naturally embroider the things they love, the cult of Elizabeth soon developed in curious directions. She was hailed as a Virgin giving birth to the Gospel of Christ.

> So there are two excellent women, one that bare Christ and another that blessed Christ; to these may we join a third that bare and blessed him both. [Elizabeth] bare him in her heart as a womb, she conceived him in faith, she brought him forth in abundance of good works. . .[25]

Along with this extravagant praise developed the extraordinary images of Elizabeth. She became St. George slaying the Dragon (figure 27), Woman of the Apocalypse—a heavenly figure framed by stars and accompanied by angels. Her triumph even extended over Time and Death.[26] To support this new ostentation, great festivals celebrating the Queen's birthday and accession day replaced the religious spectacles of the medieval church. The government had not minimized the importance of externals.[27]

It might be asked, however, how strong was this cult of the royal

23. John Jewel, *The Works*, J. Ayre, ed. (London: Parker Society), II, pp. 651–68. For a discussion of Byzantine imperial art replacing religious images, see Strong, *Portraits of Elizabeth*, p. 39. See also, John Beckwith, *The Art of Constantinople* (London: Phaidon, 1968), pp. 54–57.

24. Thomas Bilson, *The True Difference betweene Christian Subjection and Unchristian Rebellion* (Oxford, 1585), p. 552.

25. Diary of John Manningham, p. 152. Quoted in Strong, *Portraits of Elizabeth*, p. 42.

26. *Ibid.* This tradition was continued with the portraits of Charles I after his death. See M. Dorothy George, *English Political Caricature to 1792* (Oxford: Clarendon Press, 1959), I, 34–35.

27. R.C. Strong, "Elizabethan Pageantry as Propaganda" (unpublished University of London Ph.D. dissertation, 1962), pp. 74–75.

monarch on the popular imagination of Englishmen. The royal seal and other attributes were considered to be portraits of the Queen, and were generally regarded as emanations of royal power.[28] The reality which these portraits were understood to represent was attested by the belief that they partook of the nature of the sitter. Elizabeth's arms were defaced, her portrait slashed, dragged through the streets, consigned to the flames and even hanged by men opposed to her rule.[29]

The controversy over images in the English Church had progressed too far for Englishmen simply to substitute Elizabeth the Queen of England for Mary the Queen of Heaven. The cult of Elizabeth was a flexible symbol capable perhaps of being comprehended in many ways—for a church that needed an image of strength amidst the conflicts of the Elizabethan settlement; for a government unsure of its support; for a people who were accustomed to the externalization of their devotions.[30] The cult of the royal image was created in order to buttress public order at a time when the religious image had proven disruptive of that same order. Discovery of what constituted an abused image had never really been explored or clarified. The government's fear of disorder and unauthorized innovation deterred it from undertaking an investigation of this question, or from making a firm policy towards iconoclasts.

Though the government was loath to examine the larger question of images in religious worship, there were many English reformers who were eager to explore the implications of that question. Thomas Cranmer had insisted that the history of the Christian church had clarified the question of images; the primitive church had excluded them and only a decadent Rome had opted for their use. Cranmer had come to this view through utilization of the tools of history, the Fathers and Scripture.[31] These standards were still looked to in the controversies under Elizabeth, but they had by now deteriorated as

28. H. Munro Cautley, *Royal Arms and Commandments in our Churches* (Ipswich: Norman Adlard, 1934), p. 28ff.

29. Strong, *Portraits of Elizabeth*, p. 40. On the royal image of Elizabeth, see F. Yates, "Queen Elizabeth as Astraea," *Journal of Warburg and Courtauld Institutes* X (1947), 27–82.

30. *Ibid.*, pp. 76, 70, n. 3. The cult of the royal Virgin had its strength and continuance more exclusively in the literature of the period.

31. Bromily, *Thomas Cranmer, Theologian*, pp. 46f.

ways of discovering the truth. The primitive Christian church was now contemplated in the guise of what the reformers desired for in the present. For James Calfhill, one time Lady Margaret Professor of Divinity at Oxford, history became an instrument to justify current theological reforms and to overwhelm an opponent. He wrote a violent attack against one John Martiall who had attempted to defend the use of images by meeting the reformers on their own ground. Calfhill's response, being both scurrilous and pedantic, used authority to destroy the argument of his opponent through denying the validity of his citations or refuting his interpretations; through excessive concern with detail, the veracity of one's opponent could be put in doubt should points of fact be found lacking.[32]

Calfhill's arguments have been seen before—images being "great stumbling stones, not only to the simple, but also to such as will seem to be wiser."[33] His peculiar brand of iconoclasm (something shared by many sixteenth-century reformers) takes refuge in a type of pseudo-history which seeks to find a precedent from the past for the desired reforms of the present. However, when Calfhill finds the same method capable of justifying images, he counters by marshalling fuller and contradictory historical evidence to oppose what he has just confronted.

> But, on the other side, as you have brought but the bare name of three Councils for you, whereof there is none that confirmeth your error; so, if I bring three Councils indeed, as famous as they, which in plain words, by public and free assent, shall overthrow it, will ye be then content to give over?[34]

Another tactic of persuasion was the identification of English king with early Christian emperor. Jewel and other reformers were reminded that these emperors of the eighth and ninth centuries who

32. S. L. Greenslade, *The English Reformers and the Fathers of the Church* (Oxford: Clarendon Press, 1960), pp. 16–19.
33. James Calfhill, *An Answer to John Martiall's Treatise of the Cross* (Cambridge: University Press, 1845), p. 25.
34. *Ibid.*, pp. 137–38. Another technique of persuasion employed by controversalists was that of semantics. William Fulke reveals this method when he wrangles for four pages on the various meanings of "image" and "idol."
William Fulke, *A Defence . . . Against the Cavil of Gregory Martin*, ed. Charles Hartshorne (Parker Society: Cambridge: University Press, 1843), pp. 100–07, 179–216.

had called councils to rule the Church, could legitimize the power of the king to call national councils to govern the national Church; in turn, Tudor iconoclasm could then be regarded as a resurgence of imperial authority and reform clearly mirroring the destruction of images in the eighth and ninth centuries.[35]

Protestant reformers were convinced they were on solid ground, when, like Origen, Clement of Alexandria, Tertullian and other ecclesiastical writers, they decried the use of images in the Church. Jewel argued that images originally were employed in didactic narratives for the illiterate. What was then attacked, as today, he claimed, was what existed in practice: the growing cults of images as devotional objects. For many, images were only a reminder, a representation of the prototype; but for many Englishmen, it was one more step to the claim that the image chiefly exists to provide a ladder or channel of communication in approaching God: it ceased being simply an instructional tool, but became a sacramental one, like the Sacrifice of the Mass. The iconoclasm of the eighth and ninth centuries could, then, be pressed into service to justify the direction of the English Church.[36]

In practice, the "consensus of the Reformation" was another practical standard for reforming the Church. Negative feelings, spread from the continent, against all Roman practices and ceremonies, tended more and more to deny images any re-acceptance in England.[37] The attack against saints, their legends and relics continued most expeditiously when Calvin's *A Very Profitable Treatise* was published in English in 1561. The object of the attack, of course, was the practice of duplication of relics; but more significantly, the animus was directed against the inevitable idolatry that comes through traffic with the saints.

Catholic supporters of images returned these attacks with many of the same techniques employed by their opponents. The traditional arguments of Thomas Aquinas, More and Cardinal Pole were repeated and enlarged. One treatise that did not depend much on this traditionally stated Catholic position was Nicolas Sanders' *A Treatise*

35. Yates, "Astraea," pp. 40–41. Jewel, *Works*, II, 651–68; IV, 628f, 739–40.
36. Martin, *History of Iconoclastic Controversy*, pp. 18–24.
37. Tavard, *Quest for Catholicity*, pp. 26, 28–29.

of the Images of Christ. For him, everything in the world has both an immutable nature and a contingent substance or being (called a person). A man's nature can only be represented by a natural image "that is to say, by an other thing which taketh of him the same nature, which him self hath."

However, a man's person can be represented:

> The cause why the shape of our Persons may be represented by art, and not our natures, is, for that, the Artificer who worketh by his own knowledge, is able to conceive in his understanding, and afterward to form outwardly that proper shape of every thing which he perceiveth by his senses that it hath.

The painter has never seen the inward nature in itself and cannot even conceive it in his own imagination. Consequently, images do not represent our natures, but only the shape of our "persons."

An idol or "phantastical thing" has no nature to which the image can refer. However, if "it be an Image of truth," it has a direct reference to the truth of which it is an image.

> So that, if we see the Image of Christ crucified, we straight lay aside the brass, iron, or wood where upon that Image was drawn or made, and we apprehend Christ Himself, to whose person that Image doth lead us.[38]

The debate over images, however, did not take such a restrained turn as is suggested in the writings of Sanders. Off and on during the reign of Elizabeth, controversy proved as virulent as it was sarcastic.[39]

But if the cult of images was attacked in treatise and actual images were struck down, the policy against them depended on the like thinking and support of the Queen. Elizabeth herself showed a sustained interest in religious images (not unlike her father) and perhaps had felt that she had compromised too much in their removal. There was much surprise, however, when Elizabeth ordered a crucifix for the royal chapel at the very time when its use was thought to be illegal by many and visitation committees were attempting to insure

38. A. C. Southern, ed., *Elizabethan Recusant Prose, 1559–1582* (London: Sands and Co., 1950), pp. 98–100. This treatise was addressed to English readers with John Jewel as chief opponent. See Thomas Veech, *Dr. Nicholas Sanders and the English Reformation 1530–1581* (Louvain: Université de Louvain, 1935), pp. 183–90.

39. See Jewel, *Works,* IV, pp. xvii–xx. W. M. Southgate, *John Jewel and the Problem of Doctrinal Authority* (Cambridge: Harvard University Press, 1962), pp. 80–91.

adherence to the royal injunctions. Though the articles were ambiguous over what constituted in practice an abused image, a crucifix
spelled for the bishops the very things outlawed.[40]

Cox protested to the Queen that he "dare not minister in your
grace's chapel, the lights and cross remaining." Some feared that these
new trappings in the royal chapel signified a great new change in the
direction of the English reformation. And Bishop Jewel even feared
that the issue would deprive him of his bishopric, "(M)atters are
come to pass, that either the crosses of silver and tin which we have
everywhere broken in pieces, must be restored, or our bishopricks
relinquished."[41]

Whatever the Queen's reason, this precedent in the royal chapel
caused an uneasy situation that could signify a change in policy. The
bishops were unanimous against not only a change that would contradict past actions, but also would so obviously alienate supporters
who could cry "popery." Archbishop Parker and others sent a petition to the Queen listing their objections and trotting out again the
old arguments that pointed to an imageless primitive church ruled
by the second commandment. "For being a moral commandment,
and not ceremonial, it is a perpetual commandment, and bindeth us
as well as the Jews."[42] Images have their origin from the heathen and
thus can have no profit for Christians, they argued. For the learned
man, images are unnecessary, but to the ignorant, a confirmation of
his latent superstition. The petition reminded the Queen that in returning images, she would not only discredit the ministries of her
bishops, but also blemish the fame of her brother and father who had
testified to God's truth by removing all images.[43] Such plain talk and

40. Letter of Sandys to Peter Martyr, April 1560, in Hastings Robinson, ed.,
The Zurich Letters (Cambridge: University Press, 1842), I, pp. 73–74. See also *Ibid.*,
I, p. 63. Martyr's answer was by way of a strong opposition to images that was
tempered by the fact that such things were indifferent. Later, he claimed to be too
distant from the controversy to give answer. *Ibid.*, II, pp. 39, 47.

41. *Ibid.*, I, pp. 68, 63–64. Strype, *Annals*, I, ii, 500–03. See also the letter of
Peter Martyr to Thomas Sampson, March, 1560 in *Zurich Letters*, II, pp. 47–48.

42. Mathew Parker, *Correspondence*, ed. John Bruce and Thomason Perowne
(Parker Society: Cambridge: University Press, 1853), p. 81. On the dating and
authorship of this treatise, see Brook, *Parker*, p. 78.

43. Parker, *Correspondence*, p. 94. Burnet thinks this petition was drawn up
before the royal injunctions and was used to persuade the Queen of the policy
contained therein (Burnet, II, pp. 629–31; V, 530–32). Strype believes that it was

earnestness might have offended the Queen, but the prelates claimed to fear more for the religion of England.

Now to allow a most certain peril for an uncertain profit, and the greatest danger for the smallest benefit in matters of faith and religion, is a tempting of God, and a grievous offence. . .[44]

There seemed, however, to be some difference in the bishops' attitude towards images; faced with a possible crisis with the Queen, some prelates, like Parker and Cox, retreated by agreeing that images, vestments and ceremonies were "indifferent" and thus tolerable if the Queen so ordered; others like Jewel, Grindal and Sandys could claim never to agree to idolatry since admission would be a betrayal of conscience.[45]

The issue of images was important to the bishops for reasons other than theology. The Elizabethan government had aimed to unify the English Church through uniform religious practices. What was particularly dangerous to the Reformation cause was that if the Queen was dissatisfied with the religious settlement of 1559, she could use her royal chapel not only as a sign of her own independence, but as a precedent to return images to churches at large.[46]

The result of the whole controversy was, understandably, a compromise. With almost all the bishops opposed to her ideas on images, Elizabeth, who seemingly sought for unity more than anything else, retreated. Images were not returned to parish churches and the royal injunctions remained to carry out iconoclasm. Though a cross was substituted for a crucifix,[47] the royal chapel did retain its images. In fact, in 1565, the chapel was roundly described as having a rich arras and table "richly garnished with plate and jewels"; fine gilt basons, cross, cups, candlesticks, bason and ewer, two lavers, cruets and pax. Over the table, suspended against the wall, hung a cloth of silver em-

---

drawn up later and reflects a change in the Queen's position (Strype, *Annals*, I, i, 259–63, 330–32; I, ii, 198–201, 500–03).

44. Parker, *Correspondence*, pp. 79f.

45. Haugaard, *Elizabeth and the English Reformation*, p. 192. On the full story in some detail, *ibid.*, pp. 185–200, 334.

46. Collinson, *Elizabethan Puritan Movement*, p. 35.

47. This would have made no difference to Bishop Jewel; see Southgate, *Jewel*, pp. 47–48. Yet see Haugaard, *Elizabeth and the English Reformation*, p. 189, n.1.

broidered with angels in gold.[48] Consequently, this same chapel remained the last official refuge for those who sought the use of visual aids in worship; its quiet presence supported an attitude towards the liturgy which encouraged the use of religious images.

Again we must ask ourselves, had the queen a special feeling for images or were her motives politically inspired? Strype reports a conversation between the Queen and Alexander Nowell, the Dean of St. Paul's, New Years Day, 1562.

—Mr. Dean, how came it to pass that a new service book was placed on my cushion?

—May it please your majesty, I caused it to be placed there.

—Wherefore did you so?

—To present your majesty with a new-year's gift.

—You could never present me with a worse. . . You know I have an aversion to idolatry; to images of this kind.

—Wherein is the idolatry, may it please your majesty?

—In the cuts resembling angels and saints, nay, grosser absurdities, pictures resembling the blessed Trinity. . . Have you forgot our proclamations against images, pictures, and Romish relics in the churches? Was it not read in your deanery?

—It was read. But be your majesty assured I meant no harm. when I caused the cuts to be bound with the service book.

—You must needs be very ignorant to do this after our prohibition of them.

48. Elias Ashmole, *The Institution . . . of the Order of the Garter* (London, 1672), p. 369. The royal chapel seems to have had many images of the Trinity, saints and apostles. A. Peel, *Seconde Parte of a Register*, II, (Cambridge: University Press, 1915), pp. 53, 60. Yet this might be Puritan cavil. That these ornaments were obnoxious to Puritans is evident from the Admonition Controversy of 1572 which charged that this chapel was the "pattern and precedent to the people of all superstition."
It seems that the cross in the chapel royal was frequently broken ("reduced to ashes" writes Parkhurst in August, 1562). But it was replaced the following April. (*Zurich Letters*, I, pp. 122, 29). There was another attempt in March, 1568 (Bishop Parkhurst to Rudolph Gualter, Gorham, *Gleanings*, pp. 434–35). Again in 1570, the crucifix (?) was broken by Pach, the Queen's fool ("when no wiser man could be got to do it") Vernon Staley (ed.) *Hierurgia Anglicana* (London: The DeLaMore Press, 1902), I, p. 69. Apparently, Elizabeth had three crosses in silver, two of which were in use before 1583 (when they were made into new plate), while the third cross continued in use until 1600 (Oman, *Church Plate*, pp. 246–47; Collins, *Jewels and Plate*, pp. 307, 310–15).

—It being my ignorance, your majesty may the better pardon me.

—I am sorry for it; yet glad to hear it was your ignorance, rather than your opinion.[49]

Three years later, Ash Wednesday, 1565, Nowell was again humiliated by the Queen when this time he condemned the use of images in his sermon at Paul's Cross. Elizabeth was present with the Spanish ambassador and probably out of deference to him, she shouted at Nowell from her seat, "Leave that alone." Apparently the preacher did not hear for she screamed, "To your text, Mr. Dean," and with greater anger in her voice, "To your text! Leave that; we have heard enough of that! To your subject!"[50]

Elizabeth's real motives, like her father's, remain open to conjecture. Politics profoundly influenced the Queen and her actions, contradictory at time, reveal the need for accommodation with various foreign powers.

[S]he had been compelled to temporise at the beginning of her reign upon many points repugnant to her, but that God only knew the heart, and that she thought of restoring the crucifixes to churches.[51]

In reaction to continued popular disorder, Elizabeth issued another royal order in 1561 that sought greater uniformity through the organization of the physical fabric of the church. Under Edward, the roods had been destroyed, but the lofts supported by the rood screen were sometimes left. These lofts extended across the entrance to the chancel and often contained lights, reliquaries, sometimes a pulpit and even an organ; then again, if the loft was large, it supported an altar displaying the Blessed Sacrament.[52]

Under Elizabeth, the gallery fronts and the carved tabernacle work of the lofts were repugnant to reformers. It was decided that rood lofts would be taken down, but that the long beam running across the chancel would remain for the royal arms to be attached (figures 28,

49. Strype, *Annals*, I, i, pp. 408–10.
50. W. R. Matthews and W. M. Atkins, eds., *A History of St. Paul's Cathedral* (London: John Baker, 1964), p. 134.
51. The Spanish Ambassador, De Silva. Quoted in Malcolm MacColl, *The Royal Commission and the Ornaments Rubric* (London: Longmans, Green and Co., 1906), p. 62. On Elizabeth's religious attitudes, see Haugaard, *Elizabeth and the English Reformation*, pp. 186–87.
52. Francis Bond, *Screens and Galleries in English Churches* (London: Oxford University Press, 1908), p. 119.

29a, 29b). Further instructions left "the situation of the seats as well in the choir as in the church as heretofore hath been used."[53] The net result of this order was that rood lofts lost their upper portions and became merely screens. For those churches without screens, a "comely partition between chancel and nave was to be constructed."[54]

This royal order was perhaps in reaction to the destruction of screens that had survived sporadically since the Edwardian Bishop Hooper had ordered their destruction.[55] For Hooper and other reformers, screens represented the veil of the Temple in the old dispensation, separating the people from the holy chancel and symbolizing the imperfection of the old covenant to bring man to a full knowledge of God. But for Elizabeth, screens were not out of place in a Christian church. They spelled order and decency in Christian worship and were convenient ways of organizing spaces within a parish church. The Queen's insistent practicality would win over Hooper's theology.

The royal order also instructed churchwardens to return to the Edwardian policy of painting Scripture on the walls—this time, "the Tables of God's precepts. . ." over the communion table. Apparently Elizabeth felt that the bareness of the interior needed "color" for she wrote that the Ten Commandments were "not only edification, but also to give some comlye ornament and demonstration, that the same is a place of religion and prayer."[56]

In the reign of Edward, the great stone altar had been replaced by a "holy Table." A great diversity of position resulted, and continued under Elizabeth. However, the Elizabethan royal injunctions specified the table was to remain where the altar had been at the east end, except during Communion when it was to be picked up and placed at the lower end of the chancel. The people were to enter this part of the church for Communion; when finished, the table was to be re-

53. Frere, *Visitation Articles*, III, pp. 108–10.

54. Bond and Camm, *Roodscreens*, I, pp. 105–09. Although this order caused the mutilation of many screens, in reality it saved them from destruction until the nineteenth century obliterated them through renovation. Addleshaw, *Architectural Setting*, pp. 30, 37.

55. Frere, *Visitation Articles*, II, 285 (injunctions of 1551–52 for Gloucester and Worcester).

56. Cardwell, *Documentary Annals*, I, p. 296 (royal letter of January, 1561). Heylyn, *Ecclesia Restaurata*, II, p. 361. Cautley, *Royal Arms and Commandments*, pp. 109–25. J. Charles Cox, *Churchwardens' Accounts* (London: Methuen and Co., 1913), pp. 235–37.

turned to the east end.[57] The everyday placement of this table might well reveal not only important theological concepts on the meaning of Communion, but fundamental questions of its decoration. If understood to be an altar or table permanently placed against the east wall, images could always be introduced to frame its sanctity.

In practice, however, the Elizabethan table was heavy, and habit coupled with sloth soon dictated that the table would remain in that part of the church where Communion had been distributed. This practice became common throughout the reigns of both Elizabeth and James I.[58]

Further steps taken by Elizabeth included the retention of chancel steps, fonts and certain holy days which along with the injunctions concerning the holy table and rood loft, reveal an attempt to preserve certain traditional appearances. For reasons not always religious, the Queen sought to retain some accouterments of the medieval order.[59]

Consistently Elizabeth expected an outward religious conformity that expressed the allegiance of her subjects. She did not want the troubles that might result if she did persist in a complete definition of religious doctrine. Depending on the view of the government, this meant that a variety of services would exist from complete adherence to the Book of Common Prayer to interpolation of all sorts.[60]

In 1566, Elizabeth allowed the bishops to secure greater liturgical uniformity. Archbishop Parker issued his "Advertisements" which became the basis for further metropolitan visitations and episcopal visitation. No specific mention was made of images, but the articles required the wearing of surplice and cope, communicants were to be kneeling and holy tables were to be decently covered and reverently used.[61]

57. Addleshaw, *Architectural Setting*, p. 34.
58. *Ibid.*, p. 109. See Bond, *Chancel of English Churches* for pictures of Tudor and Stuart Tables, pp. 106–20.
59. Francis Bond, *Fonts and Font Covers* (London: Oxford University Press, 1908), p. 33.
60. John Strype, *The Life and Acts of Matthew Parker* (Oxford: Clarendon Press, 1821), I, p. 302. Dawley, *Whitgift*, pp. 60–61. John Aylmer, the Bishop of London claimed in 1581 that out of 350 parishes in Essex, probably only seven had identical services. A. T. Hart, The *Country Clergy* (London: Phoenix House, 1958), p. 21.
61. Dawley, *Whitgift*, pp. 75–76. Frere, *Visitation Articles*, III, pp. 171–80.

Those who refused to conform were dragged before the Court of High Commission and examined. One incident in 1567 concerns the use of authorized vestments and altar clothes that were described by some as "idolatrous geer." Melanchthon's argument that included images as things "indifferent" was employed by the government to justify these vestments.

"*Bishop Grindal*: 'That which God neither forbiddeth nor commandeth, and consisteth in things indifferent, such things Princes have authority to appoint and command.'

Prisoners: 'Prove that! Where do you find that?'

Smith: 'How can you prove those things to be indifferent which are abominable?'

Bishop Grindal: 'You mean our Caps and Tippets, which you say came from Rome.'

Watts: 'You would have us use nothing that the Papists used, then should we use no Churches, seeing the Papists used them. . .'

Lord Mayor: 'The Queen hath not established these Garments and other things for any holiness in them, only for civil order and comeliness, and because she would have Ministers known from other men, as Aldermen are known by their Tippets, Judges by their red Gowns, and Noblemen's servants by their liveries; therefore you will do well to take heed and obey.' "[62]

What proved onerous to those who refused to wear vestments was that the argument of things "indifferent" was as much a snare in the hands of a civil government or state religion as it might have been in the Catholic Church. Furthermore, the claims of civil order and comeliness still did not outweigh the claims of men's conscience which had long identified vestments with images; both were thought to be idolatrous.

The government persisted, however, in requiring vestments; though it could have used the same argument that defended vestments, to justify images, there was no general return of these things.

Parker was acting with the Queen's knowledge, but not with her legal approval. Parker, *Correspondence*, pp. 262–64, 271–72.

62. Richard Newcome, *A Memoir of Gabriel Goodman . . . and Godfrey Goodman* (Ruthin: Taliesin Press, 1825), pp. 21–22. For a similar case in 1565 where the standard arguments are repeated (i.e., those who claim to be following their own convictions on things indifferent), see Strype, *Parker*, III, 95–97.

Most royal visitations under Elizabeth continued to order the destruction of images as the "monuments of superstition and idolatry."[63]

In February, 1570, Elizabeth was declared a heretic and excommunicated by the bull *Regnans in excelsis* issued by Pius V. Though later Gregory XIII would permit English Catholics to obey their Queen in civil matters, the original excommunication rendered all English Catholics suspect as possible traitors. The Crown reacted by issuing a statute which, among more important matters, forbade the possession of crosses, pictures, and beads that were blessed by the Pope.[64] In 1578, Gregory XIII granted certain indulgences for specified devotions attached to crucifixes. The intention behind the devotion was the "preservation and delivery of Mary Queen of Scots, the leading claimant to the English throne.[65] The searches of papists' houses in the early 1580s revealed the government's concern with imagery that was in some way associated or consecrated by the Pope.[66] Those caught with such spiritual contraband were guilty of *praemunire* and severely punished by fines. Under Mary's government, images had been identified with Rome; now, treason was added to this association.

Many parishes were split by warring sides over the removal of images that had been legal under Queen Mary. Robert Goteley in East Kent warned the churchwarden who was to pull down the rood loft in 1561—"Let him take heed that his authority be good before it be pulled down, for we know what we have had, but we know not what

63. Frere, *Visitation Articles*, III, p. 169; Bentham (Coventry and Lichfield) 1565; 210: Parkhurst (Norwich) 1569; 226: Sandys (Worcester) 1569; 255, 284–85: Grindal (York) 1571; 311: Sandys (London) 1571; 332, 335: Guest (Rochester) 1571; 342, 344: Freke (Rochester) 1571; 381: Parker (Winchester) 1575. Kennedy, *Elizabethan Episcopal Administration*, II, 38: Price (Rochester) 1576; 78: Barnes (Durham) 1577; 83, 99: Sandys (York Cathedral) 1578; 111, 112: Chaderton (Chester) 1581; III, 140, 143, 150: Middleton (St. David's) 1583; 162: Overton (Lichfield) 1584; 183: Whitgift (Chichester) 1586; 210: Bickley (Chichester) 1586; 261; Piers (York) 1590; 346: Bancroft (London) 1601. J. S. Purvis, *Tudor Parish Documents of the Diocese of York* (Cambridge: University Press, 1948), pp. 4, 26, 32. It would appear that the issue was dying because of the perfunctory allusion made to images: "monuments of superstition and idolatry to be destroyed, etc." Attention is also directed to the number of visitations in 1571 that call for the removal of such picures. This is one year after the papal excommunication.

64. *13 Elizabeth c. 2* (1571). Cardwell, *Documentary Annals*, I, pp. 363–66.

65. Strype, *Annals*, II, ii, pp. 191–93.

66. *Ibid.*, II, ii, pp. 345–46. Frere, *English Church*, pp. 159–160, 210–11.

we shall have." [67] Rood lofts were first to go while the church plate that had been sold under Edward, returned under Mary, was sold again under Elizabeth. Many of these articles in the churches were offered to parishioners, though it is not clear for what purpose they were purchased. [68]

Ecclesiastical commissioners apparently followed a certain procedure for the destruction of superstitious objects. Such things were first taken to a house of a local gentleman for collection. On Sunday, there was a general confession of the wardens asking mercy for having kept images and popish books.

The whiche beinge done they . . . shall go to the same churche steele and ther burne all the Images before so many of the paryshioners as shall be ther assembled. . .[69]

Was public destruction demanded in order to insure execution of the government's orders? Certainly in some out-of-the-way places, the initial search for images was perfunctory and left much to be desired. The negligence of many churchwardens, and obstructions on the part of many parishioners forced the visitations later to be supplemented by ecclesiastical commissioners.[70] Yet hiding places were innumerable for old ways died slowly. Sometimes when the rood was removed, parishioners sketched in a cross with chalk or paint; there were reports of rood lofts still *in situ,* or of others taken down but still remaining in the church to be put up again.[71] Many of these works from the old religion were hidden against the day when it was hoped the religious tide would turn once again.

Some men flaunted the law and preserved their churches in their Marian furnishings; paintings still graced the walls of Waghen and Skirlaugh while the rector of Roos had retained both rood and acces-

---

67. *Home Countries Magazine,* X, p. 181, quoted in A. L. Rowse, *The England of Elizabeth* (New York: Macmillan, 1961), p. 417n.

68. J. E. Farmuloe and R. Nixseaman, "Elizabethan Churchwardens' Accounts," in *Bedfordshire Historical Record Society,* XXXIII (1953), xviii. Thomas Wright (ed.), *Churchwarden's Accounts of Ludlow* (Westminster: Camden Society, 1869), pp. 89–162. Machyn, *Diary,* p. 399.

69. Purvis, *Tudor Parish Documents,* pp. 144–46 (April, 1567).

70. *Ibid.,* pp. 147–48, 151, 190, 225–227.

71. *Calendar of State Papers, Domestic, Elizabeth,* IX, 71. Purvis, *Tudor Parish Documents,* pp. 148, 226–27.

sory images.[72] Reformation moved slowly in distant places such as in Wales.

I have found since I came to this country images and altars standing in churches undefaced, lwed and undecent vigils and watches observed, much pilgrimaging and many candles set up to the honour of saints, some relics yet carried about, and all the countries full of beads and knots besides divers other monuments of wilful serving of God.[73]

Some paintings were "slubbered over with a white wash that in a house may be undone, standing like a Dianaes shrine for a future hope and daily comforte of old popish beldames and young perking papists . . ." In other instances, undefaced images remained to shock those who sought complete abolition of popery.[74]

Many men complained that the trappings of Catholic worship still existed in English churches. Though it was believed that the settlement of 1559 had effected needed reforms, many Englishmen were highly critical of Elizabethan policy that tolerated much which they considered was still unscriptural, and enforced by an authority which ignored individual conscience. It was claimed that "comeliness" spelled popery and a form of worship that stressed ostentatious garments with vain gestures, signs and movements.[75]

Early in Elizabeth's reign the term "Puritan" came into use to describe those who wished to continue the reformation or purification of the English Church. The movement (for that is what it was) was ruled by the ideal of the word of God as criterion for men's lives and God's Church, with a strong dependence on Calvin and Zwingli in their theology, organization of clergy and liturgy.

The English Church, they believed, had defined its doctrines according to Scripture, but had allowed too many false Catholic practices in church order and in worship. Puritans had come to both fear and hate all or most of the traditional external signs of Christianity: not only private Communion, holy days, kneeling at Communion, surplice and cope, but the blessing of water at Baptism, the ring at

---

72. Hart, *Country Clergy*, p. 36.

73. *Calendar of State Papers, Domestic, Elizabeth*, XLIV, 27. (October, 1567).

74. Peel, *Seconde Parte* I (1584), p. 239. II, pp. 190–91 (November, 1586). See also Blensch, *Preaching*, p. 299; James Pilkington, *Works*, Parker Society: Cambridge: University Press, 1842), p. 129. "Exposition upon the Prophet Aggeus." (1562).

75. Maclure, *Paul's Cross*, p. 60. F. Trigge, *An Apologie or Defence of Our Dayes* (London, 1589), p. 24.

marriage, the sign of the cross were all Elizabethan practices singled out for condemnation. Like images, such things were considered idolatrous, confusing to the simple or simply a distraction.

Consequently Puritans argued for the absolute standard of Scripture in worship and in church government in face of the Elizabethan religious settlement which had emphasized that whatever traditions of the ancient Christian church were not expressly forbidden by Scripture, could be retained. Such practical theological differences led to distinct attitudes towards worship and the use of external signs. Anglicans retained many of the traditional adjuncts to worship that were felt to be "decent and edifying"; while such things were not prohibited by Scripture, the Church could claim to arrange the details of ceremony as suited its convenience and traditions. Indeed the Anglican emphasis on the importance of the sacraments resulted in ritualism and liturgical experimentation with observance of a reformed Christian calendar in churches whose architecture and furnishings bridged the gap between the church militant on earth and the Church triumphant in heaven.[76]

Puritan commitment to the Scriptures as liturgical criterion led to an emphasis on preaching. Anglican ceremonies of eye and ear were interpreted as compromises and distractions from man's obligations to God; they could result in weakness, impiety if not idolatry. Accordingly, Puritans worked for the removal and destruction of most of these external signs.

Toward the end of Elizabeth's reign, however, a reaction against this sort of thinking set in. There were those who protested that many of the traditional values of the English Church were being sacrificed in the removal of various medieval ceremonies and adjuncts of worship. Richard Hooker believed this and when he published his *Laws of Ecclesiastical Polity* in 1594 and 1597, his general aim was a defense of the established Church. Though Hooker does not include arguments for or against images, it is precisely in his defense of a traditional worship tolerant of Catholic practices that the return of religious images would be realized.

Like Thomas More, Hooker understood man's nature to partake of sensuous, intellectual and spiritual needs that all cried out for satis-

76. For a full explication of these differences, see New, *Anglican and Puritan*.

faction. It was the Puritan, he claimed, who aimed to abolish the first two while relegating the third to the care of Scripture. Such a view was not only an appeal to the irrational elements in human nature, but a denial of this life itself.[77] Roman Catholics have taught, insisted Hooker, that knowledge of Scripture was insufficient for salvation without the traditions of the Church. Though Puritans condemned this opinion, they moved as well to a dangerous extremity when they claimed that in Scripture is contained everything necessary for salvation.[78] Hooker believed that many things required by men for the expression of religion are not found in Scripture. The Bible, for instance, never prescribed either time or place for the celebration of the Lord's Supper, or for meeting in common prayer or the hearing of the word of God or even the day in the week most meet for the Sabbath. Furthermore, there is no word in Scripture on the rubrics of worship, Baptism or Communion.

The bounds of wisdom are large, and within them much is contained. . . Wisdom hath diversely imparted her treasures unto the world. . . Some things she openth by the sacred books of Scripture; some things by the glorious works of Nature; with some things she inspireth them from above by spiritual influence; in some things she leadeth and traineth them only by wordly experience and practice. . . (L)et all her ways be according to their place and degree adored.[79]

One such source of disagreement with the Puritans was the hallowing and sanctifying of churches. Thomas More had believed God wanted such distinctions made—that men should worship in prearranged places sanctioned by tradition and time. Hooker's point is more practical: the whole purpose of consecration is to remove churches from the disorder of life and invest God therein. This assures decency and respect. Hooker, like More, rejected any charge of paganism: Are we to forsake any true opinion because idolaters have maintained it?[80]

He argued that churches should be arranged for the purpose they

77. Peter Munz, *The Place of Hooker in the History of Thought* (London: Routledge and Kegan Paul, 1952), pp. 39–40.

78. Hooker, I, pp. 335–36.

79. *Ibid.*, I, pp. 289–90. See also, John Whitgift, J. Ayre, ed., *Works* (Parker Society; Cambridge: University Press, 1851–53), I, pp. 200f. M. Knappen, *Tudor Puritanism*, p. 301.

80. Hooker, II, pp. 48–49.

are expected to serve. Since the proper public worship of God is precisely the object of Christian piety, decoration should be tasteful and reverent. In the long run, it is true that God is served best through "affection," the place of worship being indifferent; however, the seat of our worship has great "virtue, force and efficacy, for that it serveth as a sensible help to stir up devotion, and in that respect no doubt bettereth, even our holiest and best actions in this kind." [81]

One example of this is the justification for the use of screens based on tradition, reasonableness and experience:

Our churches are places provided that the people may there assemble themselves in due and decent manner according to their several degrees and order. Which things being common unto us with Jews, we have in this respect our churches divided by certain partitions though not so many in number as theirs. . . There being in ours for local distinction between the clergy and the rest. . . but one partition, the cause whereof at the first (as it seemeth) was, that as many as were capable of the Holy Mysteries might there assemble themselves, and no other creep in amongst them. [82]

Ceremonies, Hooker felt, are always to be ruled by the end or purpose they are meant to instill in the believer. Therefore if these chosen rites signify good things, there can be no complaint against them as idolatrous, mistaken, or insignificant. [83] For good things that edify are necessary and should not be removed because of abuses. What must be taken away is the abuse. "He that will take away extreme heat by setting the body in extremity of cold, shall undoubtedly remove the disease, but together with it the diseased too." [84]

Hooker does not mention images, but he sets the stage for their acceptance and re-entry into churches. The medieval order which had appealed to the full range of human experience in the worship of God had been undermined in Reformation England. For images to return to a place of respect and authority and, in turn, to be required by the liturgy of the established church, it was necessary, in part, that a change in thinking occur. It was Hooker who was to help create this new atmosphere which was more conducive to the return of sensuous aids in the worship of the English Church.

81. Hooker, II, pp. 57–58.
82. Quoted in Bond and Camm, *Roodscreens*, I, p. 117.
83. Hooker, II, pp. 319, 321, 326–27, 337.
84. Hooker, I, p. 442.

But what Hooker yearned for, was not to be realized in the churches of Elizabeth. The greater part of this reign was concerned, as visitation records tell us, with the decay of the churches, the neglect by churchwardens, the indifference of the clergy.

It is a sin and shame to see so many churches so ruinous and so foully decayed in almost every corner. . . Suffer them not to be defiled with rain and weather, with dung of doves and owls, stares and choughs, and other filthiness, as it is foul and lamentable in many places in this country.[85]

Thus the fittings of the Elizabethan church gradually were reduced to essentials. Contrasted with the Marian church, the Elizabethan one was bare and empty.[86] The rood lofts had been removed while the tympanum's paintings were replaced with either the royal arms or a table of the Ten Commandments. A screen devoid of images and figures but one probably still finely carved separated the nave from the chancel. The altar itself had been abolished for a wooden holy table ("decently made") that often stood altar-wise when not in use. The table itself was covered with a linen cloth often made from vestments. Little ornamentation was evident; candles and stained glass served only as illumination.[87] The plate sufficient for lawful service was small: silver cup and paten and a few vessels for the wine.

Such limited furnishings, however, were in keeping with a new conception of the role of the physical fabric of the church. The parish church was no longer the physical object as a holy thing in itself, but the body of faithful or the Christian community of the parish. The Protestant return to the Bible as the basis of the spiritual life meant a change in the ordering of that life. Interest now centered in the relationships between people rather than in the underlying rhythm of Nature and God's presence.[88]

Though the Elizabethan church was still a medieval building with

85. John Jewel, Quoted in Cook, *English Medieval Parish Churches*, p. 267. Parker, *Correspondence*, pp. 132–33.

86. See the series of documents entitled *Inventorium Monumentorum Superstitionis* which graphically reveals the destruction of church furniture that had been required in the previous reign. Peacock, *English Church Furniture*. They purport to be a return made in 1566 of ornaments that were considered unnecessary or idolatrous.

87. Dawley, *Whitgift*, pp. 113–22. Kennedy, *Episcopal Administration*, I, pp. lix–lxii.

88. Davies, *Secular Use of Church Buildings*, pp. 100–02.

demarcated chancel and nave, hearing of the Divine Word through the sermon came to strengthen the place of pulpit over altar. In England churches were no longer conceived as symbolizing the order of Nature through divine sanctification; no longer would they be the holy houses of God containing the miraculous presence of His Body through the Incarnation.[89]

In the long run, the reign of Elizabeth stabilized religious forces and gave Englishmen both a relative peace and a freedom within prescribed limits that was as fresh as it was needed. If Englishmen continued to look askance at religious imagery, this was due to its political as well as religious implications; again, if Englishmen no longer identified themselves with the medieval devotional system, this was due to the changes in the patterns of English aspiration. A social as well as religious revolution was taking place; the medieval world that had found realization in alms and offerings to shrines and statues was replaced by a society that claimed no longer to need the artistic props of a world order now dead.[90]

Architecturally, the Elizabethan house had supplanted the church; the growth of secular art was an appropriate artistic change, reflecting the demise of a religious imagery that had become suspect and marking the emergence of a vigorous newly monied class displaying its wealth. Despite the excellence of such secular art in the latter sixteenth century, no new churches were built in England. The Elizabethan religious settlement of compromise had helped men to adapt the old rather than to build the new.[91]

The question still remained, however, in what direction the forces of Elizabeth accommodation and public order would move. Hooker's attempt to reconstruct the English Church was one such answer.

89. Dillistone, *Christianity and Symbolism*, pp. 69–70. A. L. Drummond, *The Church Architecture of Protestantism* (Edinburgh: T. and T. Clark, 1934), pp. 19–26.
90. Jordan, *Philanthropy in England*, pp. 145f.
91. On Elizabethan architecture, see in particular, Mark Girouard, *Robert Smythson and the Architecture of the Elizabethan Era* (London: Country Life, 1966), and W. G. Hoskins, "The Rebuilding of Rural England, 1570–1640," *Past and Present* (1953), pp. 44–59.

VII. TRANSITION

> What do I love when I love Thee. I love a certain kind of light,
> and voice, and fragrance, and a kind of food and embrace, when
> I love my God: a light, melody, fragrance, food, embrace of the
> inner man.
>
> ST. AUGUSTINE, *Confessions*, x. 6.

> And what are Ceremonies? are all vaine? are all superstitious?
> God forbid.
> > Many are tolerable, a few necessary;
> > Most are ridiculous, And some abominable.
>
> PETER SMART, from a sermon, 1628.

ELIZABETH'S CIRCUITOUS conciliation with the various religious parties in England had resulted in the royal supremacy and a common liturgy as a test of political loyalty. The English Church had
come to be understood in political rather than religious terms; as an
ecclesiastical body, it had allowed the Crown the assurance of obedience as well as faith. No wonder that in 1603 Elizabeth's successor
inherited an established church that had left too many doctrinal
questions unanswered, a clergy confused, ignorant and dispirited
and an inefficient ecclesiastical administration incapable of bringing
about a unified national expression of religious faith.

The prevailing view of the Jacobean bishops on religious images
was that there were many external signs of originating from the
medieval church that were clearly acceptable for the present. Em-
ploying Melanchthon's argument of *adiaphora*, the Jacobean clergy
believed the established church had the power to institute such "indifferent" practices in its liturgy for the strengthening of men's faith
and the edification of their minds.

. . . the kneeling on the ground, the lifting up of our hands, the knocking
of our breasts, are ceremonies significant; the first, of our humility coming
before the mighty God; the second, of our confidence and hope; the other,
of our sorrow and detestation of our sins; and these are, and may lawfully
be used.[1]

1. As reported by William Barlow, Dean of Chester in his *The Sum and Sub-*

The bishops insisted that the very sacrament of the Last Supper was proof of the validity of such signs. The abuse of ceremonies by popery did not, in their view, invalidate either their inherent worth or the fact that they had existed inviolate before Rome had tampered with them.

On the issue of images, however, both King and bishop argued that Scripture expressly forbids the worship of anything created by God or of any representation of God Himself.[2]

James I himself claimed not to be an iconoclast; he followed Henry's VIII's distinctions concerning images by accepting their commemorative nature and rejecting those representations which were worshipped or associated with any holiness ("abused"). This qualified acceptance of certain images was an ambiguous stand; it had been inherited from the Elizabethan settlement and its unwillingness to solve the question of what practically constituted an unabused image, had grown out of threatened religious disorder. And like his predecessor, James I revealed a marked contrast between public statement and private practice. Desiring "comliness," the King gave instructions in 1617 for the royal chapel at Holyrood to be decorated with gilded figures of apostles and patriarchs. When the Scottish bishops complained, the King yielded.[3]

The fate of individual religious images continued to be tempered by economic matters. Justices of the peace were empowered to search the houses of popish recusants, and, finding altars, beads or pictures, to burn them. Yet if the contraband article were a crucifix or relic of any monetary value, it was to be defaced and returned to its owner. Despite the supposed occasions for idolatry, the "rights" of property held firm; perhaps too many Englishmen had legally purchased the wealth of churches from a government eager for financial gain.[4]

---

stance of the Conference at Hampton Court in Edward Cardwell, Revision of the Book of Common Prayer (Oxford: J. H. and J. Parker, 1840), p. 197. Also see Fuller, Church History, III, pp. 172–193, on the Court Conference.

2. James I, "Premonition to All Most Mighty Monarch, Kings, Free Princes and States of Christendom," Works of James I, ed. James Montague (London: 1616), pp. 301–08. The Political Works of James I, ed. Charles H. McIlwain (Cambridge: Harvard University Press, 1918), p. 125.

3. Davis H. Willson, King James VI and I (London: Jonathan Cape, 1956), p. 391.

4. The Canons of 1604. See J. P. Kenyon, The Stuart Constitution (Cambridge:

Images were also tainted through their associations with Rome, the Marian government and, for some, the disruption of public order. Consequently, the Edwardian tradition of providing tables of the Ten Commandments at the east end of churches (sometimes in the place formerly occupied by the holy rood) was continued in the reign of James I.[5] Some wall paintings were made about this time, but they were usually emblematic or moral tales devoid of idolatrous connotations: Moses and Aaron and their association with the Ten Commandments; the symbols of the twelve tribes of Israel, and so forth.[6] Their apparent lack of ambiguity made them safe.

The general confusion over the role of religious images in public worship was mirrored in a general doctrinal drift in the established Church that produced disaffection in many parts of the country.[7] Puritans desperately sought to continue the early reforms of the Lollards by returning to Cranmer's "scriptural criterion" in judging the remaining ceremonies and adjuncts in the Church of England; they, in turn, were countered by Anglicans, who just as firmly believed reform had travelled far enough and who were now seeking the return of many traditional ceremonies of the medieval church.

Despite the complexity of Puritanism as a movement, its views on worship can be generalized;[8] many of its arguments, broadly conceived, have been seen before because Puritanism was nurtured on common theological and liturgical assumptions extending from the Lollards through the seventeenth century. Drawing their model of reform from what was believed to be the primitive Christian Church, Puritans were suspicious of everything that could not be justified

---

University Press, 1966), #39. See also Fuller, *Church History*, III, p. 187. Stuart Barton Babbage, *Puritanism and Richard Bancroft* (London: SPCK, 1962), pp. 86–102. The Code of 1603 (the 141 Canons) makes no mention of images, either in definition or prohibition; Cardwell, *Synodalia*, I, pp. 164–329.

5. Hart, *Country Clergy*, pp. 61, 67, 75.

6. See A. Caiger-Smith, *English Medieval Mural Painting* (Oxford: Clarendon Press, 1963), p. 115. (Stoke Dry, Rutland; Burton Latimer, Northants; West Walton, Norfolk; Eyam, Derbyshire).

7. H. R. Trevor-Roper, "James I and his bishops," *Historical Essays* (London: Macmillan, 1957), pp. 134–35, 143. Arthur P. Kautz, *The Jacobean Episcopate and its legacy* (unpublished dissertation, University of Minnesota, 1952), p. 3. Yet see D. E. Kennedy, "The Jacobean Episcopate," *The Historical Journal*, IV (1962), 175–81.

8. On the various meanings of the term "Puritan," see below, p. 6n9.

through Scripture.[9] They sought to exclude most aids and external elements in the worship of God, one result being their identification of worship and prayer with words and mental concentration. For Puritans, the ritual of the traditional church was too much a sensuous spectacle and therefore a distraction from God. They were convinced that beauty of ceremony inevitably caused men to think God was pacified because their hearts had been moved; worse, such images and trappings of the liturgy might cause men to confound aesthetic pleasure with supernatural grace.[10]

The Puritans believed God was not manifested in one place nor even in the bread and wine of the Communion service; his continued presence was sustained in the faith of his believers in those called to the table in communion. Consequently, since the objectivity of holy places was no longer accepted, any commodious structure could accommodate the people of God.[11] The altar was removed and replaced by the table around which the new followers of Christ could commemorate both God's gifts and human fellowship.[12] Central to all Puritan worship was the pulpit through which God could speak to man. The choir with rood screen intended to set off the sacred precinct of the canopied altar was no longer necessary. Its elimination and the destruction of its images spelled in many instances not angry iconoclasm, but the gentler sort that removed old objects because a new faith had created a different form of worship.

This was not an age of church-building despite the fact that Puritans were sometimes forced to worship elsewhere than in their own parish churches. Circumstances often forced these congregations to meet in private houses, which in the long run served their needs.

9. D. McGinn, *The Admonition Controversy* (New Brunswick: Rutgers University Press, 1949), p. 4.

10. Gregory Dix, *The Shape of the Liturgy* (Westminster: Dacre Press, 1949), p. 424. Perry Miller, *The New England Mind*, (Boston: Beacon Press, 1961), p. 46. Horton Davies, *The Worship of the English Puritans* (Westminster: Dacre Press, 1948), p. 12.

11. *Ibid.*, p. 278. See Christopher Hill, *Society and Puritanism in Pre-Revolutionary England* (New York: Schocken Books, 1964), ch. 13. Helen Rosenau, "The Synagogue and Protestant Church Architecture," *Journal of Warburg and Courtauld Institutes*, IV (1940–41), 84.

12. J. H. Nichols and Leonard Trinterud, *The Architectural Setting for Reformed Worship* (Chicago: Presbytery of Chicago, 1960), p. 15. See also J. H. Nichols, *Corporate Worship in the Reformed Tradition* (Philadelphia: Westminster Press, 1968), "Puritanism and the Anti-liturgical Movement," pp. 90–110.

However, when Puritans did meet in their own parish churches, they had to adopt the Gothic to their own needs of auricular worship; certainly existing religious art in churches was too reminiscent of dogma long disclaimed. Puritans could not be custodians of the past since these acquired associations were intellectually and spiritually unacceptable to them. When, in a few instances, they came to build their own churches, they built meeting houses whose aim was to ensure hearing and seeing to the detriment of mystery and to the denial of sacrifice.[13]

On a practical level, the Puritans rejected the arts owing to the money, time, and energy which these seemed to demand. An embellishment after all, was superfluous; when art aimed at seriousness, blasphemy often was the result. Thus it was that when confronted with art that purported to be religious, the Puritans tried to destroy it; only in divesting it of significance could they come to tolerate it.[14] The West Cheap Cross in London provides an example. It was a large market cross which had suffered varying fortunes since its construction in 1486, and had been a sumptuous affair: a large crucifix crowned by a dove, supplemented by sculptures of the Resurrection, Virgin and Child, and Edward the Confessor. In 1581, iconoclasts had defaced its figures and had attempted to pull down the whole monument. The statues were repaired, but by 1600 renovation had become necessary. To quiet Puritan objections and perhaps to render the monument "safe," a pyramid was substituted for the cross and a semi-nude statue of the pagan goddess Diana for that of the Virgin.[15] So long as images were pagan or not idolatrous in a Christian sense, Puritans were inclined to take no offense.

The Puritan hatred of images was echoed in their rejection of the Mass and the stage. Most formalized rituals, either secular or profane,

13. Arthur Drummond, *The Church Architecture of Protestantism* (Edinburgh: T. and T. Clark, 1934), pp. 19–26. Horton Davies, *Worship and Theology in England, 1690–1850* (Princeton: University Press, 1961), p. 24. Nichols, *Architectural Setting*, pp. 9, 15. Martin S. Briggs, *Puritan Architecture and its Future* (London: Lutterworth Press, 1946), p. 15.

14. John Marlowe, *The Puritan Tradition in English Life* (London: Cresset Press, 1956), p. 102.

15. However, Queen Elizabeth ordered a cross to surmount the pyramid; later the Virgin was restored but she lasted only twelve nights for she was decrowned, nearly beheaded and robbed of her Infant. Aymer Vallance, *Old Crosses and Lychgates* (London: B. T. Batsford, 1920), pp. 102, 106.

which partook of costume and external action were condemned as idolatrous.[16] Like "Bayes in windowes, new yeres guiftes, May games, dancing, pictures in churches," stage plays drew people away from more important matters. Even worse, these distractions could lead to situations inimical to religion. Like Socrates, the Puritans feared the effect of art on men unless it made them "better;" even more they feared the imagination of the artist as competitive with the demands of Scripture.[17] Ultimately, Puritans believed that a dependence on such external trappings involved the risk of temptation to believe that salvation might come by way of good works. As we have seen, the conflict about images spelled a much larger issue than the propriety of worship; the Puritan notion of justification by faith alone was clearly challenged.

Yet these views were not shared by everyone. Many Englishmen were discouraged with the inconclusive and irresolute religious context, and resisted attempts of Puritans to eliminate the few familiar images that did remain in churches. The lack of clear direction in religious affairs encouraged a return to many traditional attitudes toward worship such as those encouraged by Hooker. Late in Eliza-

16. Stage plays themselves were to be closed by the Ordinance of September of 1642 where it was decreed that such indulgences were inconsistent with the present strife of civil war. The law, at least in London, was often ignored. Another ordinance passed in October, 1647 aimed to punish all actors as rogues. Plays, however, continued as before. Leslie Hotson, *The Commonwealth and Restoration Stage* (Cambridge: Harvard University Press, 1928), p. 17. Most accounts suggest that these Puritan attacks against plays originated in the sixteenth century and were motivated by religious and moral considerations. E. K. Chambers, *The Elizabethan Stage* (Oxford: Clarendon Press, 1923), I, pp. 236–56. E. N. S. Thompson, *The Controversy between the Puritans and the Stage* (New York: Henry Holt and Co., 1903). Dover Wilson, "The Puritan Attack on the Stage," *Cambridge History of English Literature* (New York: Cambridge University Press, 1910), VI, pp. 421–31. Thornton S. Graves, "Notes on Puritanism and the Stage," *Studies in Philology*, XVIII (1921), 141–69. On the other hand, it has been suggested that the early attacks against the stage were due to changing conditions within the theaters themselves. "Attack was not led by clergy, nor were the arguments in the beginning theological; laymen took the lead in the controversy and their objections were primarily the result of social and economic conditions." Thus such an onslaught became a "middle class" assault rather than a "Puritan" attack. William Ringler, "The First Phase of the Elizabethan Attack on the Stage, 1558–79," *Huntington Library Quarterly*, V (1942), 391–418.

17. Samuel R. Gardiner (ed.), *Documents Relating to the Proceedings Against William Prynne in 1634–1637* (London: Camden Society, 1877), pp. 2–3. Lawrence A. Sasek, *The Literary Temper of the English Puritans* (Baton Rouge: Louisiana State University Press, 1961), pp. 60, 102–8.

beth's reign and continuing into the first quarter of the seventeenth century, a liturgical renewal developed within the Church of England that would confront head-on the theological and liturgical questions avoided by the Elizabethan settlement. In so doing, it would come to issue with Puritanism as a religious force and would help to create a context for the return of religious images.

This movement did not center its attention on the defense of images, but raised general questions about the nature of religious worship peculiar to the English context. In refusing to identify ceremonies and images with the abuses of Rome, some stressed how natural ought these very things to be in the life of an Englishman.

I am, I confess, naturally inclined to that which misguided Zeal terms Superstition . . . yet at my Devotion, I love to use the civility of my knee, my hat, and hand, with all those outward and sensible motions which may express or promote my invisible Devotion. I should violate my own arm rather than a Church; nor willingly deface the name of Saint or Martyr. At the sight of a Cross or Crucifix, I can dispence with my hat, but scarce with the thought or memory of my Saviour. . .[18]

Hooker and others had inclined towards a return to certain traditional ceremonies that were "indifferent" according to Melanchthon, but "necessary" according to the needs of men. Hooker had set the stage for returning images, but had not discussed them in any way save as important aids in the religious worship he was defending. It was the task of Lancelot Andrewes, the Bishop of Winchester, to develop Hooker's ideas of the necessity of beauty in the liturgy, of establishing a religious service that would give satisfaction to God and to the full man in all his needs.[19]

Andrewes looked to the past to satisfy what he felt were deficiencies in the English service; among other aids, he would discover images. He insisted that men can worship God in but three ways: through the soul, the body and the "worldly goods" we are blessed with. He urged that God be worshipped with all, "seeing there is but one reason for all."[20]

18. Sir Thomas Browne, *The Religio Medici* (London: J. M. Dent and Sons, 1962), p. 5; E. C. E. Bourne, *The Anglicanism of William Laud* (London: SPCK, 1947), pp. 59, 64.

19. Florence Higham, *Catholic and Reformed* (London: SPCK, 1962), p. 50.

20. Lancelot Andrewes, *Ninety-Six Sermons* (Oxford: John Henry Parker 1841–

But worship of the whole man was rarely seen in an England where beauty was detached from holiness and where inward faith was thought to exist apart from outward action. Did not the whole Christian tradition, Andrewes could argue, point to the fact that religion is both outward and inward?[21]

But if Andrewes was disgusted by what he saw as the failing of Christians, his policy was not to push, but to teach; and the latter he did through example. In his writings and in his own life as man of the Church, he aimed to foster a reverence and a dignity worthy of the worship of God. Such a view of course necessitated a return to some of the adjuncts of ceremony that were still associated with popery.[22]

In his controversy with Cardinal Perron, Andrewes expressed the fear that certain objects such as images and relics were laden with danger; the excess of popular devotions had often resulted in their tendency to "overshoot themselves." In fact, his comments on images are wary and cautious.

To have a story painted, for memory's sake, we hold it not unlawful, but that it might well enough be done, if the Church found it not inconvenient for her children.[23]

But Andrewes sought to emphasize the continuity between the liturgies of the early church and those of the present by admitting an external worship of God that was of "uniform and decent order;" this would entail the use not only of images and relics, but liturgies for consecrating churches, churchyards and church plate; each supported the other.

---

43), I, p. 262 (1622). Andrewes quotes Proverbs 3:9 "Honour God with your substance, for He hath blessed your state."

21. *Ibid.*, IV, p. 374 (1627); V, p. 554 (n.d.).

22. *Ibid.*, III, pp. 33–34 (1621); IV, p. 377 (1627). On Andrewes' liturgy and chapel arrangement, see Paul A. Welsby, *Lancelot Andrewes 1555–1626* (London: SPCK, 1958), pp. 127–30.

23. Lancelot Andrewes, *Two Answers to Cardinal Perron and Other Miscellaneous Works* (Oxford: John Henry Parker, 1854), pp. 21–23, 31–32. See Appendix F for a list of Andrewes' chapel furniture and ornaments, which contained a hanging of the story of Abraham and Melchisedec and part of the story of David. See also, p. 113, for his visitation articles of 1619 for Winchester; they are particularly vague on ornaments. See also William Prynne, *Canterburies Doome* (London, 1646), pp. 121–25.

Andrewes did not believe that because some ceremonies are unnecessary none are needed, for ceremonies are "the hedge that fence the substance of religion."[24] His commitment to external worship as necessary and fitting for the dignity of God and the needs of man would lead him from a cautious qualification of images to a positive defence of their use. Thus Andrewes could argue that the thrust of the Second Commandment was not against an image or a likeness of something, but against the making of artificial kinds of worship not conforming to the general dictates of worship prescribed by God.[25]

As a young man, he had voiced the opinion that in establishing what was "comely and orderly in each age and place," the authority of each church should take its own decisions. Thus, ceremonies could be changed for a variety of reasons (convenience being one); only a few precautions were necessary. The form of outward worship ought not to contradict Scripture, but be capable of expressing the "inward affections" of the worshipper.[26]

Andrewes, unlike the men who were to follow him in the administration of the Church, never forced his ideas of order and decency on others. His concern might have been with beauty, but from the dissident, he exacted only the minimum of reverence and good order. In the long run, Andrewes convinced men more through the force of personality than authority;[27] he did not really become a controversalist and did not work toward conciliation with the Puritans. Since "reverence and decency," however, had long taken on the connotations of Catholic practices and were attacked accordingly by

24. Henry McAdoo, *The Spirit of Anglicanism* (New York: Charles Scribner's Sons, 1965), pp. 327–28, 338–39.

25. Lancelot Andrewes, *The Pattern of Catechistical Doctrine* (London, 1650), p. 193. This commentary on the second commandment is Andrewes' longest argument on the doctrine of images, but one especially concerned with vocabulary and the interpretation of texts. The exposition of these ideas was probably framed by others (perhaps students' notes of his sermons). Welsby, *Andrewes*, pp. 22–23. Because of his innovations in the liturgy, Andrewes has been called "The greatest single influence on the development of English church plate during the seventeenth century." He was chiefly responsible for the development of a post-Reformation iconography that saw engravings of religious subjects on the furniture of the altar. Oman, *Church Plate*, pp. 145, 225–29. See also, Andrewes, *Two Answers*, pp. 159–63 ("Form for consecrating church plates").

26. Andrewes, *Pattern*, p. 210; *Sermons*, V, p. 60 (1592).

27. Welsby, *Andrewes*, pp. 130, 274; Oman, *Church Plate*, pp. 145–46.

Puritans, others labored actively to convince Englishmen of the importance of these ideas.

John Donne, for instance, could not see why the identification of a beautiful service with Catholicism should render these practices unacceptable and hence illegal. "It is a perverse way, rather to abolish Things and Names (for vehement zeale will work upon Names as well as Things) because they have been abused, then to reduce them to their right use."[28]

Made Dean of St. Paul's in 1620, Donne became in time the most eminent preacher in England; he surpassed Andrewes in fluency but shared that prelate's liturgical sympathies and supported his general policies of worship.[29] He believed that ceremonies in themselves are "indifferent," but where there is no obedience nor ritual, religion necessarily will vanish.[30]

When Christ devested, or supprest the Majesty of his outward appearance, at his Ressurection, *Mary Magdalen* took him but for a *Gardiner*. Ecclesiastical persons in secular habits, lose their respect. Though the very habit be but a Ceremony, yet the distinction of habits is rooted in nature, and in morality: And when the particular habit is enjoyed by lawful Authority, obedience is rooted in nature, and in morality too. In a Watch, the string moves nothing, but yet it conserves the regularity of the motion of all. Ritual and Ceremonial things move not God, but they exalt that Devotion, and they conserve that Order, which does move him.[31]

The early church recognized, Donne reasoned, the need for both order and dignity and encouraged many of the ceremonies that God had bestowed on the Jews. That these things had been once profaned was no reason to abolish them, for the primitive church had returned them again to good use. Even in the Reformation, care was taken

28. John Donne, *The Sermons*, eds. Evelyn Simpson and George Potter (Berkeley and Los Angeles: University of California Press, 1954–62), VII, p. 325. For Donne as a good Anglican of Laudian temperament, see: Evelyn M. Simpson, *A Study of the Prose Works of John Donne* (Oxford: Clarendon Press, 1962), pp. 73–111; A. S. P. Woodhouse, *The Poet and His Faith* (Chicago: University Press, 1965), pp. 55–66; H. J. C. Grierson, "John Donne and the 'Via Media'," *Modern Language Review*, XLIII (1948), 313–14.

29. Augustus Jessopp, *John Donne* (London: Methuen and Co., 1897), pp. 183–86; Edmund Gosse, *The Life and Letters of John Donne* (New York: Dodd, Mead and Co., 1899), II, p. 234.

30. Donne, *Sermons*, X, p. 116.

31. *Ibid.*, VII, p. 430. See also, V, p. 108.

that ceremonies corrupted by Rome were not to be abolished, but resurrected to valid service.[32] The abuse of ceremonies occurs when they are no longer used as simple means for the instruction and edification of the unlettered or "weaker sort;" in time, such abuses can become essential parts of a service to which meritorious grace is assigned. This corruption consists in transferring to religious images attributes and characteristics that never existed; ultimately, it meant bestowing on the image the honor due to God alone through such encumbrances as myths, daily miracles and the like.[33]

But that which was sound in its origins can always be abused in practice; the conclusion that people be denied all ceremonies because of these abuses, is rejected by Donne as it had been by Thomas More.

And this is true, that where there is a frequent preaching, there is *no necessity* of pictures; but will not every man add this, That if the true use of Pictures be preached unto them, there is *no danger* of an abuse; and so, *as Remembrances* of that which hath been taught in the Pulpit, they may be retained.[34]

Though Donne felt that existing disagreements within the English Church should be settled by lawful authority, he was quite put off by the Puritans' refusal to accept images: "Woe to such peremptory abhorrers of Pictures, and to such uncharitable condemners of all those who admit any use of them, as had rather throw down a Church, then let a Picture stand." Donne's curse, however, was balanced with an appeal to conciliation for such things as images were in their nature "indifferent" and should be discussed by both sides.[35] He wished the drive towards decency and order in the English service should not be an isolated example like Andrewes' chapel, but inex-

32. *Ibid.*, VII, pp. 325–56.
33. *Ibid.*, VII, pp. 432–33.
34. *Ibid.*, VII, pp. 431–32; X, pp. 90–91. Yet Donne the poet could write:
"Marke in my heart, O Soule, where thou dost dwell, / The picture of Christ crucified, and tell / Whether that countenance can thee affright, / Teares in his eyes quench the amasing light, / Blood fills his frownes, which from his pierc'd head fell. / And can that tongue adjudge thee unto hell, / Which pray'd forgivenes for his foes fierce spight? / No, no; but as in my idolatrie / I said to all my profane mistresses, / Beauty, of pitty, foulnesse onely is / A signe of rigour: so I say to thee, / To wicked spirits are horrid shapes assign'd, / This beauteous forme assures a pitious minde."
("Thirteenth Holy Sonnet"); Herbert J. C. Grierson, ed., *The Poems of John Donne* (Oxford: Clarendon Press, 1912), I, p. 328.
35. *Sermons*, VII, pp. 162, 174f.

perienced throughout the realm, in parish church as well as episcopal chapel.

The patience of Andrewes and conciliatory attitudes made by Donne were not completely shared by others;[36] the movement was to be neither halted nor weakened by compromise or tolerance. It gained momentum in the provinces where many clergymen restored the "decency" and order of worship that also spelled the return of images. That images accompanied this general return of ceremony and traditional practices of the medieval church can be illustrated by one specific example outside of London.

John Cosin, the prebend or Canon of Durham, who, after the Restoration was to become Bishop of Durham, shared substantially the views of Andrewes and Donne on images. Though he had vigorously condemned the excessive veneration of images for the standard reasons seen before, Cosin qualified these views. He insisted that proper respect has not been given God unless worshippers "fall . . . lowly down before His presence, religiously to adore Him as well with their bodies as their souls."[37] This desire to use sensuous experience in the worship of God, while not countenancing idolatrous images, nevertheless fostered ceremonies and attitudes of aspiration inimical to Puritanism. For such forms of worship it was feared, inevitably would pave the way for the return of images.

Brought by Puritans before the Durham Assizes, a common law court, in 1628 and again in 1629 Cosin was charged with ritualistic and doctrinal innovations. Apparently along with the ornaments of beauty, images had crept in. The articles of inquiry charged that images, candles and "sundry other popish and superstitious rites" were leading people to idolatry.[38]

36. A most vocal one being Richard Montague (or Mountague) *A Gagg for the new Gospell? No! A New Gagg for An Old Goose* (London: 1624), pp. 299–319; *Appello Caesarem, A Just Appeale From Two Unjust Informers* (London, 1625), pp. 248–65. Also, the Bishop of Gloucester, Godfrey Goodman, *The Creatures Praysing God, or the Religion of dumbe creatures* (London, 1622), pp. 28, 32.

37. John Cosin, *Works* (Oxford: John Henry and James Parker, 1855), II, pp. 1–16, 114–15. See also Giles Widdowes, *The Schismatical Puritan* (Oxford, 1630), p. 13.

38. John Cosin, *Correspondence*, ed. George Ornsby (Durham: Surtees Society, 1869), I, p. 162. Peter Smart, another prebend, was behind this attack. See his *The Vanitie and Downe-fall of Superstitious Popish Ceremonies* (Edinburgh, 1628). G. Kitchin, *Seven Sages of Durham* (London: T. Fisher Unwin, 1911), pp. 99–132.

Particularly offensive to his Puritan accusers was the great baptismal font with canopy that Cosin and the chapter had erected. It was a sumptuous piece, made of wood and stone, decorated with images of the Holy Ghost (in the form of a dove) accompanied by a representation of the sun. There were even images of Christ, St. John the Baptist, and the four evangelists at the font "which 6 pictures cost 20^{li}., as the painter told me." [39]

Cosin's accusers alleged that these ceremonies were opposed to the Act of Uniformity. The decision of the court, however, revealed the strength of the liturgical movement: the indictments were rejected and Cosin and his followers were commended for bringing "decencie and order" to God's service. [40] What Cosin attempted to do on a local level would be matched in time throughout the realm; his ideas were not new, but his willingness to push and in the process, to face charges of "innovation" showed the progress of the "new Anglicanism."

In William Laud, the thrust towards "decency and order" received its greatest champion and the strongest churchmen since Wolsey. [41] This busy prelate had travelled rapidly from the presidency of St. John's College, Oxford to the bishoprics of St. David's and London. Along this route, he was rewarded with the Deanery of the royal chapel and the office of privy councillor. In 1633 he would become Archbishop of Canterbury and primate of all England.

Under James, the English Church had arrived at a point where it might indeed assert its independent existence apart from Rome or Geneva. Hooker, Jewel and Andrewes had sought to defend this separate existence through an appeal to Scripture and a use of the primitive Christian Church as a model. They rejected the two roads of Roman Catholicism and Calvinism seeing in the Old Testament idea

---

39. Cosin, *Correspondence*, I, p. 168. See also Prynne, *Canterburies Doome*, pp. 73–74; Margaret Whinney and Oliver Miller, *English Art 1625–1714* (Oxford: Clarendon Press, 1957), pp. 58–59, plate IIa; J. Charles Wall, *Porches and Fonts* (London: Wells, Gardener and Darton, 1912), pp. 223–24, 331.

40. Cosin, *Correspondence*, I, pp. 144–45. In the second case (1629), Cosin and others were indicted but there was "no such direct law whereon to ground them." (Cosin, *Correspondence*, I, xxv). See Bond and Camm, *Roodscreens*, I, pp. 117–18 on the screen Cosin will later be accused of erecting at Durham.

41. Not an unjust comparison; see a *True Relation, or Rather Parallel, between Cardinal Wolsey ... and William Laud* (London, 1641).

of a godly prince a means to maintain the English Church against the pretensions of both.

In William Laud, the Crown had not only an honest administrator, but a strong advocate of kingly power. In was under this protection of the Crown that Laud would attempt to return to the order and discipline of Andrewes, but the implications of Laud's reforms would go considerably beyond that imagined or desired by his predecessors.[42]

Laud claimed, however, that it was not his desire to innovate. He accepted the primatial office with full intention of "seeing that the Prayer Book was observed and that the royal injunctions for the maintenance of order in the Church were carried out."[43] In reality, he aimed at the removal of Puritanism as an effective religious force and a return of Catholic order in worship through the uniformity of clergy and laity alike. In furtherance of this aim, he would depend on those bishops of like persuasion—Neile of York, Juxon of London, and Wren of Ely.[44]

Laud could legally defend the traditional established form of worship—the Elizabethan settlement—and at the same time, emphasize qualities latent within the service. In 1622, his reservation on religious imagery had been similar to Bishop Andrewes's; during his conference with the Jesuit Fisher, he argued that the doctrine of images was unknown in the ancient church and that Rome was too pagan in the practice of iconolatry. Clarification is necessary because

42. Paul Welsby, *George Abbot* (London: SPCK, 1962), pp. 121, 148–49. William Lamont, *Godly Rule, Politics and Religion 1603–60* (New York: St. Martin's Press, 1969), pp. 56–77.

43. C. H. Simpkinson, *Life and Times of William Laud* (London: John Murray, 1894), pp. 78, 91. See also William Laud, *The Works*, ed. W. Scott and J. Bliss (Oxford: John Henry Parker, 1847–60), VI, pp. 46–70, in which he deals with the problem of innovations.

44. The first visitation articles of Wren of Norwich show agreement in matters of faith and discipline with Laud. (Cardwell, *Documentary Annals*, II, pp. 251–58). Later Wren will be accused of idolatry and superstition by the House of Commons, December, 1640. See the visitation articles of Juxon, 1634, in William H. Hutton, *The English Church 1625–1714* (London: Macmillan, 1903), pp. 56–57; Trevor-Roper, *Laud*, p. 39. See the rich inventory of Neile as Dean of Westminster Abbey, 1617–29 in Perkins, *Westminster Abbey*, III, pp. 205–13. Later the list of Laud's "followers" will be expanded to Pierce of Bath and Wells, Lindsay of Peterborough, Montague of Chichester and Skinner of Bristol. Prynne, *Canterburies Doome*, p. 93.

"the doctrine . . . is so full of danger, that it works strongly, both upon the learned and unlearned, to the scandal of religion, and the perverting of truth." The problem, Laud believed, occurs when people believe that there is an intrinsic divinity residing in the image. As in all cases, ". . . ceremonies do not hurt the people, but profit them, so there be a mean kept, and the bye be not put for the main; that is, so we place not the principal part of our piety in them."[45]

But if Laud was reserved in his attitude toward images themselves, his wariness evaporated when he spoke of the contemplated building scheme of St. Paul's Cathedral that would reflect the earthly glory of the Church. In a sermon at court in June of 1621, Laud compared King James to Solomon—for would he not, like that Hebrew king, build a new Jerusalem? Such a designation would reflect the unity of God's abode and the king's dwelling—united just as was the English Church and state.

Therefore when you sit down to consult, you must not forget the church; And when we kneele down to pray, we must not forget the State: both are but one Jerusalem.[46]

If Laud's purpose was to buttress his plans for liturgical renewal (St. Paul's being one of them) with the support of the government, the center of his reform revolved around the Eucharist; this was to his supporters "the whole content of the Christian religion and far greater lessons than even the best of sermons can provide."[47] Consequently, Laud argued that order and respect was due the holy table upon which the Eucharist was displayed. Andrewes's chapel reflected the basic premise that the liturgy must encompass the whole of man's nature—an appeal to the senses as well as to the soul. Thus it was that Andrewes's chapel was taken as a guide and model of Laudian reform: holy table covered with an embroidered carpet, candlesticks, sacred vessels, incense, copes and in time, images.[48]

Since King Edward's time, the altar had become a table; as the lat-

45. Laud, Works, II, pp. 308–12.
46. Quoted in Per Palme, Triumph of Peace, a study of the Whitehall Banqueting House (Stockholm: Almquist and Wiksell, 1956), pp. 23–24.
47. Herbert Thorndike, The Theological Works (Oxford: John Henry Parker, 1853), I, pp. 274–75, 833.
48. G. W. O. Addleshaw, The High Church Tradition (London: Faber and Faber, 1941), p. 77. Cosin, Works, V, pp. 14–15. Andrewes, Sermons, I, pp. 263–64.

ter had been moved into the lower end of the chancel, certain abuses had crept into the divine service. The table was used as a convenient place to throw a coat or set a lunch. Though this arrangement had some advantages in allowing a larger number of communicants to participate more easily in the service, Laud's view was that the overall effect of over-familiarity with something that should be kept sacred was detrimental to reverence.[49] Convenience had made the holy mundane, and this had led to contempt with dismal implications for the beauty of worship itself.

As Dean of Gloucester, Laud had effected in 1616–1617 a reform wherein the altar was permanently placed at the upper end of the choir; this had been the precedent of Andrewes in his own chapel; it had also been the precedent in certain cathedrals and in the royal chapel.[50] Placing the communion table back where the altar had stood carried with it not only implications of the mass, but "the corollary that the manner in which it was arrayed mattered very much more." [51] To insure respect and reverence, images, light and incense would be introduced; the altar was then enclosed with a fixed railing (figure 30) which opened in the front or side. Rails themselves were an innovation, except for a few Elizabethan churches which had used them as a substitute for chancel screens (figure 31).[52] After 1617, scattered parishes imitated Laud's arrangement and adopted the program that would bring with it striking changes in the liturgy; this in turn would affect the physical appearance of churches in the direction of allowing more images.[53]

Under James, the liturgical renewal could develop only so far without threating the compromise of the Elizabethan settlement. Laud

49. Addleshaw, *Architectural Setting*, pp. 116, 118.

50. Oman, *Church Plate*, pp. 175–76. Such a precedent was also followed in principle by other Laudians: C. Wren, *Parentalia* (London: T. Osborn, 1750), pp. 81, 83.

51. Oman, *Church Plate*, p. 156.

52. Addleshaw, *Architectural Setting*, pp. 117, 121; Laud, *Works*, VI, pp. 59–60; Bond, *Chancel*, p. 131. Cautley, *Suffolk Churches*, pp. 187–88. Cox, *Churchwardens' Accounts*, p. 104. The earliest account of rails in England is 1574.

53. Addleshaw, *Architectural Setting*, p. 122. For one example, see the brief flowering of woodwork in Cornwall in the 1620s. Brown, *Cornwall*, pp. 54–55. The early visitation articles of Laud in Works, V, pp. 381–95 (St. David's 1622), V, 399–418 (London, 1628) tell us less than one would expect in regard to these changes. Trevor-Roper, *Essays*, p. 144.

himself had moved from a guarded view of images to a respectful tolerance to an enthusiasm that hoped to carry out substantial religious changes throughout the realm; time would show that he would get such an opportunity.

VIII. THE NEW ANGLICANISM

I stress dignity and external worship.

WILLIAM LAUD, *The History of the Troubles and Trial.*

But you can't expect a government to know what original art is.

JOYCE CARY, *The Horse's Mouth*

DISSATISFACTION over the English Church had been widespread under James I; with the commencement of the reign of his son, Charles I in 1625, many Englishmen continued to be saddened by the disrepute of the established church, its unclarified doctrines and practices, the decay of its physical fabric.[1] Disagreement existed not so much about the need for change but about the form and nature it should take. The Puritans, wishing for further reformation in the direction of that occurring on the Continent, sought the strong rule of Scripture as criterion for the various ceremonies and practices of the Church. The Laudian party claimed to support the Elizabethan settlement but in reality aimed at a new reformation that would direct England away from the biblicism of the early Reformation and toward many of the traditional practices of the medieval church.

When Laud became Primate of all England in 1633, he wished to propagate the liturgical reforms with which his party had only experimented in different parts of the realm. He also wished to initiate a definition of these reforms which he hoped would become a permanent part of the laws and traditions of the English Church. While Andrewes had aimed at persuasion through example, and appeal to reason and convenience in matters of worship, Laud demanded obedience and thought he would gain it through coercion.[2] The Reformation had laid violent hands on churches and their ornaments; rapid changes in religious doctrine had furthermore brought confusion and, worst of all, disrespect to the adjuncts of God's worship. Little

1. Under Archbishop Abbot, discipline and uniformity had become lax, resulting in a great variety of services. After October, 1627, Abbott was sequestered and commissioners (Laud being one of them) directed the affairs of the Church.
2. George, *Protestant Mind and the English Reformation*, p. 362.

wonder that Laud could later conclude that churches lay "very nastily."[3]

Laud's favorite example of irreverence and sacrilege was an incident on Christmas Day, 1630 at Tadlow in Cambridgeshire, when a dog stole the bread meant for the Eucharist. It was a lesson in the need to protect the sanctity of the chancel with rails.[4]

For further evidence of this disrespect to God and Church, Laud could point to the nave of St. Paul's in London which had long been used as a promenade for the idle and a shop for the business man ("Paul's Walk"). Porters carried through their produce and merchants loitered with their associates to clinch business deals; advertising was displayed on the walls and pillars of the nave. The noise was intense—"like that of bees, a strange humming or buzz mixed, of walking, tongues and feet; it is a kind of still roar or loud whisper."[5] Servants even waited for expected employment at one of the piers called appropriately, "The serving-man's pillar."[6] Even Falstaff had engaged Bardolph as his servant in the very precincts of the cathedral.[7]

Laud believed not only that this commercialism was part of a larger disrespect to the Church and its ceremonies, but that in times past, secular activities in God's house had been far less conspicuous than they were currently in England. Most important, he insisted that such disrespect produced a concomitant spiritual indifference that resulted in a decline of true faith. He considered it essential that Englishmen again be taught the correct attitude and behavior towards holy things; Laud's interest in images was due to this understanding of them as important aids in the public services of the Church which, in turn, nurtured faith. Consequently it was necessary to reinforce if not defend the very things then abused because they

3. Laud, *Works*, IV, p. 283.
4. Cox, *Churchwardens' Accounts*, pp. 307–09. Addleshaw, *Architectural Setting*, p. 188.
5. W. R. Matthews and W. M. Atkins (eds.), *A History of St. Paul's Cathedral* (London: John Baker, 1964), p. 109. *Documents Illustrating the History of St. Paul's Cathedral*, ed., W. Sparrow Simpson (London: Camden Society, 1880). p. L.
6. George H. Cook, *Old St. Paul's Cathedral* (London: Phoenix House, 1955), p. 19. The best treatment of Paul's Walk is in Davies, *Secular Use of Church Building*, pp. 142–54.
7. Shakespeare, *2 Henry IV*, I, ii.

would aid in returning beauty and decency to English worship. Nowhere does the archbishop show any independent aesthetic interest in images, but always considered their importance in the context of the liturgy. Consequently, he raised the question of images within a broader view of worship than hitherto had been entertained since the reign of Henry VIII. In the late sixteenth century, Richard Hooker had discussed the implications of this kind of worship that depended on material means for the realization of spiritual ends. Laud meant to carry out Hooker's ideas and to work for a uniformity of religious practices throughout the realm.

It must be remembered, however, that for the Puritan, no church or place signified special holiness; this was also true of altars or images for things in themselves are never holy they believed; it is only in their use for holy purposes that dignity occurs.[8]

However, for Laud, the church was hallowed ground. He believed that every detail of the service ought to be directed to the worship of God. If beauty was the result of order imposed on chaos, then Laud insisted that man's religious actions were furthered, ordered and made understandable through visible and audible signs. These things were simply the natural and inevitable outward reflections of a true inward faith.

As has been seen, Laud thought the altar the most important piece of church furniture and thought it considerably above the pulpit in dignity; at the former is said, *Hoc est corpus meum*, while in the latter, merely *Hoc est verbum meum*. A greater reverence, he believed, was due to the body than to the word of Christ.[9] This opinion of the altar or table did not imply a Real Presence at Communion. Though others like Richard Montague might have moved in this direction,

<hr>

8. *Mercurius Rusticus* (1646), p. 216; Peter Hall (ed.), *Reliquiae Liturgicae: Documents connected with the Liturgy of the Church of England.* (Bath: Binns and Goodwin, 1847), III, p. 82 (Westminster Directory).

9. For the then developing literature on altar worship at the east end of churches and the distinctions between table and altar, see Peter Heylyn, *A Coale from the Altar* (London, 1636), which was answered by John Pocklington, *Altare Christianum or the Dead Vicar's Plea* (London, 1637). The latter was in turn answered by Laud's chaplain, William Bray, *A sermon of the Lord's Supper* (London, 1641). See also the controversy, John Williams, *The Holy Table, Name and Thing* (London, 1637), and Heylyn's *Antidorum Lincolniense, or an Answer to a Book, called 'The Holy Table, Name and Things'* (London, 1637). Cardwell, *Synodalia*, I, pp. 404–06. Laud, *Works*, VI, pp. 59, 61.

Laud's views were eventually summed up in the seventh canon of 1640:

This situation of the Holy Table doth not imply that it is, or ought to be esteemed, a true and proper altar, whereon Christ is again really sacrificed, but it is and may be called an altar . . . in that sense in which the primitive Church called it an altar, and in no other.[10]

In order to underline this sanctity which instills holy reverence in the worshipper, altars were decorated with tapestries, sculptures of saints, crucifixes and colored glass; the whole chancel received carved and decorated rails while a canopy was often erected over the altar itself.[11]

Despite these adjuncts to the service which had not been seen for sometime in England, Laud claimed to walk a middle path between "overburdening the service of God," and leaving it "naked." He refused, like Hooker and Donne, to identify these things with Rome. For are not ceremonies "the hedge that fence the substance of religion from all the indignities which profaneness and sacrilege too commonly put upon it?"[12]

Since the time of Edward VI, attempts at uniformity in the English Church had developed through enforcing a common liturgy rather than through a strict definition of doctrine. Laud clearly understood that if the rite of Communion spelled fundamental theological ideas on worship, the placement of the table would be crucial in determining these ideas. Moving the table to the east end, for instance, would argue for its greater identification with altars and special holiness; images, candles and church plate would be introduced as necessary accessories. Moving the table into the nave, however, would reinforce the communal bond that required no ornaments.

Neither the Prayer Book under Edward VI, nor the Elizabethan Injunctions nor even the Canons of 1604 of James I had decided this

10. Queen Elizabeth's injunctions had not impugned or forbidden altars; since the Lord's Supper was called a sacrifice, "so may the Holy Table be called an altar, and consequently set up in the place where the altar stood." Heylyn, *A Coale from the Altar*; Cardwell, *Documentary Annals*, I, pp. 233–34.

11. Addleshaw, *Architectural Setting*, pp. 138–39, 145.

12. William Hutton, *William Laud* (Boston: Houghton, Mifflin, 1895), pp. 31, 64–66, 70, 99–103. Peter Heylyn, *Cyprianus Anglicus* (Dublin: John Hyde and Robert Owen, 1719), p. 8. Hall, *Works*, VII, p. 474.

matter of the table; in practice, the decision had remained with churchwardens and parishioners in individual parishes. If the archbishop could dispute their control, he could transfer this power to bishops of his own choosing. Authority to determine the place of the altar would be only the first step in the direction of furthering practices favored by Laud; other liturgical changes such as the return of images, incense and special devotions would follow in the wake of the renewal of traditional ceremonies and objects.[13]

Laud's test case came in 1633. It was the legally constituted authority of the King to decide ecclesiastical matters except when his discretionary power was limited by acts of Parliament. In the church of St. Gregory-by-Paul's, it was judged that it would be the bishop in his diocese who would determine the place of the altar. Charles I, as Head of the Church, had acted in making this decision and had solved a problem which Elizabeth, for political reasons, had purposely left vague.

In the controversy over the cross in the Queen's chapel, the Elizabethan bishops had discovered the dangers of differing with the legal head of the Church. Under Charles I, the coincidence of the Laudian bishops' liturgical ideas with the king's would make it possible for them to resurrect many of the traditional Catholic practices in the established religion. The reforms of ceremony reflected doctrinal issues; uniformity on all points could be achieved through the sympathy and powers of the Crown. Churchwardens would soon be ordered "to place the communion table under the eastern wall of the chancel, where formerly the altar stood; to set a decent rail before it to avoid profaneness. . ."[14]

To enforce the decision recently made by the King and by implication to exercise greater uniformity in the English Church, Laud acted to re-establish the law of visitation. This was, as has been seen, an inquiry into the customs and practices of the diocese, parish by parish —to find out if conformity existed. A metropolitan visitation was thus undertaken from 1633–1636 under the direction of Laud's energetic

13. See Addleshaw, *Architectural Setting*, p. 127. Bishop Andrewes' chapel was emulated, but its ornaments were only endorsed by the primate. Laud, *Works*, IV, p. 251.

14. Heylyn, *Cyprianus Anglicus*, p. 285.

vicar-general, Sir Nathaniel Brent. He and his agents were empowered to investigate every parish, little or great, by questioning and probing for ecclesiastical abuses, needed repairs to the church fabrics and general problems of conformity and discipline.[15]

Much neglect and ruin of the fabric of the churches and their furnishings during the past fifty years was noted; many plans for restoring them were laid, for the archbishop's concern for liturgical uniformity was backed up and sustained by the power of the king.[16] There is no specific mention of images in these visitation articles possibly because, given their past history, prudence dictated no direct reference be made to them. On the other hand, images were identified and subsumed within the larger ideas of consecration and the position of the altar. Once these essentials were accepted, images and other matters would follow.[17]

The arguments based on history and tradition which had been used by the Puritans to argue for iconoclasm were now appealed to in defense of iconolatry.[18] Laud was convinced that popery had been vanquished in England because its people were at last sufficiently instructed in the dangers of worshipping images; consequently, paint-

15. Allen French, *Charles I and the Puritan Upheaval* (London: George Allen and Unwin, 1955), p. 273. There is relatively little information about parochial conditions as contained in the records of the metropolitan visitation. Yet see E. R. C. Brinkworth, "The Laudian Church in Buckinghamshire," *University of Birmingham Historical Journal*, V (1955), 31–59, where the visitation books of the archdeacon of Buckingham show an effective tightening up of discipline. For the effects of Archbishop Neile's visitations in York, see Ronald Marchant, *The Puritans and Church Courts in the Diocese of York, 1560–1642* (London: Longmans, Green and Co., 1960), pp. 56, 63.

16. Hart, *Country Clergy*, p. 94. Laud's accounts of the state of his province were sent to Charles who initialed specific problems that Laud wanted the King to know about. The two worked well together. Laud, *Works*, V, pp. 317–70 (1633–39).

17. *Ibid.*, V, pp. 421–35. There is also little mention of rails in Laud's visitation articles, but we know they were being imposed on parishes on account of the various complaints of parishioners. *Ibid.*, V, pp. 342–43, 362; VI, pp. 477–79. Many objected because there was no law or canon to sustain such innovations, Laud thought "for decency sake," they should be used. *Ibid.*, V, p. 360. Consequently, the visitation articles of Laud are more important for what is left out or implied than what is stated explicitly. The same can be said of Wren's *Articles to be inquired of within the Diocese of Norwich* (London, 1636). *Articles . . . Ely* (London, 1638).

18. Laud, *Works*, IV, p. 8.

ings and sculpture could be lawfully used in churches without fear of idolatry. Laud also claimed that early Protestant reformers never felt the need to enjoin obedience by specific rules or particular rubrics because many practices witnessed under Roman Catholicism were clearly acceptable and still in use. For beneath all such ceremonies lay this rule:

> . . . that all such Rites as had been practised in the Church of Rome, and not abolished, nor disclaimed by any Doctrine, Law or Canon of the first Reformers, were to continue in the same state in which they found them.[19]

Yet Laud was hard to pin down; his answers to complaints could be as circuitous as the Puritans' scriptural justification of iconoclasm. For instance, he could argue that Queen Elizabeth and her Council, in all their laws and injunctions, had never meant to eliminate all images, but only those abused pictures of "false and feigned Miracles, as had no truth of being or existed in Nature."[20] Very frequently, the archbishop's arguments justifying this or that ceremony were subsumed if not lost in the larger arguments justifying the authority of the Church. Laud was not about to defend publicly individual ceremonies and props that were all in the legitimate domain of his ecclesiastical power. The Sherfield case was clear on this.

In February of 1632, the recorder of Salisbury, Henry Sherfield, was censured in the Court of Star Chamber. Disapproving of a window portraying God creating the world, Sherfield had received permission from the vestry to take it down.[21] The Bishop of Salisbury heard about this and indignantly vetoed the whole idea. Thereupon the recorder gained entry to the church and in the act of breaking the window with a pike-staff, fell and hurt himself (his wounds took a month to heal). The event proved of momentous interest throughout England for it struck against the episcopal authority supported by the Crown. This interest increased when the attorney-general initiated proceedings against Sherfield in Star Chamber with twenty-two privy councillors in attendance. Not only was Laud's policy on wor-

19. Laud, *Works*, IV, pp. 11–12; III, p. 341. Heylyn, *Cyprianus Anglicus*, IV, p. 9.
20. Laud, *Works*, IV, p. 9.
21. Cox, *Churchwardens' Accounts*, pp. 88.

ship under review, but the case clearly underlined the Puritan objection to an art that was not literal. Sherfield was particularly upset that the window was not a true representation of creation:

[F]or that it contained divers forms of little old men in blue and red coats, and naked in the heads, feet and hands, for the picture of God the Father; and that in one place he was set forth with a pair of compasses in his hands, laying them upon the sun and moon; and the painter had set Him forth creating the birds on the third day, and had placed the picture of beasts and men and women on the fifth day—the man was a naked man, and the woman naked in some part, as much from the knees upwards, rising out of the man.[22]

What was intolerable to Sherfield, apparently, was that the artist seemed to extrapolate from the Bible and did not base his representation of creation on what was there literally described; the window confused more than it instructed, Sherfield insisted.

Laud, however, refused to countenance the vestry's removing or displaying "anything in the church that is doubtful." Thus its order was invalid and Sherfield's action was sacrilegious and criminal. But this opinion impelled Laud to defend the proper use of images. His claim was that religious representations were used two hundred years after Christ and that even the Fathers had accepted them. But of course, the images in church are not meant for adoration—otherwise they would be idols.

I do not think it lawful to make the picture of God the Father; but 'tis lawful to make the picture of Christ, and Christ is called the express images of His Father. I don't mean to say that the picture of Christ as God the Son may be made; for the Deity cannot be portrayed or pictured, though the humanity may.[23]

But Laud refused to develop his ideas. Within the context, his concern was not whether the broken window might be superstitious, but the fact that it was removed. He even refused to discuss whether the picture should have been removed. ("And I shall crave liberty not to declare my opinion at this time. . .") The whole problem is

22. Quoted in Hugh Shortt (ed.), *City of Salisbury* (London: Phoenix House, 1957), p. 70.
23. Laud, *Works*, VI, i, pp. 16–17. See William Prynne's treatment of the case in *Canterburies Doome*, pp. 102–03.

this: did Sherfield break the window in contempt of the Church's authority?

Laud's defense of images is not elaborated essentially because images are seen within the context of the proper jurisdiction of the Church to be used for the sake of beauty and decency of worship. Laud could support images through defending the bishop's power to make such decisions. In the Sherfield case, what was really under attack according to Laud was not the use of images, but the very real power of the Church. Images are employed because of the decency of worship; they are defended because of their identification with the authority of the archbishop. Lord Protector Somerset had employed the same argument (that of exercising legitimate power in the interest of public order) to get rid of images.

The reasons of order and good taste had been used by Elizabeth to enforce certain practices and objects in the English service; the Laudians, however, were more ambitious. In order to support their commitment to uniformity in the established church and to disseminate graphically their theological and liturgical ideas, they undertook a large and extensive building program that sought the beautification of churches and the refurbishing of the liturgy through painting and sculpture. Chancels were again divided from the church proper by newly constructed "grates of wood curiously carved or of iron, or of brass cast into comely works." Communion tables were decorated with rich carpets, precious silks and linens. Images framed the sacred table.[24]

A quality of sumptuousness prevailed; images lent both dignity and beauty to the holy. After the remodelling of the church of St. Katherine Kree in London, it was consecrated by Laud with great pomp in 1630.

At the Bishop's approaching near the west door of the church, the hangbies of the Bishop cried out with a loud voice, "Open, open, ye everlasting doors, that the King of glory may enter in": and presently (as by miracle) the doors flew open, and the Bishop . . . entered in; as soon as they were in the church, the Bishop fell down upon his knees, with his eyes lifted up and his hands and arms spread abroad, uttering many words, and saying, "This place is holy, and this ground is holy: in the name of the Father, the Son,

24. *De Templis: A Treatise of Temples*, by N. T. (London, 1638), pp. 184–201.

and the Holy Ghost, I pronounce it holy," and then he took up some of the earth or dust, and threw it up in the air.[25]

Parish churches were beautified with newly glazed windows of rich decorative figures. Paintings and statuary depicting the history of the saints were brought in to decorate new altars of cedar and inlaid woods; colorful tapestries, candlesticks of precious metals, Turkish carpets and rich plate completed the picture. A statue of the Virgin with Child was placed in the new porch of the Church of St. Mary the Virgin, Oxford (figure 32), in spite of Puritan objections. Magdalen College chapel received a new black and white marble floor and new stalls, while classical orders and festoons adorned the Gothic tracery. Such ornamentation had made the chapel a worthy place for worship and as the work was completed, the altar was put at the east end and adorned with crucifix and tapestries depicting the life of Christ.[26]

The church of St. Giles in the Fields, London, was particularly sumptuous. The interior was divided into three parts: the chancel, set off by a large screen with gate, had two large pillars and three statues: St. Paul with his sword, Barnabas with his book and Peter with his keys. These figures were, in turn, framed by winged cherubs and lions. A reading desk near the altar, draped with a covering of purple and gold, held two large books of needlework portraying Christ and the Virgin.[27]

Others who sympathized with Laudian objectives carried this tradition and industry into the provinces. Robert Wright had blotted out the inscriptions of the Ten Commandments in his cathedral at Lich-

---

25. William Prynne, *Canterburies Doome*, p. 113. William Prynne, *A Quench-Coal* (London, 1637), p. 197. On Bishop Wren's liturgical policies, see C. Wren, *Parentalia* (London: T. Osborn, 1750), pp. 73–114. The church of St. Katherine Kree has since undergone much interior reconstruction in 1732, 1874, 1880, 1960. T. F. Bumpus, *Ancient London Churches* (London: T. Werner Laurie, n.d.), pp. 241–49. Pevsner, *London*, pp. 145–46. Philip Norman, "The Church of St. Catherine Cree," *St. Paul's Ecclesiological Society*, vol. 190.

26. Alfred Clapham, "The Survival of Gothic in Seventeenth Century England," *The Archaeological Journal*, CVI, Supplement (1952), 5. J. Lees-Milne, *The Age of Inigo Jones* (London: B. T. Batsford, 1953), p. 148–49. Laud, *Works*, V, pp. 62, 84, 99, 115, 123, 142–43. VII, 191f. Trevor-Roper, *Laud*, pp. 284–85.

27. *Petition by the Puritans to Parliament against the Rector, Dr. Heywood, 1640. Some account of the Hospital and Parish of St. Giles in the Fields* (London, 1640), p. 201.

field just as Edwardian reformers had blotted out the medieval paintings with letters. Wright added a large crucifix "as big and large as
any three men," above the altar.[28] James Montague, in finding his
church at Bath in great disrepair, left it a symbol of the Laudian revival. At Cambridge, the victory of the Laudian party in the 1630s
soon transformed the faces of the colleges; Matthew Wren, himself
the Master of Peterhouse, inspired a great burst of building activity.[29]

What inspired much of this beautification was what was considered
by the Laudians the return of religion to its rightful relation to nature. For Godfrey Goodman, Bishop of Gloucester, the Incarnation
of Christ had as its logical extension in time the Christian Church
which took to herself the things of this life and deemed them good:

> Thus in Christian religion, if our ceremonies were first invented by Pagans,
> if our prayers were first composed by Heathen, yet still we may lawfully use
> them; for when we prefixe, *In nomine Patris & Filii, & Spiritus Sancti*, or
> when we shut up our prayers with *Per Christum Dominum Nostrum*, then
> we give them the tincture of Christianity.

Donne had said as much but Laud, it must be remembered, had
defended images for their ability to communicate historical events of
a religious nature. Laud's matter-of-fact view of religious representations was not shared by Goodman, who believed that natural signs
could depict an invisible, spiritual world. Goodman opened up the
possibility of images enlargening our experience since all of natural
life is sanctified for man's use. It is in these things, he claimed, that
men find "the visible signes of invisible graces;"

> Suppose the foure Elements, The Fire, when as God appeared like fire in a
> bramblebush, and the Holy descended in fiery tongues; The Aire, when as
> Christ together with his own breath, breathed out his Spirit: The Water, in
> our baptisme: The Earth, in her fruits: Bread and Wine in the Eucharist.
> Thus they share in our sacraments, according to the capacity of their
> nature. . .[30]

---

28. Prynne, *A Looking Glasse for all Lordly Prelates* (1636), p. 43.

29. Lees-Milne, *Inigo Jones*, pp. 154–157. The history of Peterhouse College
Chapel (consecrated in 1632) is confusing; see R. Willis and J. Clark, *The Architectural History of the University of Cambridge* (Cambridge: University Press,
1886), I, 31–34, 40–43; II, 50–61. On Cosin's building program, see N. Pevsner,
County Durham (Baltimore: Penguin, 1953), pp. 31–33, 61, 207–08. On the chapel
of the Ferrar family at Little Gidding, see Nicholas Ferrar, *The Story Books of
Little Gidding* (London: Charles J. Thynne, 1913), p. xxv.

30. Goodman, *The Creatures Praysing God*, pp. 28, 32.

Goodman was concerned that this union of grace and nature had not prevailed for some time in the established Church. Fonts where Christians are baptized and make profession of the Trinity and Incarnation are pulled down. Fasting and the observance of religious events like Easter and Good Friday are neglected. Even the memorials of Christ's Passion—the harmless wayside crosses are destroyed.

I found no honour was given to the name of Jesus, no settled Form of Prayer, but everyone left to his own inventions.[31]

In his diocese of Gloucester, Goodman turned Communion tables into altars and railed them, frequently adorning them with tapers, crucifixes and images. At Windsor, he erected a large cross with a richly gilded Christ crucified on one side and a Christ resurrected on the other.[32] Apparently such repairs caused consternation for in August, 1635, the mayor of Windsor wrote Goodman a letter of both thanks and inquiry. The marketplace of that city had never contained a cross before; since the recent act was done without the King's knowledge and license, would this cause trouble for the city corporation? "(F)or no man by law can erect or paint a Crucifix or a Cross in a public place without his Majesty's license as I am informed. . ." Goodman's reply was not really an answer to the question, but an opportunity to argue for the significance of symbols: "The Cross is the sign and badge of Christianity, and implies in effect the whole mystery of our redemption."[33]

The legality of images rested with the power of the Crown. It was in Charles I's acceptance of these things that ultimately made Goodman's actions possible—if not the whole Laudian program itself. With Laud, the King believed in religious conformity defined by a well-composed liturgy that appealed to all the senses.[34] Early in his reign,

---

31. Richard Newcome, *A Memoir of . . . Godfrey Goodman* (Ruthin: Taliesin Press, 1825), pp. 77–78.

32. William Prynne, *The Second Part of the Antipathy* (London: 1641), pp. 316–17. The cross would fall to an iconoclastic mob by 1642.

33. Geoffrey Soden, *Godfrey Goodman Bishop of Gloucester* (London: SPCK, 1953), pp. 238–39. It is significant that Goodman was a secret Roman Catholic after 1636 and was leaning toward Rome before then. Trevor-Roper, *Laud*, pp. 174–78.

34. Philip A. Knachel (ed.), *Eikon Basilike, The Portraiture of His Sacred Majesty in His Solitudes and Sufferings* (Ithaca: Cornell University Press, 1966), p. 96. See also, A. Mayer, "Charles I and Rome," *American Historical Review*, XIX (1914), 13–26.

Charles had commissioned John Cosin to edit a prayer book that would provide the English service with a richer ceremonial than the Book of Common Prayer. Cosin's *Manual of Private Prayer*, published in 1627, for all practical purposes fulfilled this requirement and produced an English equivalent of a Roman service.[35]

Eventually, many Englishmen might claim to see no difference between the services at the Queen's Chapel (Roman Catholic) and those in the King's Chapel (Church of England). In fact, those who flocked to the Queen's Chapel at Somerset House could enjoy a full Baroque illusionism which combined all the arts to create a dramatic service. In order to display the Holy Sacrament, Francois Dieussart had built a machine which recreated a large oval paradise, forty feet high, supported by pillars, ornamented by prophets. Ranged behind the high altar were seven rows of clouds and a good two hundred angels, some adoring the Sacrament while others played musical instruments.[36]

The King's interest in the Laudian program was not based simply on common liturgical objectives; Charles's enthusiasm and support for images and other ornaments were clearly related to the greater context of English art collecting and connoisseurship in the early seventeenth century.[37]

35. John Cosin, *A Collection of Private Devotions* (ed. P. G. Stanwood, Oxford: Clarendon Press, 1967), p. xvi. For the Puritan interpretation, see William Prynne, *A Briefe Survay and Censure of Mr. Cozens His Couzening Devotions* (London, 1628). Martin Havran, *The Catholics in Caroline England* (Stanford: University Press, 1962), pp. 51–52.

36. Cyprien de Gamache, *Memoirs of the Mission in England of the Capuchin Friars of the Province of Paris from the year 1630 to 1669 . . .* trans. in Thomas Birch, *The Court and Time of Charles I* (London, 1849), II, p. 310f.

37. The literature here is voluminous. Claude Phillips, *The Picture Gallery of Charles I* (London: Seeley and Co., 1896). G. F. Waagen, *Works of Art and Artists in England* (London: John Murray, 1838), I, pp. 24–30. Lionel Cust, "Notes on Pictures in the Royal Collections," *Burlington Magazine*, XIX (1911), 127–33. Oliver Millar (ed.), "Abraham Van Der Doort's Catalogue of the Collections of Charles I," *Walpole Society*, XXXVII (1958–60). W. G. Blaikie Murdoch, *The Royal Stuarts in Their Connection with Art and Letters* (Edinburgh: J. and J. Gray Co., 1908). M. B. Pickel, *Charles I as Patron of Poetry and Drama* (London: Frederick Muller, 1936). William B. Rye, *England as seen by Foreigners* (London: John Russell Smith, 1865), pp. 157–67 (pictures in the royal collection in 1613). Henry G. Hewlett, "Charles the First as a Picture Collector," *The Nineteenth Century*, XXVIII (August, 1890), 201–17. Francis Henry Taylor, *The Taste of Angels* (Boston: Little Brown and Co., 1948), pp. 208–34. Francis Haskell, *Patrons and Painters* (New York: Alfred A. Knopf, 1963), pp. 177–79. F. Grossman, "Notes

Charles's artistic interests were not, however, shared by his arch-bishop. As has been seen, Laud encouraged the use of painting, sculp-ture and architecture for their ability to bring men to understand ideas which were religious in character; he cultivated works of art more for the dignity and propriety it gave to the Church and its liturgy than for any aesthetic interest. His tastes were conservative, preferring to support established styles such as Gothic and Roma-nesque rather than initiating any artistic innovation.[38] Thus, the products of his program show no high degree of taste, but a myriad of architectural styles and internal fittings whose richness sought to mirror the richness of Laudian devotions.

Fundamentally, Laud was untouched by the inward mysteries of Christianity and his emotional attitude toward the liturgy was postu-lated on the solidity of formal loveliness. Material adjuncts, whether brick, mortar, paint or glass, were as important to him in worship as visitations and ruthlessness were to his reorganization of the Church. If Charles's and Laud's motives did not exactly coalesce, at least their cooperation produced results.[39]

St. Paul's Cathedral in London, for example, received considerable attention from both King and primate. Former commissions ap-pointed to look into the cathedral's decayed fabric had done little; the new commission that came into being in April, 1631, was sus-tained by the enthusiasm of Laud and the devotion of Charles.[40] Both

on the Arundel and Imstenraedt Collections," *Burlington Magazine*, LXXXIV–V (1944), 151–54, 173–76. Mary Hervey, *The Life, Correspondence and Collections of Thomas Howard, Earl of Arundel* (Cambridge: University Press, 1921). Francis C. Springell, *Connoisseur and Diplomat* (London: Maggs Bros., Ltd., 1963). M. R. Toynbee, "Some Early Portraits of Charles I," *Burlington Magazine* XCI (1949), 4–9. K. A. Esdaile, "The Busts and Statues of Charles I," *Burlington Magazine* XCI (1949), 9–14. Michael Levey, *The Later Italian Pictures in the collection of Her Majesty the Queen.* (London: Phaidon Press, 1964), pp. 9–19. Oliver Millar, *The Tudor-Stuart and Early Georgian Pictures in the Collection of Her Majesty the Queen* (London: Phaidon Press, 1963), I, pp. 13–20.

38. Lees-Milne, *Age of Inigo Jones*, pp. 147–48. John Summerson, *Architecture in Britain, 1530–1830* (London: Penguin Books, 1953), p. 100; W. C. Costin, *The History of St. John's College* (Oxford: Clarendon Press, 1958), pp. 40–45. John E. Stocks, "The Church of St. John the Evangelist, Leeds," *The Publication of the Thoresby Society*, XXIV (1919), 190–224.

39. Trevor-Roper, *Laud*, pp. 125–26. Wilkins, *Concilia*, IV, p. 492.

40. William Dugdale, *The History of St. Paul's Cathedral* (London: Lackington, Hughes, Harding, etc., 1818), pp. 104–09.

men sought in this reconstructed cathedral a reflection of religious stability which they felt had long been lacking since the Reformation. (Figure 33 shows the reconstruction by Inigo Jones of the north elevation.)

Since no Parliament or Convocation was summoned between the years 1629–1640, there were few official protests against the policies and accomplishments of the Laudians. It was perhaps due to this eleven-year hiatus, or "personal rule" of the King, that made the Laudian program appear a success. Early in the reign of James I, this movement had been hesitant and its building program was less imitated than it was condemned; evidence is not complete, but it would appear that by the late 1630s, the use of images and other liturgical aids had become relatively widespread.[41]

The issue of the placement of the Communion table which had been used initially by Laud to effect control over churchwardens and parishioners was hotly contested as a matter of theological importance. The Puritans emphasized a view of the Eucharist as a commemorative event: they refused to kneel at the altar rails or even to enter the chancel. They wished the Communion table to be carried into the nave and set east-west, with Communion administered to those sitting around it.[42] Many feared the changes that were being introduced by Laud as a kind of "backsliding" that moved the English Church away from the Puritan interpretation of the Elizabethan settlement.[43]

Puritans came to see not only the employ of altars as both unscriptural and idolatrous, but they also questioned the consecration of churches and hallowing of images which Laud found consistent with his attitude towards altars. Much Puritan vehemence against church furniture and consecrated buildings was thus a reaction against ex-

41. Peter King, "Bishop Wren and the Suppression of the Norwich Lecturers," *The Historical Journal* XI (1968), 237–54. Hutton, *Laud,* p. 77. Brinkworth, "Laudian Church in Buckinghamshire," *University of Birmingham Historical Journal* V (1955), 46, 59. In Somerset alone, Laud's disciples restored more than 150 altars to the east end in one year (1634). A. K. Wickham, *Churches of Somerset* (London: Phoenix House, 1952), pp. 68–70. "Laudian Documents," *Somerset Record Society,* XXXXIII (1928), 182–85.

42. F. Bond, *The Chancel of English Churches* (Oxford: University Press, 1916), p. 116.

43. Prynne, *Quench-Coal,* p. 5.

ternalization of the holy. When the Laudians maintained that churches succeeded to the same degree of sanctity as the Tabernacle of Moses and the Temple of Solomon, the Puritans insisted that these churches were closer to the holiness of the Jewish synagogues and to which a reverence was due only insofar as they were publicly destined for use in divine service.[44]

Peter Smart in a sermon in Durham Cathedral spoke out against "the continuall increase of Popish and unlawfull ceremonies" introduced by the Laudian party. The church is filled with vestments, crosses, images, altars and all sorts of baggage, he claimed. The superstitious vanities are born of the hand and mind of men; they undermine and overthrow the Law of England and the Gospel of Christ. Through ceremonies, Smart insisted, God had taught men obedience in ancient Israel; but this external observation was only to be until the coming of Christ "who was the end, the complement, the consummation of Ceremonies."[45]

Many chancery records attest to the complaints of Puritans against Laudian innovations. One such incident took place in 1639 in the parish of All Hallows Barking, London. Some of the parishioners sent a petition to the bishop of London in protest against a new font with "certain carved images, the picture of the Holy Ghost and a cross over it" and a Communion table that had images placed on the rail around it. They desired the images to be taken down. Much confusion and disputation followed the meetings of the vestry, with the peace of the parish being disrupted. The compromise was that the rails remained, the altar was kept in place, but the imagery was taken down.[46]

Part of the expenses in the rebuilding of St. Paul's had been defrayed through the fines imposed by the hated prerogative courts;

44. Cardwell, *Documentary Annals*, II, p. 237–39 (1633). Fuller, *Church History*, III, pp. 381–82. C. H. Firth and H. S. Rait (eds.), *Acts and Ordinances of the Interregnum* (London: Statute Law Committee, 1911), I, p. 607.

45. Peter Smart, *The Vanitie and Downe-Fall of Superstitious Popish Ceremonies, a sermon preached in the cathedral church of Durham* . . . (Edinburgh, 1628), pp. 2, 18.

46. *Great Britain, Privy Council Register: Charles I*, IX, p. 304. The "Resolutions on Religion presented by a Commission of the House of Commons," in 1629 complains of changes and innovations in religion. Popery and popish ceremonies are feared. See S. R. Gardiner, *Constitutional Documents of the Puritan Revolution* (Oxford: Clarendon Press, 1966), pp. 77–83.

this brought public ill-will to the project and association with the government. Even after the King offered to pay for the whole west end, contributors remained unmoved. The initial excitement of the plans had produced fairly large contributions; after 1635, the offerings declined, owing to a growing distaste for the government and its involvement in the affairs of the Church.[47]

The Laudian insistence on order went against the Elizabethan establishment which had been a commodious house with room for many points of view. Those who disagreed with Laud were seen by him as rebels; countless Puritans became permanently alienated from the national church which increasingly sought conformity over peace and unity.[48] The fundamental stand on the rejection of images, developed by Tyndale, Hooper, Cranmer and Parker, was adopted by the Puritan "faction" in the Church of England; William Perkins was one who had inherited such a view.

Though he lived in the reign of Elizabeth and was known more as a preacher than theologian, Perkins exerted his greatest influence in the early seventeenth century.[49] The Puritans consulted his writings and in their growing confrontation with Laud and his policies, could find support for their iconoclasm. Though Laud's stand on images was rarely made public or defined and was explicitly interwoven with the problems of reverence and "holy beauty," the strength of Perkins's view was not lost. Laud could ignore it as long as he held office; but even then, such ideas remained a living force to counter everything the archbishop worked for and believed in.

Perkins readily admits to accepting Christian images and pictures, but for him these images reside essentially in the sermons and the right administration of the Sacraments. "For in them Christ is de-

47. Wilkins, *Concilia*, IV, pp. 123, 196, 346. Clarendon, Edward Hyde, Earl of, *The History of the Rebellion and Civil Wars in England*, Edited W. D. Mcray (Oxford: Clarendon Press, 1888), I, p. 125.

48. Laud, *Works*, VI, p. 42. John White, *The First Century of Scandalous Malignant Priests* . . . (London, 1643).

49. William Haller, *The Rise of Puritanism* (New York: Harper Torch, 1957), pp. 65, 91–92. Knappen, *Tudor Puritanism*, pp. 374–75. Rosemary Sisson, "William Perkins, Apologist for the Elizabethan Church of England," *Modern Language Review* XLVII (1952), 495–502. The definitive English edition of Perkins' works was published in Cambridge in 1608–09 and reprinted 1612–13, 1616–18. See H. C. Porter (ed.), *Puritanism in Tudor England* (London: Macmillan, 1970), pp. 265–270.

scribed and painted out unto us." Unlikely many iconoclasts, Perkins is more willing to admit the symbolic importance of ceremonies, as when the minister brings his parishioners to know the crucifixion and agony of Christ, a knowledge he transmits not through dead art but through living words, gestures and actions. So, too, the administration of the Last Supper lives on through its re-enactment in Communion.[50]

Perkins develops the idea of idolatry as "when something that is not God is set up in the roome of God"—for example, when divinity or any of its qualities is ascribed to a creature. This is false worship of God by means of "devised worship"—such as through images.[51] Though Perkins's basic ground for rejecting such images is scriptural,[52] he is not unwilling to make distinctions in terms of images as a whole. He comments on them generally and accepts their "civill use." He is enthusiastic about nonreligious pictures and approves of them because they correctly serve their purpose in the adornment of buildings, on coins, or as portraits of the king. "Images serve to keepe in memory friends deceased, whom wee reverence."

Indeed, public edification is so important that Perkins consents to images representing acts of history—divine or human. The history of the Bible may be painted but he suggests it be shown only in private places. ". . . (I)t is lawfull to make an image to testifie the proference or the effects of the majestie of God, namely, when God himself gives any special commandment so to do."[53] But good Puritan that he is, Perkins returns to his original opinion that the really best image of Christ is not pictorial but dynamic—either in sermons or in the lives of fellow Christians.

Perkins also attacked some of the traditional medieval arguments for iconolatry. One argument in support of images was based on the Incarnation and maintained that since God appeared as man, so he may be represented. Perkins rejects this idea; God apparently can

50. William Perkins, *The Workes* (London, 1626, 31), II, pp. 222–23.
51. *Ibid.*, II, pp. 331, 521–24. See also I, p. 674; III, p. 507.
52. *Ibid.*, I, pp. 35–42; I, pp. 587–89; III, p. 506. See William Ames, *A Fresh Suit Against Human Ceremonies in Gods Worship* (Rotterdam, 1633), pp. 295–304, 369–78.
53. Such as the brasen serpent.

appear in any way he pleases; therefore it does not follow that man should recreate God in human form.

... [W]hen God appeared in the forme of a man, that forme was a signe of God's presence onely for the time where God appeared, and no longer; as the bread and wine in the Sacrament are signes of Christ's body and blood, not for ever, but for the time of administration. . .[54]

The argument of analogy (which was used by Thomas More) states that since we kneel before the arms of the king, therefore how much more it is right that we kneel before the image of God. Perkins rejects this analogy as a false proposition. He suggests the analogy breaks down because the reverence is on different planes.

To kneele to the chaire of estate, is no more but a civil testimonie or signe of civill reverence, by which all good subjects when occasion is offered, show their loyalties and subjection to their lawfull princes.[55]

Though Perkins systematically refuted the arguments of his opponents and laid a strong groundwork for the continued rejection of religious images, it was not his opinion that immediately prevailed.

In 1640, Laud attempted to secure a firmer legal basis for his innovations and past policies. The canons which he rammed through the Convocation of Canterbury defended the authority of the Crown along with the legality of the Laudian liturgical practices; the latter depended on the former. The preface of the canons argued that the current rites of the Church of England were not popish in origin but based on the Book of Common Prayer of Edward and Elizabeth. In fact, the articles claimed that there was greater orthodoxy in the royal chapel than at large, since many of the legal and accepted rites had fallen into disuse throughout England.[56] Obedience and conformity were demanded. Article VII repeated the Elizabethan injunction of required altars at the east end except during Communion; rails were necessary to avoid profanation.[57]

---

54. Perkins, *Workes*, I, p. 588.

55. *Ibid.*, I, p. 589. See also I, pp. 683–84.

56. Cardwell, *Synodalia*, II, pp. 380–89. Charles I had subscribed to the 39 articles in 1627. Cardwell, *Documentary Annals*, II, pp. 221–25; Laud, *Works*, V, pp. 624–26.

57. Cardwell, *Synodalia*, II, pp. 404–06. Hutton, *Laud*, pp. 80–84.

These canons, however, were rejected by the Short Parliament which had been summoned in response to the Scottish revolt. James I had re-established episcopacy in that land but he had not tampered with either Calvinist ideas or the Presbyterian form of church government it implied; above all, he had not insisted on the use of the Book of Common Prayer in that country. Charles I, however, had pressed for the uniformity in religion that England had officially experienced under Laud. A new set of canons had been prepared for the Scottish Church in 1636; the next step was the introduction of a prayer book much like that used in England.

War soon broke out between the two lands. As soon as the Long Parliament met in response to this crisis, the pentup resentment in England against the Laudian movement which had resulted in the return of images, brought about the trial, impeachment and eventual execution of William Laud. It was not only the archbishop who was indicted, but his liturgical revival and program as well.

The Laudian ceremonies, images and administrations were heaped together and considered by many Englishmen to be both illegal to the law established by the Elizabethan settlement and blasphemous to God. In December of 1640, a petition signed by thousands of Londoners was presented to the House of Commons. It spelled out, among other things, the dangers of the Laudian reform.

11. The growth of Popery and increase of Papists, priests and Jesuits in sundry places, but especially about London since the Reformation; the frequent venting of crucifixes and Popish pictures both engraved and printed, and the placing of such in Bibles.

14. The great conformity and likeness both continued and increased of our Church to the Church of Rome, in vestures, postures, ceremonies and administrations, namely as bishops' rotchets and the lawn-sleeves, the four-cornered cap, the cope and surplice, the tippet, the hood and the canonical coat, the pulpits clothes, especially now of late, with the Jesuits' badge upon them every way.

15. The standing up at *Gloria Patri*, and at the reading of the Gospel, praying towards the east, bowing at the name of Jesus, the bowing to the altar towards the east, cross in baptism, the kneeling at the Communion.

16. The turning of the Communion Table altarwise, setting images, crucifixes and conceits over them, and tapers and books upon them, and bowing

or adoring to, or before, them, . . . which is a plain device to usher in the Mass.[58]

In that same month, the House of Commons rejected the canons recently passed by Convocation and declared them illegal since Parliament had not approved them. Three days later, William Laud was impeached and deprived of his freedom.

Specifically, Laud was accused of

. . . countenancing the setting up of images in churches, churchwindows, and other places of religious worship. That in his own chapel at Lambeth he had repaired the Popish windows, that had been destroyed at the Reformation. . . That he had caused divers crucifixes to be set up in churches over the communion-table, in his chapel at Lambeth, at Whitehall, and at the university at Oxford, of which he was Chancellor.[59]

He was especially guilty, said his accusers, of acting contrary to the statute of *3, 4 Edward VI* and the injunctions of Elizabeth which directed all images and monuments of idolatry to be destroyed.

At his trial, Laud's defense revealed a sympathy with Bishop Gardiner's view of images. That sixteenth-century prelate had viewed the attack on images as an assault on authority; he had also claimed that images and other tangible signs, if correctly used, serve man in his understanding of spiritual matters. No new arguments are encountered; Laud's defense proves rather to confirm what had been said before:

I do not approve of images of God the Father, though some will justify them from Daniel VII but as for the images of things visible, they are of use, not only for the beautifying and adorning the places of divine worship,

58. Kenyon, *Stuart Constitution*, pp. 173–74. The Root and Branch Petition.

59. Daniel Neal, *The History of the Puritans* (London: Longman, Hurst, Rees, Orne, Brown, 1837), p. 300. On the general charges against the primate, see Prynne, *Canterburies Doome*, pp. 25–28. Prynne claims that Laud owned images and supported their use: *Ibid.*, pp. 58–62, 66–78, 93, 102–110, 462–80, 487. The scurrilous and often amusing pamphlets that attacked Laud are voluminous: *A Prophecie of the Life, Reigne, and Death of William Laud* . . . (London, 1644); *Canterbury's Will, with A serious Conference betweene His Scrivener and Him* (London, 1641); *Romes ABC, Being a Short Perambulation, Or Rather Articular Accusation of a late Tyrannical Oppressour* . . . (London, 1641); *A New Play called Canterburie His Change of Diet* (London, 1641). For a survey of these pamphlets, see R. Coffin, *Laud, Storn Center of Stuart England* (New York: Brentano's 1930), pp. 256–75.

but for admonition and instruction; and can only be an offence to none but such as would have God served slovenly and meanly, under a pretence of avoiding superstition.[60]

To the charge that he kept popish windows and a crucifix in his chapel at Lambeth, the archbishop's defense was both circuitous and straightforward. He claimed only to have repaired the ornaments of his chapel. He had set up neither window nor crucifix. So far as the intrinsic merits of the windows were concerned (depicting the creation of the world to the Day of Judgment), Laud could see neither crime nor superstition.

[T]hough Calvin does not approve images in churches, yet he doth approve very well of them which contain a history; and says plainly, that these have their use *in docendo et admonendo*, in teaching and admonishing the people: and if they have their use, why they may not instruct in the Church, as well as out, I know not.[61]

The prosecution denied this and cited the law of Edward VI which demanded the destruction of abused images.[62] Laud answered that the wording of the law did not include images in windows. He felt that "contemporary practice," which is the best expounder of the meaning of any law, neither destroyed them in Elizabeth's reign, nor abstained from setting them up in James I's time. Even if the homilies which were confirmed by Church and state spoke of the destruction of images, good Englishmen must decide for themselves in matters indifferent to the general settlement. The Edwardine laws were passed at a time when men were "new weaned from the worship of images." Now apparently, the threat was no longer alive.[63]

To the charge that he had popish paintings in his house, Laud answered again out of Calvin, "That it is lawful to make and have the picture of any things *quorum sint capaces oculi*, which may be seen."[64] For should Christians be denied representations of Christ simply because such images could not show his soul, it would follow that no one could have any picture of any man. "Who ever drew a

---

60. Neal, *History of Puritans*, p. 301; Prynne, *Canterburies Doome*, p. 462f.
61. Laud, *Works*, IV, pp. 198–99.
62. *3–4 Edward VI c. 10.*
63. Laud, *Works*, IV, p. 200; Heylyn, *Cypriannus Anglicus*, p. 9.
64. Laud, *Works*, IV, p. 204.

picture of the soul?" So a painting of Christ shows his humanity and certainly this can be lawfully done.[65]

It would appear that Laud was not afraid of idolatry in the educated as much as profanation in the ignorant. Charged with allowing Bibles with pictures to be sold, he claimed that with the advice of the Privy Council, they were sold only to "learned and discreet men."

For pictures themselves are things indifferent; not simply good, nor simply bad, but as they are used. And therefore they were not to be sold to all comers, because they may be abused, and become evil; yet might be sold to learned and discreet men, who might turn them to good.[66]

In so many respects, then, Laud reveals an attitude that is akin to Gardiner and Hooker. Superstitious ceremonies were never urged; what was enjoyed was the external beauty of worship premised on the knowledge that the contempt for externals would soon cause internal faith to decline. In all of the ceremonies and ornaments resurrected by Laud, there were no innovations, but "restorations of the ancient approved ceremonies, in, and from the beginning of the Reformation, and settled either by law or custom. . ."[67]

But Laud had also been influenced by Melanchthon's theory of things "indifferent." Just as the power of Henry VIII had condemned images in the sixteenth century, so through the power of Charles I, images were returned to England in the seventeenth century; each action, though contradictory, could be defended or justified through the claims of the legitimate kingly power to determine religious practices that were "indifferent" to Scripture.

And since Laud was no longer protected by his king, he was mercilessly interrogated, his papers were rifled and finally he was executed. Even his defense did not escape scurrilous refutation. Other supporters of the Laudian establishment were indicted, their popish innovations elaborated with exactness tempered by indignation. The Laudians were accused of destroying the Book of Common Prayer

65. For other accusations dragged up to prove the charges of innovation, see Laud, *Works*, III, pp. 314; IV, 207, 209, 221, 229, 236.

66. *Ibid.*, IV, pp. 239, 400.

67. *Ibid.*, III, pp. 407–08. See Fuller's distinctions between innovation and "renovation" and the charge that Laud tampered with the Book of Common Prayer; Fuller, *Church History*, III, p. 369; Thomas Lathbury, *A History of the Convocations of the Church of England* (London: J. Leslie, 1853), pp. 270–75.

through their innovations, and in its place setting up altars "with all manner of superstitious altar-furniture, crosses, crucifixes, candles, candlesticks, etc."[68]

In 1628 and again in 1629, John Cosin, as prebend or canon at Durham, had been accused of being "our young Apollo, who repaireth the Quire and set it out gayly with strange Babylonian ornaments." Though he had been twice brought before a common-law court, he was acquitted. With the fall of Laud, however, Cosin's old enemies had at last their chance for revenge: the old accusations of idolatry and popery were again dragged out.

Specifically, Cosin was accused of taking away the Communion table in the cathedral church. In its place he had built a marble altar with columns and cherubim, framed by a carved screen, richly gilded. Cosin's "extravagance" extended also to popish vestments, embroidered with depictions of the Trinity in the form of an old man, a crucifix and a dove. Cosin and others of like thinking had also erected many religious paintings and sculpture; one statue "represented the picture of Christ, with a golden beard, a blue cap, and sun-rays upon his head."[69]

In this context of accusations, the ultimate indictment was that

---

68. *The Petition and Articles exhibited in Parliament against Dr. Haywood, by the Parishioners of St. Giles's-in-the-Fields* (London, 1641), pp. 3–9. The innovators or "Arminian faction" were reported to be Bishops Laud, Lindsell, Corbet, Wren, Montague, Howson, Goodman, Manwaring, White, Field, Wright, Harsnet and Neale. Peter Smart, *A Short Treatise of Altars, Altar-Furniture. . .* (London, 1643). The political and religious complexion of the bishops and others in the royal household, underwent change. Not all were Laudians; see Peter King, "The episcopate during the Civil Wars, 1642–1649," *English Historical Review*, LXXXIII (1968), 526f.

On the articles of impeachment against Bishop Wren, see John Nalson, *An Impartial Collection of the Great Affairs of State* (London, 1682–83), II, pp. 398–402. William Shaw, *A History of the English Church, 1640–60* (London: Longmans, Green, 1900), I, 103–110; Wren's case, however, never came up.

69. *Articles of the Commons' Declaration and Impeachment upon the complaint of Peter Smart, against John Cosin* (London, 1643), pp. 7–10. See Peter Smart, *A catalogue of superstitious innovations. . .* (London, 1642). Most of these accusations are probably Puritan cavil. Cosin's main defence, however, rests upon the fact that many of these "innovations" were in use before his time: "beyond the memory of man." Cosin, *Correspondence*, I, p. 170n.; C. Hunter, *An Illustration of Mr. Daniel Neal's History of the Puritans* (Durham: J. Ross, 1736), 90–131. Cosin also insists that when he was bowing, it was not to the table, but to "God Almighty." *Ibid.*, pp. 93–94.

charged to the Cheapside Cross in London. Along with Laud, Cosin and others, this old market cross was accused of seducing good Englishmen to Rome,

> At which sad Newes the Crosse began to shake,
> And all the pictures there began to quake . . .
> In this affright the Virgin lost her Crown.
> Hands they flew off, and legs came tubling downe.
> The Crosier staffe was broke, which might have kept
> His Holinesse from dogs, while he had slept. . . .[70]

The Laudian program had visibly and profoundly changed the Church in England. It had alienated many of the King's subjects from the established religion and had helped to identify this Church with the government of Charles I. Laud and his supporters had tried to justify most of their innovations by way of theology, history, and in some ways, by English law. Charles had declared himself for the Laudian revival; his authority as king came from God, resulting in a responsibility for the spiritual and material welfare of everyone in the realm. To realize these ends, it was reasoned by royalists, Charles's power in church and state had to be absolute. "Belief in a divine right of kings meant belief in God."[71]

Laud had taken full advantage of the Elizabethan settlement which had allowed a wide doctrinal latitude within a fixed, though sometimes vague, liturgical practice. In spite of the arguments of Hooker and the curious fate of the Queen's own chapel, the use of religious images in the Elizabethan Church remained suspect. The new Anglicanism of the seventeenth century, however, had centered its service around the decency and beauty of the altar; this suggested to the Puritans sacerdotalism, ritualism and worse, the underpinings for a return to Roman Catholic attitudes to Salvation through good works. Such views, Puritans argued, would lead to the economic support and

70. R. Overton, *Articles of High Treason Exhibited against Cheapside Crosse, with the last Will and Testament of the said Crosse* (London, 1642), p. 4. See also *The dolefull Lamentation of Cheapside Crosse: Or old England sick of the Staggers* (London, 1641). *Thorny Ailo's Verses upon the defacing of Cheapside Crosse. . .* (London, 1642).

71. Margaret Judson, *The Crisis of the Constitution* (New York: Octagon Books, 1964), pp. 111, 177. Judson also points out that this insistence on law was matched by counter arguments also based on law. *Ibid.*, p. 13.

the theological defense of religious representations. Furthermore, the Laudian reform sought to remake England through coercion.[72] It is no wonder that Puritans discerned in their government and in their established Church the relics of popery. For, if Laud saw in images the return of decency and order supported by legitimate authority, Puritans could say that what actually resulted was the invasion of a "counter-Reformation" that in name the archbishop had disclaimed.[73]

72. W. R. Fryer, " 'The High Churchmen' of the Earlier Seventeenth Century," *Renaissance and Modern Studies*, V (1961), 124.

73. See Christopher Hill, *Economic Problems of the Church* (Oxford: Clarendon Press, 1963), p. 337, for the social factors that accompanied Laud's religious program.

IX. THE PURITAN REACTION

I hate traditions; I do not trust them—They are popish all. . .
Please the profane, to grieve the godly.

> ANANIAS (BEN JONSON, *The Alchemist*)

. . . we tear what we cannot loose, and eject what we happen
not to understand.

> SAMUEL JOHNSON, Preface to *Shakespeare's Works*

THE LAUDIAN CAMPAIGN for general religious uniformity in the English Church was soon opposed by the alliance of Parliament and Puritan. Where such attempts at uniformity had been effected by the ordering of the liturgy and its furnishings, these very things were now attacked as symbols of ecclesiastical oppression. Iconoclasm was to be the answer to royalist iconolatry.

At Laud's trial, the arguments of his accusers presaged the future and fate of religious images in England. The Puritan, William Prynne, long the enemy of Laud, rejected Laud's defense that much of the religious imagery still existing in the realm was due to the archbishop's predecessors. Even if this were true, Prynne felt it was no justification for images nor for any mitigation of responsibility. Since Laud as bishop was a spiritual leader, claimed Prynne, his policies would be followed: he should have struck down what obviously was popish.[1]

First, himselfe introduced Crucifixes with other Popish Innovations into [his chapel] which he afterwards by way of imitation prescribed to Cathedralls; and then being charged with this practise in Cathedralls, he justifies himselfe by His Majesties Chapell, where he takes Sanctuary; just as if a Cutpurse should justifie the cutting of a mans purse in Pauls Cathedrall because hee formerly picked another mans pocket in Whit-Hall Chapell. . . .[2]

Prynne's own view on religious images are those encountered in Perkins and others: God cannot be depicted by visible means because

---

1. Prynne, *Canterburies Doome*, pp. 472–74.
2. *Ibid.*, pp. 487, 492. Prynne felt that rails do not conform to Elizabeth's injunctions since the altar could not be moved into the nave.

he has no similitude.[3] The early church had no images and this was recognized by the statute of Edward (*3 Edward VI c. 10*) which condemned all religious images, no matter what the material. "(P)opery may creep in at a glasse window, as well as at a door."[4]

Particularly galling for Prynne was Laud's misreading of Calvin. Prynne correctly pointed out that Calvin only says it is lawful to make images of men or beasts for civil use. The archbishop had inferred from Calvin's contentions that it was also lawful to make pictures of religious subjects so long as they were clothed in human or natural forms. Through such reasoning, which Prynne suggested is false, Christ's nativity, the Last Supper, God the Father as an old man or the Holy Ghost as a dove would be acceptable representations.[5]

The issue of imagery, so important in Laud's trial, could not be side-stepped. The Long Parliament, once called, proceeded to act with haste and resentment against considered abuses of the past.[6] The House of Commons issued an order in January, 1641, directing commissioners to be sent into several counties "to demolish and remove out of churches and chapels all images, altars, or tables turned altarwise, crucifixes, superstitious pictures, and other monuments and relics of idolatry."[7]

The King still possessed the power to issue proclamations on his own authority. Parliament, in need of insuring the legality of its own deliberations, hit on the "ordinance" (or law passed while the King was "absent" from London). The first ordinance of the Long Parliament concerning images was not made until August, 1643.[8] It stated

3. William Prynne, *Histrio-Maxtix* (London, 1633), pp. 894–904.

4. Prynne, *Canterburies Doome*, pp. 464–66.

5. *Ibid.*, pp. 463–64. See Calvin, *Institutes of the Christian Religion*, I, p. 110.

6. Gee and Hardy, *Documents illustrative of English Church History*, pp. 537–45 (articles 11, 16).

7. Along with removing the communion table from the east end and taking away the rails, leveling the chancel, another injunction was included: "That all crucifixes, scandalous pictures of any one or more of the Trinity, and all images of the Virgin Mary, shall be taken away and abolished." *Journal of the House of Commons*, II, p. 279 ("Resolutions of the House of Commons on Ecclesiastical innovations, September, 1641"). The Lords did not agree that this order should be put into effect at once. Nevertheless, it was circulated and became law. Hutton, *English Church*, p. 90. Frederick Varley, *Cambridge during the Civil War 1642–1646* (Cambridge: W. Heffer, 1935), pp. 32. Steel, *Proclamations*, I, ciii.

8. Firth, *Acts and Ordinances*, I, pp. 265–66. Much like *3–4 Edward VI c. 10*, this ordinance did not extend to pictures of people not reputed to be saints. See Addleshaw, *Architectural Setting*, p. 145.

that all altars and tables of stone were to be taken away and demolished, all tapers, candlesticks, crucifixes, crosses, images and pictures, all inscriptions should be destroyed. Rails were to be broken. Communion tables were to be taken from the east end and placed in "some other fit convenient place." This ordinance was later supplemented in May, 1644 and authorized the removal of copes, surplices, fonts, screens and organs.[9] As to what objects were treated in these ordinances, there was no ambiguity such as existed in previous royal injunctions; executing the order, however, witnessed the same latitude and widespread confusion as in the past.

Obedience to these Parliamentary ordinances depended not on legality, but on sympathy to the Parliament's aims and victory of its armies.[10] The resultant destruction accounted for much of whatever was left of the physical fabric of medieval churches and of the Laudian program of church beautification.

When I came to Oxford crucifixes were common in the glass in the studies' window; and in the chamber windows were cannonised saints (for example, in my chamber window, St. Gregory the Great) . . . But after 1647 they were all broken. Down went Dagon. Now no religion is to be found.[11]

Some of this reformation was carried out voluntarily. However, to insure compliance, committees for demolishing monuments of superstition were established.[12] An example of one such committees can be found in the counties of the Eastern Association. Here the Earl of Manchester issued a commission to one William Dowsing to fulfill the articles of the ordinance.[13]

Dowsing kept a journal wherein he methodically described his ac-

9. Firth, *Acts and Ordinances*, I, pp. 425–26; Shaw, *English Church*, I, pp. 103–10; Cox, *Churchwardens*, pp. 153–55; Bonds, *Fonts*, pp. 275–79. Surprisingly, the greatest amount of destruction to screens took place in the nineteenth century. That century was so eager to achieve the true congregational idea of worship that screens were sawed down to the rails or suffered complete removal. Bond and Camm, *Roodscreens*, I, pp. 118, 120–21.

10. Bruno Ryves, *Mercurius Rusticus* (London, 1685), p. 26. C. V. Wedgwood, *The King's War 1641–1647* (New York: MacMillan, 1959), pp. 148–49.

11. John Aubrey, *Brief Lives and Other Selected Writings* (ed. Anthony Powell) (London: Cresset Press, 1949), p. 8.

12. Firth, *Acts and Ordinances*, I, pp. 371–72, 755–77, 926, 1143; II, p. 1461.

13. Dowsing received the commission from Manchester in December of 1643. Alan Everitt (ed.), "Suffolk and the Great Rebellion 1640–60," *Suffolk Record Society*, III (1960), p. 62. Varley, *Cambridge*, p. 36.

complishments in the counties of Suffolk and Cambridge. This note-book was not typical of other commissions, nor for that matter, was it complete on the counties it covered. It was the sort of rough note-book kept by an author who perhaps had hopes of later writing up a report.[14] The journal itself plainly shows that the ordinance was carried out:

[In] Sudbury . . . We brake down a picture of God the Father, 2 crucifix's, and Pictures of Christ, about an hundred in all; and gave order to take down a Cross off the Steeple; and diverse Angels, 20 at least, on the Roof of the Church. . . Dunstal . . . We brake down 60 Superstitious Pictures; and brake in pieces the Rails; and gave order to pull down the Steps.[15]

At Blythburgh, Suffolk, he even pulled up the brasses of gravestones in the floor of the Church (figure 34). In some cases, Dowsing met with resistance on the part of churchwardens who used delaying tac-tics to save their churches; to be sure, some parishes had been cleared of idolatrous objects before his arrival.[16] How much destruction he committed is open to conjecture. Berwick reports that it was consid-erable at Cambridge, and Dowsing's journal itself mentions that Clare College chapel was deprived of a thousand superstitious pic-tures (counting, perhaps, each figure within the window).

At Clare . . . We brake down 1000 Pictures superstitious; I brake down 200; 3 of God the Father, and 3 of Christ, and the Holy Lamb, and 3 of the Holy Ghost like a Dove with Wings. . .

College records, however, show no extensive repairs were neces-sary after Dowsing's visit;[17] this makes it difficult to estimate the damage done by these visitations. Dowsing's journal would suggest he destroyed all adjuncts of the old religion, but apparently his icono-

14. *Ibid.*, pp. 29–45.
15. William Dowsing, *The Journal*, ed. C. H. Evelyn White (Ipswich: Pawsey and Hayes, 1885), pp. 15, 17.
16. *Ibid.*, pp. 18, 26, 27, 50, etc.
17. G. B. Tatham, *The Puritans in Power* (Cambridge: University Press, 1913), pp. 110–11; Dowsing, *Journal*, p. 17; John Berwick, *Querela Cantabrigrensis* (Ox-ford, 1646), pp. 17–18; Robert Masters, *History of the College of Corpus Christi* (London: John Murray, 1831), pp. 46–47; Willis and Clark, *Architectural History of Cambridge*, I, pp. 511–12; Charles Henry Cooper, *Annals of Cambridge* (Cam-bridge: Warwick and Co., 1845), III, pp. 338–39. J. G. Chesire, "William Dowsing's Destructions in Cambridgeshire," *Transactions of Cambridgeshire and Hunting-donshire Archaeological Society*, III (1914), 78f.

clasm was tempered by the lack of time for a thorough "reformation," his dependence on others to do his bidding and most important, his apparent exaggeration to demonstrate his zeal. Then again the visitation was not as extensive in area (350 churches in Suffolk alone went unvisited) as it might have been. Probably much of the destruction was aimed at the cheap pictures on panels, canvas or paper that had become portable adjuncts to the Laudian service's aim for beautification.[18]

The county committees appointed by Parliament with powers of sequestration, assessment and martial law consisted of men with determined resolve in their search for "pictures and trumpery." For one committeeman in Kent, Sir William Springate, this included searching the houses of relatives. When he visited his wife's uncle, Sir Edward Partheriche, also a member of the committee of Kent, he saw what he believed to be several superstitious pictures, such as the crucifixion of Christ, and one of the resurrection. His response was to draw his sword and cut them all out of the frames. Then, sticking them upon his sword's point, he went into the parlour and presented the remains to the wife of his host.[19]

In the case of Richard Baxter, the vicar of Kidderminster, the destruction of objectionable images was left to the churchwardens who had to face the protective instincts of the parish.

A crew of the riotous party of the town (poor journeymen and servants) took the alarm, and run together with weapons to defend the crucifix and the church images.[20]

The intent to carry out the law could divide parishes and cause disruption and hostility among different sympathizers. When one Mr. Sherman, the churchwarden of All Hallows Barking in London, was chided for allowing the figure of St. Michael to remain, he could

18. It is possible that Dowsing was provided with a "sort of 'black list' of churches to be visited" wherein it was known popish innovations had been introduced. Varley, *Cambridge*, pp. 40–43. On Dowsing and the problem of his manuscripts, his motivation and extent of destruction, see *East Anglian, Notes and Queries* VII (1897–98), 1–5; XII (1907–08), pp. 49–53, 71–73, 90–93.

19. A. M. Everitt, *The County Committee of Kent in the Civil War* (Leicester: University College, 1957), pp. 24–25.

20. Richard Baxter, *Autobiography*, ed., J. M. Thomas (London: J. M. Dent and Sons, 1925), p. 38.

answer, "It stood there so many years, and had done no miracle, therefore we conceived it could not be a saint." Pressure forced him to burn it, but others in the parish condemned him for this act. Since Mr. Sherman was conciliatory, he proposed, "Now . . . let's go to the Tavern, and merrily discourse what all of us can say farther upon this matter."[21]

As fighting continued and great expanses of England were progressively dominated by Parliamentary forces, parishioners imitated their ancestors and anticipated changes in religious requirements by trying to salvage what they could. In some places, the rector and churchwardens attempted to conform to the ordinances by removing the more objectionable ornaments; but then, the parishioners themselves often considered this insufficient and carried out further reformation.[22]

Images which had been saved and secreted away during the dissolution of the monasteries were again threatened and sometimes rescued. The painted window of the crucifixion that had been preserved by the last abbot of Waltham in 1540 and removed to the chapel of New Hall, later came into the possession of General George Monk. "(H)aving more taste than fell to the lot of most generals of his time," he buried the window underground during the Commonwealth and replaced it at the Restoration.[23] Probably much stained glass was saved this way. Empty windows could be shown to the Parliamentary visitors while the glass itself could be hidden. The glass at Denbigh, Suffolk, for instance, was packed away in a chest and buried.[24]

Most of these accounts seem gossipy and fragmentary. Unfortunately, they represent the little that is left of the larger story of destruction. They do show, however, the contradictory nature of many human actions; compromise would frequently prevail over law and religious zeal.

21. Quoted in Elizabeth and Wayland Young, *Old London Churches* (London: Faber and Faber, 1956), pp. 45–46.

22. Thomas Wright, *The History and Topography of the County of Essex* (London: George Virtue, 1836), I, pp. 77–78. Sometimes the images were not destroyed but sold. See *Archaeologia*, L (1887), 40.

23. Wright, *Essex*, I, p. 105; Francis Blomefield, *An Essay towards a Topographical History of the County of Norfolk* (London: William Miller, 1805), I, pp. 70, 112.

24. Cautley, *Suffolk*, p. 29.

But this is not to deny that religious zeal inspired many to commit destructive acts. If a legally tenured iconoclasm had been ordered by Parliament because of images' association with the hated liturgical program of Laud and the government of Charles I, nonetheless deep religious antagonism to images also still existed. Puritan insistence on a "naked Christ" provided significant impetus for a theological as well as a practical justification of iconoclasm. Iconoclasm became the cause of God.

> He that will clothe the gospel now, intimates plainly that the gospel is naked, uncomely, that I may not say reproachful. Do not, ye church maskers, while Christ is clothing upon our barrenness with his righteous garment to make us acceptable in his Father's sight; do not, as ye do, cover and hide his righteous verity with the polluted clothing of your ceremonies, to make it seem more decent in your own eyes.[25]

This was simply and wholly the argument: the Word is perfect; nothing may be added to or taken from it without offense to God.[26] Religious images all too graphically reminded Puritans of the altars, vestments, rails and ecclesiastical courts that had been imposed on England with the aid of the King.

The Puritan, Richard Culmer, was himself reminded of such associations. When he was appointed by Parliament to detect and demolish superstitious images at Canterbury, he proved as methodical as Dowsing. However, because of the religious basis to his iconoclasm, Culmer's actions proved more thorough and determined. In 1642, he obediently reported his findings at Canterbury to Parliament so "that you may more perfectly cure the malignant disease, called the Cathedrall evill." The cathedral authorities, however, had refused to execute the ordinances that demanded the suppression of popery: "They loved their cathedral Jezebel the better because she was painted." When Culmer and the appointed Commissioners arrived to carry out the ordinances at the Cathedral, they discovered so many images that they believed the building "had been built for no

---

25. John Milton, *Reason of Church Government Urged*, Book II, Chapter II. See also his *Of Reformation in England* (1641).

26. Anthony Burges, *The Difficulty and the Encouragements to a Reformation. A Sermon preached before . . . House of Commons* (London, 1643), pp. 5–6.

other end, but to be a stable for idols."[27] Systematic destruction com-
menced; tapestries, sculpture, paintings were all cast down. Stained
glass windows that had been exempted from the Elizabethan injunctions along with the newer ones from the Laudian revival had made
Canterbury a haven of colored splendor. Culmer was determined to
end this forthwith.

In spite of the outcries from the clergy present, he climbed to the
top of the ladder in order to batter down the large window to the
left of the choir: "the picture of God the Father, and of Christ, besides
a large crucifix, and the picture of the Holy Ghost in the form of a
dove, and of the twelve apostles." No one else wanted to climb to
such heights, but Culmer considered it an honor to strike down
"proud Becket's glassy bones."

Then he turned his attention to the large stone image of Christ
standing over the south gate; this was pulled down with ropes and
Culmer congratulated himself that, as Christ had driven the merchants from the Temple, so he ejected from churches the idols which
had defiled the worship of God.[28] Where there was once to be heard
the "roaring-boyes, tooting and squeaking" of organs and the weight
of gilded images, pictures and "dumb idols," Puritans could rejoice
that the assembly of God's congregation resigned, "O our God! what
a rich and rare alteration! what a strange choice is this indeed!"[29]

Even when altars and screens were not embellished with images,
they were frequently destroyed or mutilated. At Peterborough Cathedral, the Communion table was destroyed along with a stone
screen setting off the rear of the chancel. It was apparently a most
magnificent piece, painted and gilded with three lofty spires which

27. Richard Culmer, *Cathedrall Newes from Canterbury* (London, 1644), dedication, pp. 19–24.

28. Richard Culmer (*fils*), *A Parish Looking-glasse* (London, 1657), p. 6. Culmer,
Canterbury, pp. 23–24. J. W. Legg and W. H. St. John Hope (eds.), *Inventories of
Christ Church Canterbury* (Westminster: Archibald Constable and Co., 1902), pp.
266–69. Compare the inventory of 1634 (pp. 243–65) with that of 1662 (pp. 266–
77). Culmer's *Cathedrall Newes from Canterbury*, 1644, was attacked by the anonymous, *The Razing of the Record or, an Order to forbid any Thanksgiving for the
Canterbury Newes publisht by Richard Culmer* (Oxford, 1644), and *Antidotum
Culmerianum* (Oxford, 1644). Richard Culmer, *fils*, subsequently answered both
and aimed to vindicate his father in his *Parish Looking-glasse* (London, 1657).

29. John Vicars, "God's ark overtopping the world's waves," *England's parlia-
mentarie chronicle* (London, 1643–6), p. 184.

rose almost as high as the roof of the church. No imagery decorated it, "or anything else that might justly give offence"; yet, it bore the name of altar, and was thus laid low.[30]

On the other hand, paintings, sculpture, buildings, vestments, along with nonrepresentational carvings, were indiscriminately destroyed in the larger context of military operations, in the violence of inflamed mobs and soldiers, and through popular confusion and sport. Much of this destruction, however, cannot be described as having been committed by those who had specific views on images. The physical conditions of war itself was impetus enough for the destruction that ensued.[31]

In the sixteenth and seventeenth centuries, churches were felt to have lost their religious character if they were used for military purposes: "then may we beate them downe, not onlie as beinge hindered, but as beinge endamaged and endangered by them."[32] There are shot marks in the church porch of Ashton, Devon, and near the west door of Berkeley, Gloucestershire; at Alton, Hants, the royalists had fought behind a barricade of pews so that bullet-holes on the door and on the piers of the nave remain as testament.[33]

Once the churches were emptied of marksmen, they were turned by both sides into prisons, hospitals, storehouses, rest places or stables. Again, the safety of the physical fabric and its furnishings was threatened.[34] Three thousand Scottish prisoners were detained in Durham

30. *History of the Church of Peterborough* (London: 1686), p. 334.

31. Scotland witnessed similar conditions; see David McRoberts, "Material Destruction caused by the Scottish Reformation," *Essays on the Scottish Reformation 1513–1625* (Glasgow: Burns, 1962), pp. 415–62.

32. Hayward, *Annals* (1560), pp. 58–59. C. G. Cruickshank, *Elizabeth's Army* (Oxford: Clarendon Press, 1966), p. 225.

33. See also, Thomas Mace's account at York Minster, F. Harrison, *The Painted Glass of York* (London: SPCK, 1927), p. 2. Joshua Sprigge, *Angelia Rediviva* (London, 1647), pp. 55, 143, 159; D. R. Guttery, *The Great Civil War in Midland Parishes* (Birmingham: Cornish Brothers, Ltd., 1950), pp. 77, 80; Lucy Hutchinson, *Memoirs of the Life of Colonel Hutchinson* (London: Henry G. Bohn, 1854), pp. 177, 184; Alfred H. Burne and Peter Young, *The Great Civil War, a military history of the First Civil War 1642–1646* (London: Eyre and Spottiswoode, 1959), pp. 86, 122.

34. Alfred Kingston, *Hertfordshire during the Great Civil War and the Long Parliament* (London: Eliot Stock, 1894), pp. 87–88. Evelyn, *Diary*, December 18, 1648; Sprigge, *Anglia Rediviva*, pp. 45, 80, 186–87, 192; Frederick John Varley, *Mercurius Aulicus* (Oxford: Basil Blackwell, 1948), p. 34; Frederick John Varley, *The Siege of Oxford* (Oxford: University Press, 1932), p. 89; Wedgwood, *King's*

Cathedral after their defeat at Dunbar in 1646. For warmth, these men made bonfires of the woodwork of the choir; they knocked out colored glass and wrought havoc with the chapels and tombs.[35]

Once a town or fortress was taken, material destruction was the rule, for custom had given the victorious the lawful right of plunder. The soldiers got little in value from these spoils if they sold them, but the extent of the destruction was enormous.[36] Sometimes conquering troops were given a gratuity by the townspeople in place of the opportunity of plunder ("storm-money"). Throughout the war, discipline readily broke down and infected both Cavalier and Roundhead.[37]

Special books were designed to supplement the work of the army chaplains in enforcing discipline. In 1644, one Robert Ram, the minister of Spalding published *The Soldiers' Catechism*, wherein he discussed not only the ideal soldier but the justice of the Parliamentary side. Commensurate with this picture, Ram defends the iconoclastic zeal of the soldiers and at least indicates that such behavior was winked at, if not encouraged by the chaplains and officers.[38]

Is it well done of some of your Souldiers (which seem to be religious) to break down crosses and images where they meet with any?

1. I confesse that nothing ought to be done in a tumultous manner.

2. But seeing God hath put the Sword of Reformation into the Soldiers hand, I thinke it is not amisse that they should concell and demolish those Monuments of Superstition and Idolatry, especially seeing the Magistrate and the Minister that should have done it formerly, neglected it.[39]

War, pp. 175, 189; Arthur Leach, *The History of the Civil War in Pembrokeshire* (London: H. F. and G. Witherby, 1937), p. 155.

35. Cook, *English Cathedrals*, pp. 323–24; Varley, *Cambridge*, p. 44. Richard Symonds, *Diary of the Marches of the Royal Army during the Great Civil War*, ed., C. E. Long (London: Camden Society, 1859), pp. 67–68. C. M. Doe, "The Blowing Up of Great Torrington Church," *Devon Association Transactions*, XXVI (1894). J. W. Willis Bund, *The Civil War in Worcestershire* (Birmingham: Midland Editions, 1905), p. 50.

36. Berwick, *Querela*, p. 13.

37. Francis Drake, *Eboracum or the History and Antiquities of the City of York* (York, 1788), I, p. 210; Sprigge, *Anglis Rediviva*, pp. 103, 237, 267; Bund, *Worcestershire*, pp. 49–50; Leach, *Pembrokeshire*, p. 187. Henry Ellis (ed.), "Letters from a Subaltern Officer of the Earl of Essex's Army" *Archaeologia* XXXV (1853), pp. 310–334; Firth, *Cromwell's Army*, pp. 191–93, 277–78.

38. *The Soldiers' Catechism*, however, was not an official compilation. *English Historical Review*, XV (1900), 585.

39. (Robert Ram?), *Cromwell's Soldiers' Catechism*, ed. Walter Begley (London: Elliot Stock, 1900), pp. 20–21.

But the general destruction during the Civil War was engendered by a variety of motives. The soldiers inevitably got out-of-hand, as they delighted themselves with malicious mischief or ran merrily up and down the church "with swords drawn, defacing the Monuments of the dead, hacking and hewing the Seats, and stalls, scratching and scraping the painted walls."[40] Every day the Parliamentary soldiers would hunt cats with hounds in the Cathedral of Lichfield, "delighting themselves in the echo from the goodly vaulted roofs."[41] At Exeter, the soldiers' iconoclasm was a mixture of sport and obedience to the ordinances against images. This prompts one to ask whether decapitating statues was a way of destroying the religious reality of the sculpture (as when one kills a man, one destroys his life) or did it merely signify a prank?

They strook off the heads of all the statues, on all Monuments in the Church, especially they deface the Bishops Tombs, leaving one without a head, another without a Nose, one without a hand, and another without an Arme . . . they pluck down and deface the Statue of an Ancient Queen, the wife of Edward the Confessor . . . mistaking it for the Statue of the blessed Virgin Mary. . . .[42]

There was a tremendous exaggeration of destruction for purposes of propaganda. *Mercurius Rusticus* and other newspapers were dedicated almost exclusively to the narration of atrocities committed by Parliamentary armies. It was the intention of these royalist papers to attract the neutral by the tale of heinous facts frequently invented by the editors to bolster the cause of the royalist armies and to sow dissension in the enemy.[43]

Consequently, there were extensive reports of profanation of churches by the Parliamentary army. Royalists claimed that the lower parts of churches were made stables with chancels as slaughter houses. Puritans were charged with hanging on pulpits the carcasses of

40. Hill, *Tudor and Stuart Lincoln*, p. 163; *Lincolnshire Notes and Queries*, VIII (1904–5), pp. 173–74.

41. Tatham, *Puritans in Power*, p. 253; Guttery, *Midland*, p. 38.

42. *Mercurius Rusticus* (1646), p. 220. However, when the Bishop of Norwich's chapel was attacked in 1647, he pleaded for the safety of his images by offering to remove the heads of certain religious representatives "since I knew the bodies could not offend." Joseph Hall, *Works* (Oxford: D. A. Talboys, 1837), I, liv.

43. Unfortunately much of what little we know of iconoclasm in England at this time is based on these newspapers. Hence, their inclusion despite their limitations.

slaughtered meat which had been butchered on Communion tables. The floors of churches were frequently covered with dung and the blood of animals: "in contempt of God and his holy Temple, they defile each part and corner both of Church and Chancel with their own Excrements."[44] The rebels, after all, were rebels not only because they had revolted against the King, but, royalists claimed, against God as well.

As the King's side grew more desperate, papers like *Mercurius Aulicus* used whatever material was available: "the rumor, the loaded anecdote, the counterstory, the truth." The desecration of churches continued to be one of their favorite weapons.[45] Absolute profanation was witnessed, it was claimed, when Parliamentary soldiers at Canterbury Cathedral in 1642, "began a fight with God himselfe." They toppled the Communion table, its rails and seats, defaced the screen and its tabernacle work and finished by ripping a tapestry of the life of Christ. One iconoclast, it was reported, said "here is Christ, and swore that he would rip up his bowells."[46]

In the reign of Edward VI, Bishop Gardiner had warned Somerset that religious iconoclasm would produce destruction of the badges and images of royalty. This fear had been realized in some ways under Elizabeth when many secular tombs were mutilated. During the war between Parliament and King, Gardiner's admonition was particularly fulfilled. At Chichester Cathedral, in 1642, rebels "picked out the eyes of King Edward VI's picture saying, "That all this mischief came from him, when he established the booke of Common Prayer."[47]

Some destruction of secular images occurred because soldiers erased

44. *Mercurius Rusticus* (1685), pp. 37–38, 69–70.
45. Joseph Frank, *The Beginnings of the English Newspaper 1620–1660*, Cambridge: Harvard University Press, 1961), pp. 41, 74. K. Roosevelt, "Propaganda Techniques of the English Civil War and the Propaganda Psychosis of Today," *Pacific Historical Review* XII (1943), 369–79. See also, W. L. Sachse, "English Pamphlet Support for Charles I, November 1648–January 1649," *Conflict in Stuart England* (eds. W. A. Aiken and B. D. Henning) (London: Jonathan Cape, 1960), 147–68.
46. *Mercurius Rusticus* (1646), pp. 184–85.
47. *Ibid.*, p. 203. See also the destruction of royal monuments in the Abbey Church of Westminster, 1643–44. Carpenter, *House of Kings*, pp. 168, 169, 171. Arthur Stanley, *Historical Memorials of Westminster Abbey* (London: John Murray, 1886), pp. 150–51, 428–29.

the images of their enemy. In December of 1642, Parliamentary soldiers at Winchester Cathedral tried to deface the monument of the Earl of Portland, but since its brass withstood their beating, they turned to his father's monument of stone.

Mistaking a Judge for a Bishop, led into error by the resemblance or counterfeit of a square cap on the head of the statue, they strike off not only the cap, but also the head too of the statue, and so leave it.[48]

It was claimed by royalists that the statues of James I and Charles I by Hubert Le Sueur at the entrance to the choir of Winchester Cathedral were first mutilated, then hacked to pieces. The iconoclasts were heard to have said that they would bring Charles I back to his Parliament.[49] This is a clear example of royalist exaggeration. The statues of Charles and James in question were not destroyed as reported, but stolen in December of 1642. They escaped because of their commercial value, for it was hoped that they would later fetch a good price on the Continent.

How many of these accounts are true, of course, will probably never be known. Too much in way of previous destruction under Thomas Cromwell, Edward VI and Elizabeth and the Restoration and changes which were to follow, combined with the lack of good descriptive inventories, have blocked the possibility of fully assessing the destruction.

However, the iconoclasm of the seventeenth century stands distinctly apart from that of the sixteenth. The destruction of images during the Civil War was more virulent and comprehensive in its attack when compared to the sixteenth-century variety. Religious visitations and inspections were undertaken by zealous men backed

48. *Mercurius Rusticus* (1646), pp. 208–09.
49. *Ibid.*, pp. 209–14. The statues were later returned after the Restoration. Vallance, *Great English Church Screens*, pp. 51–52. On the destruction of the sculpture in Winchester Cathedral, see T. D. Atkinson, "Medieval Figure Sculpture in Winchester Cathedral," *Archaeologia*, LXXXV (1935), 159–67. Even the tapestries from Canterbury Cathedral which had been defaced in 1642, were sold in Paris between 1653–56 and eventually acquired for the choir of the cathedral church in Aix-in-Provence. Aymer Vallance, "The Tapestries from Canterbury Cathedral," *Archaeologia Cantiana*, XLIV (1932), 67–78. The worst damage was probably to the Cathedral Muniment Room. W. R. W. Stephens and F. T. Madge (eds.), "Documents relating to the History of the Cathedral of Winchester in the seventeenth century," *Hampshire Record Society* XIV (1897), 57–70.

by a strong Parliament which was winning a war in the name of the destruction of superstition. Acts of iconoclasm committed by the Parliamentary army frequently had the taint of intended profanation. Puritans, it can be recalled, had sternly rejected any consecration or hallowing of things. No church or place signified special holiness for them; this was also true of articles like altars or Communion cups for things in themselves are never holy. Puritans believed that it is only in their use for holy purposes that dignity accrues.[50]

The damage, destruction, and sacrilege that ensued during the Civil War resulted from many factors: the irrational, the contradictory and impulsive motives showed themselves along with highly devised schemes of destruction. It would take the coming years of the Commonwealth and Protectorate to water down this energy and bring about the cessation of hostilities.

When the Puritan party led by Oliver Cromwell achieved victory in 1648, the religious settlement that was reached was not as unified as one would have expected. Within the Puritan camp itself, controversy raged on all points of polity, theology and worship. Since there was little attempt on the part of the new government to find solidarity on traditional lines, what unity of religion remained stemmed from the survival of parochial institutions, clerical identification and the remnant of the old ecclesiastical structure.

The state did not regulate religious doctrine and worship, but seems to have allowed for almost complete toleration of opinion.[51] Church life itself was congregational with parish activity and functions reflecting the views of the minister or parishoners. The inaction of the government removed the threat any one group held over another and helped to retain a brief if tenuous peace. Again, it was the issue of public order that prevented further destruction of images. As time progressed and men forgot the recent war, the pressures against the Anglican clergy were removed and in rural areas, the

50. *Mercurius Rusticus* (1646), p. 216; Peter Hall (ed.) *Reliquiae Liturgicae: Documents connected with the Liturgy of the Church of England* (Bath: Binne and Goodwin, 1847), III, p. 82. (Westminster Directory).

51. Robert S. Bosher, *The Making of the Restoration Settlement* (Westminster: Dacre Press, 1951), pp. 6–8. J. A. Dodd, "Troubles in a City Parish under the Protectorate," *English Historical Review* X (1895), 41–54.

traditional services of the Book of Common Prayer were conducted without threat of harassment.[52]

It is open to question, however, what ornaments of worship remained within these churches. A considerable religious reformation had taken place during the war and now that peace had come with Puritan triumph, official policy came to reflect an iconoclasm that would be diluted by time. The cathedrals, to be sure, remained victims of the recent war; since they stood as symbols of the past, it was only natural that there would be attempts to remove them. In February of 1651, a proposal was introduced in the House of Commons that "all Cathedral churches, where there are other churches or chapels sufficient for the people to meet in for the worship of God, be surveyed . . . pulled down, and sold, and be employed for a stock for the use of the poor."[53]

The motion was never carried, but the threat remained. Demolition itself was begun in Lichfield Cathedral, but advanced only to the stripping of the lead from the roof. When petitioners sought to save Winchester, their pleas took the form of a defense of the fabric for preaching and never alluded to beauty or history.[54]

St. Paul's in London probably suffered the most; this was undoubtedly due to its proximity to Puritanism's center and to the fact that it was still undergoing repairs when the war broke out. The scaffolding for the Laudian renovations was taken down to be sold, but since it supported parts of the roof, a collapse of the stone vaulting in the south resulted.[55] Such activity was contagious and soon St. Paul's appeared good for easy pickings. In 1654, the Lord Mayor and Alderman of London petitioned Cromwell.

Within the last six months part of the roof (on the south side) of Paul's Church fell down, with the lead that covered it. The City is in great want of water, and as to procure a further supply which will be very chargeable. We beg the lead towards making pipes for its conveyance.[56]

52. W. K. Jordan, *Religious Toleration in England* (Cambridge: Harvard University Press, 1936), III, pp. 195–200.
53. Stephens and Madge, "Documents relating to the History of the Cathedral Church of Winchester in the Seventeenth Century," p. 256.
54. *Ibid.*, p. 97.
55. Jane Lang, *Rebuilding St. Paul's after the Great Fire of London* (Oxford: University Press, 1956), p. 6.
56. *Calendar of State Papers, Domestic*, LXXV, #1 (August 23, 1654).

The carved work of Inigo Jones' western portico was damaged and the whole edifice was turned to secular uses. Rows of mean little shops were rented out or taken over by men who proceeded to make themselves comfortable by mutilating the columns. Statues were hurled down and even Paul's Cross was not saved from removal.[57]

The statues of James I and Charles I at the west end of the Cathedral were broken up and the inscriptions on the stonework defaced. The image of Charles at the Exchange lost its head and scepter, but earned a new inscription: "Exit tyrannus Regum ultimus, anno primo restitute liberatis Angliae 1648."[58]

The nave was utilized as a cavalry barracks with part of it a stable quartering up to eight hundred horses. Romping and exercising of horses, brawling and rowdiness effected great harm to the fabric. But in the long run, the majority of the cathedrals suffered less than St. Paul's and reflected the hesitancy of the government's religious settlement.[59]

The royal collections were, like the churches of England, threatened by the same lukewarm iconoclasm, now growing colder. If the Stuart holdings of paintings, sculpture and tapestries were thought to be idolatrous, they were also valuable and could fetch high prices. Even in 1645, Parliament had undertaken to sell some pictures at York House; superstitious works of art were to be destroyed, but this order was never carried out.[60] In March, 1648, the House of Commons voted to confiscate the personal estate of the royal family.

57. Evelyn, *Diary*, 23 July, 1643; Tatham, *Puritans in Power*, p. 258; Cook, *Old St. Paul's Cathedral*, p. 85.
58. *Calendar of State Papers, Domestic*, IX (July 31, 1650), #7.
59. See Celia Fiennes, *Through England on a Side Saddle* (London: Field and Tuer, 1888).
60. Claude Phillips, *The Picture Gallery of Charles I*, p. 47. Horace Walpole claims that the Puritan appeals to superstition were merely a subterfuge for disguising their real distaste for art: its association with the court. "The arts were, in a manner, expelled with the royal family from Britain. The anecdotes of a civil war are the history of destruction. In all ages the mob have vented their hatred to tyrants on the pomp of tyranny. The magnificence the people have envied, they grow to detest, and mistaking consequences for causes, the first objects of their fury are the palaces of their masters. . . The arts that civilize society are not calculated for men who mean to rise on the ruins of established order." Horace Walpole, *Anecdotes of Painting in England* (London: Henry Bohn, 1862), II, p. 426. See also I, pp. 282f.

Commissioners were delegated the authority to inventory, appraise and sell such objects for the express purpose of discharging public debts, settling of arrears of salaries by now unemployed officials of the court and for general needs of the state.[61]

In the beginning there was some mismanagement because the House forbade its members to participate in the commission. Though an incomplete catalogue of the goods was drawn up, much was probably secreted away or privately sold.[62] Nothing was peddled by direct auction for all transactions were negotiated with private persons or, for those who feared identification with the upstart government, through their agents.

More than £118,00 was obtained this way until Cromwell himself put an end to the sale of Stuart treasures. When the Council of Officers decreed in 1656 that the government of the Commonwealth would reside in one man, Cromwell not only halted the sale, but even detained recent purchases.[63] Clearly the focus on one person necessitated a recovery or at least a stay on the sale of now required pomp. Royal furniture was recovered and certain ornaments were reserved for Cromwell's official residences. Mantegna's "Triumph of Julius Caesar" was hung in the Long Gallery at Hampton Court, tapestries were displayed in public apartments, while the Protector's own bedroom received paintings of Vulcan, Mars and Venus. Even new decorations were needed and the Council of State sent ten panels by Mantegna as cartoons to the royal tapestry works at Mortlake.[64]

For such extravagance, however, Puritans chided the Protector and

61. *Ibid.*, I, p. 284. Wilhelm Treue, *Art Plunder, the fate of works of art in war, revolution and peace* (London: Methuen and Co., 1960), p. 98. H. R. Trevor-Roper, *The Plunder of the Arts in the Seventeenth Century* (London: Thames and Hudson, 1970), pp. 53–58.

The fullest treatment of this matter is in Oliver Millar's introduction to "The Inventories and Valuations of the King's Goods 1649–1651" *The Walpole Society* XXXXIII (1970–72), xi–xxv.

62. Hutchinson, *Life of Colonel Hutchinson*, p. 367. For extracts of the inventories, see *Nineteenth Century* (August, 1890), 211–17. See also W. Nuttall, "King Charles I's Pictures and the Commonwealth Sale," *Apollo*, LXXXI (1965), 302–09.

63. Walpole, *Anecdotes* I, 289.

64. C. H. Firth, "The Court of Cromwell," *The Cornhill Magazine*, III, n.s. (September, 1897), 351. Phillips, *Picture Gallery*, pp. 48–49. *Calendar of Clarendon State Papers*, II, 217. *Calendar of State Papers Domestic, 1653–54*, p. 111; *1654*; pp. 291, 338, 456f.

sent him stern letters of objurgation. Disapproving of the naked antique marbles in the Privy Garden at Hampton Court, Mrs. Mary Netheway wrote:

This one thing I desire of you, to demolish those monsters which are set up as ornaments in Privy Garden, for whilst they stand, though you see no evil in them, yet there is much evil in it, for whilst the groves and altars of the idols remained untaken away in Jerusalem, the wrath of God continued against Israel.[65]

Cromwell's life did not last long and the half-hearted official iconoclasm of the Protectorate dwindled to little. Even if the resurrected Rump Parliament tried to sell Whitehall and its furnishings in 1659, the return of Charles II to kingly power one year later soon put a stop to all depredations of churches and their images.[66] Whitehall was readied for its royal master and the official policy of iconoclasm was overturned.

65. Firth, "Court of Cromwell," pp. 363–64.
66. *Journal of the House of Commons*, VII, 613f (March 16, 1659).

EPILOGUE

Mr. Lely, I desire you would use all your skill to paint my picture truly like me, and not flatter me at all; but remark all these
roughnesses, pimples, and warts, and everything as you see me,
otherwise I never will pay a farthing for it.

        —Oliver Cromwell to the painter, Peter Lely
    HORACE WALPOLE, *Anecdotes of Painting in England*

A fundamental revision of man's attitude towards life is apt to
find its first expression in artistic creation and scientific theory.

    JOSE ORTEGA Y GASSET, *The Dehumanization of Art*

THE REFORMATION of images in England entailed the beating down
of walls and church fittings, the smashing of stained glass and
sculpture, the ripping and tearing of paintings and tapestries; it included the destruction of objects whose only offense was that they
were ornamental or decorative; it ended in quiet reconstruction as
well as in violent civil disorders.

The reformation of images was again something more in that it
signified changing attitudes about the role of religious images in the
larger context of the Reformation. Both Catholics and Protestants
had agreed that the second commandment forbids idolatry; yet each
disagreed over the issue of when an image becomes idolatrous. At no
time was it possible in practice to prove that idolatry was taking
place, since the worship of a created thing in place of God occurs in
the mind of the worshipper rather than in the image addressed.

The arguments justifying or condemning images are not impres-
sive. They are repetitive formulas based on different views of salvation and religious worship. In fact, similar arguments could have
been invoked by both sides to arrive at opposite conclusions. The
primitive church was not an institution to be studied whose attitudes
toward images could be applied to the present; instead, the primitive
church was painted in colors appropriate to contemporaneous needs
and requirements. Melanchthon's doctrine of things "indifferent" was

inexact and potentially a blank ledger wherein different reformers could fill out what they might consider appropriately "indifferent." It was, in part, the failure of religious debate to make legitimate distinctions that ultimately allowed other forces to determine the fate of images.

It has been the purpose of this essay to understand the reformation of images in relation to these other forces. Along with the specific religious traditions and assumptions of Roman Catholicism, the medieval image of Christ and his saints was inextricably bound up in a whole philosophical fabric of political and social order. A blow aimed at one aspect of this fabric was essentially a blow against all. Therefore, the destruction of an object (whether cruifix, statue of saint or consecrated object) was, *de facto*, an attempt to destroy that which the object symbolized religiously, which in turn was inseparable from the fabric and basis of the political state (ordained by God through his vicar and invested in the monarch). It is not surprising, then, that the reformation of images in England was defined by the larger needs of church and state as institutions and by some profound changes in human consciousness rather than by any genuine intellectual discretion concerning the properties of images. Recall that Henry VIII had tried to distinguish what images were acceptable from those which he considered abused; the eventual fate of monastic images, however, was determined not by these distinctions, but by the economic and political needs of the Crown. Indeed, in Henry's and subsequent reigns, divergent factors combined to influence the eventual outcome of destruction. The reformation of images was as complex and contradictory as the movement today described as the Reformation.

I have tried to place English iconoclasm in this larger context of the Reformation without minimizing either the importance of published religious debate or the acts of physical destruction. Yet because images were tied to the traditional ecclesiastical and civil authority now rejected, such objects evoked, and in that sense possessed, the very real power that their supporters and detractors attributed to them. Therefore, in the long run the breaking of these images was an expression of a highly developed order of daring philosophical violence within the setting of profound social and political change. The more mundane and deplorable facts of the joys of destruction are the reprehensible but secondary effects of the attitudes of iconoclasm.[1]

Thomas Aquinas had argued that spiritual ideas are understood by material manifestations—that all our knowledge has its origins in sense. If this is true, the breaking of images helped in breaking up the fundamental intellectual presuppositions of political government, ecclesiastical organization, religious devotion and artistic representation. The net result was the development of new modes of human experience and thought.

Religious images were important to Englishmen because they spelled out in graphic terms the fundamental rites of passage from birth through life to death. Religion was not so much a system of doctrine as it was a ritual way of life; such experiences were significantly defined by the images that soon were to be overthrown.

Changes taking place in Tudor-Stuart England were those involved with the way men spoke to God, in their intellectual and emotional responses to the liturgy. For the sake of religious unity, Bishop George Day of Chichester was willing to jettison his belief in transubstantiation. But he renounced his diocese and accepted imprisonment under Edward VI rather than consent to the replacement of altars with tables. The physical altar of stone or wood was in Melanchthon's terms, "indifferent," but Day argued that to make an altar into a table was to transform the Mass as sacrifice into a communion.[2]

The Elizabethan Separatist Henry Barrow was just as convinced that the actual physical experiences of worship determine the intellectual premises of faith. He argued for the complete elimination of church buildings because implicit in these structures are "magical notions" that must be destroyed. "The idolatrous shape so cleaveth to every stone, as it by no means can be severed from them whiles there is a stone left standing upon a stone."[3]

1. Yates, *Art of Memory*, pp. 235, 277–78.
2. Smith, *Henry VIII*, p. 124.
3. L. H. Carlson (ed.), *The Writings of Henry Barrow*, 1587–90, p. 478.

Early in the sixteenth century, Englishmen were still convinced that their monarch was anointed by God to be his vicar on earth, responsible for administering divine justice to men. For all practical purposes, while this idea persisted throughout the century and into the next, Englishmen disagreed on the specific means by which the ruler should exercise his divine responsibility. Nevertheless, this political and social order that set king over subject was revealed in the conception of the world as an organic unity given meaning by the creating God. This idea found its fullest expression in metaphors of the microcosm reflecting the macrocosm and in the use of visual images. These metaphors and images were taken from the everyday world of human activity, and related to a larger political, social and religious condition. This extension admits a profound belief in the correspondence of the material world to the supernatural, of the individual to the political or social orders. Consequently, the arguments of the social and political order in defense of religious images were linked with the acceptance of the king as arbiter of God's justice.

When Henry VIII destroyed monasteries and confiscated income and properties, he believed he was appropriating religious imperial rights for the monarchy; one result, however, was that he acted in paradoxical opposition to the very institution upon which the monarchy was founded, in a sense undoing by his own hand the institutions which sanctioned his right to do so. The monarch, we must remember, was held to have received his authority to rule from God and was ordained in this capacity by God's vicar on earth, the Pope. Therefore, the attack upon the institutions of Catholicism by Henry was tantamount to attacking the foundations of his own royal authority.

The effect of Henry's campaign was to establish the beginning of a civil-religious ambience whereby Englishmen could be loyal to God and king, and with clear conscience circumvent the loyalty to Rome and the institutions of Roman Catholicism, thereby supporting the monarchy without losing hope of Heaven. The divine right of kingship was not renounced. Instead, it was defined outside the context of Roman and Catholic defense and authority. The images which had formerly cemented the spiritual and political unity of the nation were now jettisoned; other symbols were found. Royal arms replaced the crucifixes and other distinctly Roman Catholic images; the implication was that the English monarch was still as ordained by God as he had ever been.[4]

Likewise, royal portraits of Elizabeth I were not intended to be merely physical likenesses of the Queen, but were badges of royalty that assured the legitimacy of her royal power. Elizabethan symbolism resided in the imperial theory that monarchs have religious and political rights within their own domains. Thus to depict a ruler whose image and arms would supplant those of Christ and his saints was to conceive of such images as possessing the hieratic detachment and iconlike mask of the God-ordained ruler.[5] Portraits of the monarch were thus understood in the context of the concept of divine right as being holy images supplanting those of traditional saints, with their unacceptable associations with Roman piety and an allegiance that provoked political, as well as religious, conflict. Indeed, even many of the Virgin Mary's symbols were appropriated by Elizabeth, the "Virgin Queen"—Rose, Star, Moon, Phoenix, Ermine, Pearl —"Long Live Eliza." instead of "Hail, Mary."[6]

Calvinism in the guise of Puritanism had helped to transfer men's political and religious allegiance from Rome to the prince; in time, it would seek to transfer the same allegiance from the prince to the saint. This meant that the Puritans were committed to the establishment of a Holy Commonwealth that no longer depended on the traditional workings of royal and ecclesiastical power. "The saints saw themselves as divine instruments and theirs was the politics of wreckers, architects, and builders—hard at work upon the political world."[7]

Consequently, in order to accomplish the replacement of devotion to king and church with loyalty to God and the nation, iconoclasm became an essential element in the protestantization of England that, in part, resulted in the Revolution of 1642.[8] Indeed, the ultimate

4. The earliest known royal arms so placed are those of Henry VIII at Rushbrooke in Suffolk.
5. Strong, *Portraits of Elizabeth*, p. 36.
6. Yates, "Astraea," pp. 74–75, 81–82. Strong, *Portraits of Elizabeth* p. 10.
7. Walzer, *Revolution of the Saints*, p. 3.
8. In the French Revolution, iconoclasm was evidenced, but also a growing cult of pagan festivals that sustained the idea of revolution. See David Dowd, *Pageant-Master of the Republic, Jacques-Louis David and the French Revolution* (Lincoln: University of Nebraska Press, 1948), chapter III.

desire to reform all aspects of society required the elimination of
those images that spoke for other religious and political allegiances.

Reformation must be universal [exhorted the Puritan minister, Thomas
Case] . . . reform all places, all persons and callings. . . Reform the univer-
sities, reform the cities . . . the Sabbath, reform the ordinances, the worship
of God . . . Every plant which my heavenly father hath not planted shall be
rooted up.[9]

Possibly the fullest example of revolutionary reform demanded by
Puritans was the replacement of the sacramental priesthood with a
preaching ministry of educated men free of the allegiance to crown
and episcopal appointment. In fact, their dependence on the purity
of the Word revealed their freedom from the traditional corporate
church; their simple, undecorated clothing and churches would, furthermore, suggest this restored supremacy of Word over image and
ceremony. Long before the Puritans launched a frontal assault on
the traditional political orthodoxy of the crown and the prevailing
pattern of human relations, they had undermined its foundations in
image and symbol. Just as the seventeenth century witnessed subtle
but significant shifts in imagery and manner of political and social
argument, so, too, the old traditions and their associations of ideas
and experiences (if not doctrines) were denied, then discarded. Iconoclasm produced a vacuum that human nature abhors with the result
that new images were made to represent new ideas—or at least to
represent the removal of the old ideas.[10] A new political discipline
was forged—not dependent on hierarchy, patronage and image, but
a voluntary contract of individual and collective acceptance.

Iconoclasm destroyed an artistic heritage, but in the breach caused
by that destruction, a new kind of relationship of ruler, subject and
the state grew. Thus far more was swept away than art objects, according to our contemporary understanding of art-historical verities.
But unlike mere wanton destruction, the ground exposed was not
left barren.

Indeed, the violence done to religious art in this period was soon

9. Thomas Case, *Two Sermons Lately Preached* (London, 1642), II, 13, 16.
Quoted in Walzer, *Revolution of the Saints*, pp. 10–11.
10. See Walzer, *op. cit.*, chapter 6, "The New World of Discipline and Work."

followed by changes in the art forms themselves. By the end of Henry VIII's reign in 1547, there was a collapse of a court culture and with it active royal patronage. The English Church was separated from Rome, its monasteries and shrines dissolved and confiscated; the fate of the physical fabric of every church and its furnishings were already threatened by new acts of iconoclasm soon to ensue. Given the very special economic and political problems of the country and certainly, the controversy surrounding images, neither state nor established church could sponsor religious art.

In fact, the virtual disappearance of subject painting and the emergence of a curious kind of Elizabethan and Jacobean portraiture is a result of this campaign against religious art. Portrait painting at this time reveals an attitude toward the human body in an "isolated, strong, exotic and anti-naturalistic style" more suggestive of Byzantine art, itself the result of iconoclast movements, than the art of Renaissance Italy.[11]

The arts in England were taken over by the patronage of the nobility and the gentry. Scholarship, connoisseurship and antiquarianism became the attributes of the gentleman, and these, in turn, redeemed poetry and painting as important subjects in the educational scheme.[12] The visual arts were identified with the liberal arts and became ornaments in one's respite from the more practical occupations of life. Interest focused on the revelation of the sitter's social status and notoriety. Enhancing this interest was the use of emblematic devices and color symbolism which expressed the general hopes and human aspirations of the gentleman or lady in question.[13] It was the world of Bacon, Digby and Boyle.

God and his saints were no longer mentioned: the new art that came into being purported to be spiritual while not being religious.

11. Roy Strong, *The English Icon: Elizabethan and Jacobean Portraiture* (New Haven: Yale University Press, 1969), p. 3.

12. Henry Peacham, *The Complete Gentleman* (Ithaca: Cornell University Press, 1962), p. 120. Walter Houghton, "The English Virtuoso in the Seventeenth Century," *Journal of the History of Ideas*, III (1942), 57. W. Lee Ustick, "Changing Ideals of Aristocratic Character and Conduct in Seventeenth Century England," *Modern Philology* XXX (1932-3), 147-166.

13. Strong, *Icon*, pp. 30-31. See his important qualification that most portraiture at this time was "crude face recording," p. 37.

It aimed at an ideal imitation of human life that in the rejection of nature as it *is*, claimed to depict it as it *should* be.[14] The artist was expected to follow both the canons of classical art and the "perfection of an inward image made up in his mind by a most earnest and assiduous observation of all such bodies as in their owne kind are most excelling."[15] This portrayal of the superior forms of nature found its expression not in devotional stories of the medieval church, but in Scriptural and classical themes from history and mythology; its true home was not in churches and shrines, but at court and country manor.

In contrast, the medieval Catholic Church as well as the Counter Reformation had understood religious images as an important assistance to salvation through their teaching of the mysteries of religion. Such representations confirmed Christians in remembering their articles of faith and ultimately in ordering "their lives and manners in imitation of the Saints . . . to adore and love God . . ."[16]

The advent of iconoclasm in the sixteenth and early seventeenth centuries spelled the end of this union between art and religion. Gone were the correspondences of the natural world to the supernatural, of the world we know as reality to the world of true Reality. Such metaphors and images had been possible only in a material world graced by the medieval view of the Incarnation of Christ and guided by the traditions of the Church. It is not how things appear to the senses, Puritans argued, but what they mean; this is opposed to where the details of the natural world were to be explored for the sake of a higher knowledge. Ignorance of the natural world is an attitude nourishing and nourished by a mistrust of "appearances" and a denial of the physical universe for the sake of a "truer" or "more real" world.

Nothing was quite the same again; if religious images spelled idola-

14. John Pope-Hennessy, "Nicholas Hilliard and Mannerist Art Theory," *Journal of Warburg and Courtauld Institutes*, VI (1943), 90. D. J. Gorgon, "Poet and Architect: the intellectual setting of the quarrel between Ben Johnson and Inigo Jones," *Journal of the Warburg and Courtauld Institutes*, XII (1949), 152–78. Luigi Salerno, "English Seventeenth Century Literature on Painting," *Journal of the Warburg and Courtauld Institutes*, XIV (1951), 235–38.

15. Francis Junius, *The Painting of the Ancients* (London, 1638), Book I, p. 2. R. W. Lee, "Ut Pictura Poesis: The Humanistic Theory of Painting," *Art Bulletin*, XXII (1940), 197–269.

16. Canons and Decrees of the Council of Trent, Session XXV, Tit. 2.

try to Protestant reformers, an occasion for plunder to most people, then the tangible legacy of iconoclasm would outlast these two centuries. For it was the violence done to religious art in this period through both destruction as well as controversy that helped to mold the character of the art that was to follow. The arts went their separate ways from religion because in great part Protestantism no longer really desired the assistance of visual aids in teaching the mysteries of faith. The lives of the Saints were ignored; the Mass and its devotions anathemized. Scripture and the pulpit prevailed.[17]

Of course, it can be argued that the move from art as a handmaiden of religion to its conception as an autonomous activity in the seventeenth century is explainable without the story of the reformation of images. But the rupture (for that is what it is) between the two conceptions of art in England existed at the very time when the ecclesiastical art of the Middle Ages was theologically undermined, liturgically repressed, politically identified with Rome and economically broken.

What could more hasten the way for art to move free of religion than the Protestant insistence on Scripture as a restraint to artistic imagination or the "safe" kind of decorative art that offends no one, least of all instructs? (". . . but if they will have anything painted, [let] . . . it be either branches, flowers, or posies [mottoes, texts] taken out of Holy Scripture.")[18] The suddenness of the change between art as a means of expressing the mysteries of faith and art as a means of creating the most beautiful forms of nature according to the principles of human reason was not really so sudden. The former declined and disappeared in the early sixteenth century with the repression in England of the Church that sustained it. Despite its brief reappearances during the reigns of Mary and Charles I, when it was supported by Gardiner, Andrewes and Laud, such art was not revived. The

17. *Visitations Articles and Injunctions*, II, 289, article 28. Hooper's injunctions for Gloucester and Worcester, 1551–52.

18. The Reformation, however, must not be seen as simply an iconoclastic movement, but which, at least in other countries nourished its own kind of art and artist. In fact, in Germany and the Netherlands, the direct effect of "Protestant doctrine on artistic productivity does seem to affect expressive form and intrinsic content in addition to iconographical subject matter." Erwin Panofsky, "Comments on Art and Reformation," in Craig Harbison (ed.), *Symbols in Transformation, Iconographical Themes at the Time of the Reformation* (Princeton: Art Museum, 1969), pp. 9–14.

hiatus was filled with a religion that sought not visual images, but words. The new art that came to be looked outside this religious context for nourishment. In England, at least, Christ remained "naked" —without images; iconoclasm had triumphed.

210

SELECTED BIBLIOGRAPHY

Addleshaw, G. W. O. *The High Church Tradition*. London: Faber and Faber, 1941.

Addleshaw, G. W. O., and Etchells, Frederick. *The Architectural Setting of Anglican Worship*. London: Faber and Faber, 1958.

Alexander, Paul J. *The Patriarch Nicephorus of Constantinople*. Oxford: Clarendon Press, 1958.

Allison, C. F. *The Rise of Moralism*. London: S.P.C.K., 1966.

Ames, William. *A Fresh Suit Against Human Ceremonies in God's Worship*. Rotterdam, 1633.

Andrewes, Lancelot. *Ninety-Six Sermons*. 5 vols. Oxford: John Henry Parker, 1841–43.

——. *The Pattern of Catechistical Doctrine*. London, 1650.

——. *Two Answers to Cardinal Perron and Other Miscellaneous Works*. Oxford: John Henry Parker, 1854.

Bale, John. *A Declaration of Edmonde Bonners Articles, concerning the Cleargye of London Dyocese*. London, 1561.

——. *Select Works*. Edited for the Parker Society by Henry Christmas. Cambridge: Cambridge University Press, 1849.

Barnes, Robert. *The Whole Workes of W. Tyndall, John Frith and Doctor Barnes, Three Worthy Martyrs*. London, 1573.

Baynes, Norman H. "The Icons before Iconoclasm," *Harvard Theological Review* XLIV (1951). 93–106.

Beny, Roloff, *Pleasure of Ruins*. ed. C. B. Smith. London: Thames and Hudson, 1964.

Bieler, André. *Architecture in Worship, the Christian Place of Worship*. Edinburgh and London: Oliver and Boyd, 1965.

Blench, J. W. *Preaching in England in the Late Fifteenth and Sixteenth Centuries*. Oxford: Basil Blackwell, 1964.

Bond, Francis. *The Chancel of English Churches*. London: Oxford University Press, 1916.

——. *Fonts and Font Covers*. London: Oxford University Press, 1908.

——. *Screens and Galleries in English Churches*. London: Oxford University Press, 1908.

——. *Westminster Abbey*. London: Oxford University Press, 1909.

Bond, Frederick and Camm, Dom Bede. *Roodscreens and Roodlofts*. 2 vols. New York: Charles Scribner's Sons, 1909.

Bonner, Edmund. *A Profitable and Necessary Doctrine, with Certayne Homelyes Adioyned Therunto*. London, 1555.

Bosher, Robert S. *The Making of the Restoration Settlement*. Westminster: Dacre Press, 1951.

Bourne, E. C. E. *The Anglicanism of William Laud*. London: SPCK, 1947.

Bromiley, G. W. *Thomas Cranmer Theologian*. New York: Oxford University Press, 1956.

Brook, V. J. K. *A Life of Archbishop Parker*. Oxford: Clarendon Press, 1962.

Buchholz, Friedrich. *Protestantismus und Kunst im Sechzehnten Jahrhundert*. Leipzig: Dieterich'sche Verlagsbuchhadnlung, 1928.

T. Buddensieg, "Gregory the Great, the destroyer of Pagan idols," *Journal of Warburg and Courtauld Institutes* XXVIII (1965) 44–65.

Bullinger, Henry. *The Decades*. 4 vols. Edited for the Parker Society by Thomas Harding. Cambridge: Cambridge University Press, 1849–52.

Burnet, Gilbert. *The History of the Reformation of the Church of England*. Edited by Nicholas Pecock. 7 vols. Oxford: Clarendon Press, 1865.

Bush, Douglas. *The Renaissance and English Humanism*. Toronto: University Press, 1939.

Calfhill, James. *An Answer to John Martialls's Treatise of the Cross*. Edited for the Parker Society by Richard Gibbings. Cambridge: Cambridge University Press, 1846.

Calvin, John. *Institutes of the Christian Religion*. Translated by John Allen. 2 vols. Philadelphia: Presbyterian Board of Christian Education, 1930.

———. *Tracts and Treatises*. 3 vols. Grand Rapids: B. Eerdmans Publishing Company, 1958.

Cardwell, Edward (ed.). *Documentary Annals of the Reformed Church of England (1546–1716)*. 2 vols. Oxford: Oxford University Press, 1844.

———. *A History of Conferences and Other Proceedings Connected with the Revision of the Book of Common Prayer*. Oxford: J. H. and J. Parker, 1840.

———. (ed.) *Synodalia, a Collection of Articles of Religion, Canons and Proceedings in the Convocations in the Province of Canterbury*. 2 vols. Oxford: Oxford University Press, 1842.

Cheshire, J. G. "William Dowsing's Destructions in Cambridgeshire," *Cambridgeshire and Huntingdon Archaeological Society Transactions*, III (1909–14).

Clebsch, William. *England's Earliest Protestants*. New Haven: Yale University Press, 1964.

Cobb, Cyril S. (ed.) *The Rationale of Ceremonial 1540–43*. London: Longmans, Green and Company, 1910.

Collier, Jeremy. *An Ecclesiastical History of Great Britain*. Edited by Thomas Lathbury. 9 vols. London: William Straker, 1852.

Collins, A. J. (ed.) *Jewels and Plate of Queen Elizabeth I*. London: British Museum, 1955.

Collins, William Edward (ed.). *Lectures on Archbishop Laud*. London: A. Southey and Company, 1895.

Collinson, Patrick. *The Elizabethan Puritan Movement*. Berkeley: University of California Press, 1967.

Constant, G. *The Reformation in England*. Trans. by E. I. Watkin. 2 vols. New York: Sheed and Ward, 1942.

Cook, G. H. *The English Cathedral Through the Centuries*. London: Phoenix House, 1957.

―――. *The English Medieval Parish Church*. London: Phoenix House, 1954.

―――. *English Monasteries in the Middle Ages*. London: Phoenix House, 1961.

―――. (ed.) *Letters to Cromwell and others on the Suppression of the Monasteries*. London: John Baker, 1965.

―――. *Mediaeval Chantries and Chantry Chapels*. London: Phoenix House, 1963.

Cosin, John. *Correspondence*. 2 vols. Edited by George Ornsby. Durham: Surtees Society, 1869.

―――. *Works*. 5 vols. Oxford: John Henry and James Parker, 1855.

Coulton, G. G. *Art and the Reformation*. Cambridge: Cambridge University Press, 1953.

―――. *Five Centuries of Religion*. 5 vols. Cambridge: Cambridge University Press, 1923.

―――. *Ten Medieval Studies*. Cambridge: Cambridge University Press, 1930.

―――. "The High Ancestry of Puritanism," *Ten Medieval Studies*. Boston: Beacon Press, 1959.

Cox, J. Charles. *Churchwardens' Accounts*. London: Methuen and Company, 1913.

―――. *The Parish Registers of England*. London: Methuen and Company, 1910.

Cox, J. Charles and Ford, Charles Bradley. *The Parish Churches of England*. New York: Charles Scribner's Sons, 1935.

Cox, J. Charles and Harvey, Alfred. *English Church Furniture*. London: Methuen and Company, 1908.

Cranmer, Thomas. *The Miscellaneous Writings and Letters*. Edited for the Parker Society by John E. Cox. 2 vols. Cambridge: Cambridge University Press, 1846.

Cromwell, Oliver. *The Writings and Speeches*. Edited by Wilbur C. Abbott. 4 vols. Cambridge: Harvard University Press, 1937–47.

Crouch, Joseph. *Puritanism and Art*. London and New York: Cassell, 1910.

Cruttwell, Patrick. *The Shakespearean Moment*. New York: Random House, 1960.

Davies, Horton, *Worship and Theology in England From Cranmer to Hooker. 1534–1603*. Princeton: University Press, 1970.

Davies, J. G. *The Secular Use of Church Building*. New York: Seabury Press, 1968.

Davis, Eliza J. "The Transformation of London," in R. W. Seton-Watson, *Tudor Studies*. London: Longmans Green and Company, 1924. pp. 287–314.

———. *The Worship of the English Puritans*. Westminster: Dacre Press, 1948.

Davis, J. F., "Lollards, Reformers and St. Thomas of Canterbury," *University of Birmingham Historical Journal* IX (1963–4) 1–15.

Dickens, A. G. *The English Reformation*. London: B. T. Batsford, 1964.

———. *The Marian Reaction in the Diocese of York*. London: St. Anthony's Hall Publications, 1957.

Donne, John. *The Sermons*. Edited by Evelyn M. Simpson and George R. Popper. 10 vols. Berkeley and Los Angeles: University of California Press, 1953–62.

Dowden, Edward. *Puritan and Anglican, Studies in Literature*. London: K. Paul, Trench, Truebner and Company, 1901.

Dowsing, William. *The Cambridge Journal*. Cambridge: History Teacher's Miscellany, 1926.

———. *The Journal*. Edited by C. H. Evelyn White. Ipswich: Pawsey and Hayes, 1885.

Drummond, Andrew L. *The Church Architecture of Protestantism*. Edinburgh: T. and T. Clark, 1934.

Dugdale, William. *The History of St. Paul's Cathedral*. London: Lockington, Hughes, Harding, 1818.

Dugmore, C. W., Charles Duggan, G. J. Cuming (eds.). *Studies in Church History*. London: Thomas Nelson and Sons, 1964–65.

Dugmore, Clifford. *The Mass and the English Reformers*. London: Macmillan, 1958.

Edward VI. *The Chronicle and Political Papers*. Edited by W. K. Jordan, Ithaca: Cornell University Press, 1966.

Eikon Basilike. Edited by Philip Knachel. Ithaca: Cornell University Press, 1966.

Erasmus, Desiderius. *The Colloquies*. Translated by Craig R. Thompson. Chicago: University of Chicago Press, 1965.

———. *Enchiridion Militis Christiani*. Notre Dame: Fides, 1962.

Firth, C. H. and Rait, R. S. (ed.) *Acts and Ordinances of the Interregnum 1642–1660*. London: Statue Law Committee, 1911. 3 vols.

Floyd, Charles (ed.). *Formularies of Faith put forth by Authority during the Reign of Henry VIII*. Oxford: Oxford University Press, 1856.

Foxe, John. *The Acts and Monuments*. Edited by Stephen Reed Cattley. 9 vols. London: R. B. Seeley and W. Burnside, 1837–41.

Frere, W. H. *The English Church in the Reigns of Elizabeth and James I*. London: Macmillan, 1904.

————. (ed.) *Visitation Articles and Injunctions.* 3 vols. London: Longmans, Green and Company, 1910.

Fryer, W. R. "The 'High Churchmen' of the Earlier Seventeenth Century," *Renaissance and Modern Studies* V (1961), 106–48.

Gairdner, James. *The English Church in the Sixteenth Century.* London: Macmillan, 1902.

Gardiner, Samuel R. *The Constitutional Documents of the Puritan Revolution 1625–1660.* Oxford: Clarendon Press, 1906.

————. *History of the Commonwealth and Protectorate 1649–60.* 3 vols. London: Longmans, Green and Company, 1901.

————. *History of England From the Accession of James I to the Outbreak of the Civil War.* 10 vols. London: Longmans, Green and Company, 1884–91.

Gardiner, Stephen. *Letters.* Edited by James Arthur Muller. Cambridge: Cambridge University Press, 1933.

Garside, Charles. *Zwingli and the Arts.* New Haven: Yale University Press, 1966.

Gee, Henry and Hardy, William J. (ed.). *Documents Illustrative of English Church History.* London: Macmillan and Company, 1914.

George, Charles H. and Katherine. *The Protestant Mind of the English Reformation.* Princeton: Princeton University Press, 1961.

Gibson, Edmund (ed.). *Codex Juris Ecclesiastici Anglicani or the Statues, Constitutions, Canons, Rubricks and Articles of the Church of England.* 2 vols. Oxford: Clarendon Press, 1761.

Goodman, Godfrey. *The Creatures Praysing God, or the Religion of Dumbe Creatures. London,* 1622.

Grabar, André. *L'iconoclasme byzantin.* Paris: Collège de France, 1957.

Great Britain. *Acts of the Privy Council of England.* London: H. M. Stationery Office, 1921.

Great Britain. Public Record Office. *Calendar of State Papers, Domestic series of the Reigns of Edward VI, Mary and Elizabeth.* Edited by Robert Lemon and M.A.E. Green. 12 vols. London: H. M. Stationery Office, 1856–72.

Great Britain. Public Record Office, *Calendar of State Papers, Domestic Series of the Reign of James I.* 4 vols. London: H. M. Stationery Office, 1857–59.

Great Britain. Public Record Office. *Calendar of State Papers, Domestic Series of the Reign of Charles I.* 22 vols. London: H. M. Stationery Office, 1858–93.

Great Britain. *Statutes of the Realm.* Edited by A. Luders, T. E. Tomlins, J. Raithby. 11 vols. London: H. M. Stationery Office, 1810–28.

Hall, D. J. *English Mediaeval Pilgrimage.* London: Routledge and Kegan Paul, 1966.

Hall, Joseph. *The Works*. Edited by D. A. Talboys. 12 vols. Oxford: Oxford University Press, 1837–39.

Haller, William. *Liberty and Reformation in the Puritan Revolution*. New York: Columbia University Press, 1955.

———. *The Rise of Puritanism*. New York: Harper Torch, 1957.

Hayward, John. *Annals of the First Four Years of the Reign of Queen Elizabeth*. Edited by John Bruce. London: Camden Society, 1840.

Heylyn, Peter. *Cryprianus Anglicus or the History of the Life and Death of . . . William, by Divine Providence, Lord Archbishop of Canterbury*. Dublin: John Hyde and Robert Owen, 1719.

Heylyn, Peter. *Ecclesia Restaurata*. 2 vols. Cambridge: Cambridge University Press, Ecclesiastical History Society, 1849.

Hill, Christopher. *Puritanism and Revolution*. New York: Schocken Books, 1964.

Hooker, Richard. *Works*. Edited by John Keble. 3 vols. Oxford: Clarendon Press, 1874.

Hooper, John. *Early Writings*. Edited for the Parker Society by Samuel Carr. Cambridge: Cambridge University Press, 1843.

Hughes, Paul and Larkin, James (eds.). *Tudor Royal Proclamations*. New Haven: Yale University Press, 1964.

Hutton, William H. *The English Church, 1625–1714*. London: Macmillan, 1903.

———. *William Laud*. Boston and New York: Houghton Mifflin, 1895.

James I. *The Political Works*. Edited by Charles H. McIlwain. Cambridge: Harvard University Press, 1918.

———. *Works*. Edited by James Montague. London, 1616.

Jewel, John. *The Works*. Edited for the Parker Society by John Ayre. 4 vols. Cambridge: Cambridge University Press, 1850.

John of Damascus. *Writings*. Translated by Frederic H. Chase. New York: Fathers of the Church, 1958.

Jordan, W. K. *Edward VI: The Threshold of Power*. London: George Allen and Unwin, 1970.

———. *Edward VI—The Young King*. Cambridge: Harvard University Press, 1968.

Kenyon, J. P. (ed.). *The Stuart Constitution 1603–1688*. Cambridge: Cambridge University Press, 1966.

Kitzinger, Ernst, "The Cult of Images in the Age before Iconoclasm," *Dumbarton Oaks Papers*, VIII (1954), 83–150.

Knappen, M. M. *Tudor Puritanism, a Chapter in the History of Idealism*. Gloucester, Mass.: Peter Smith, 1963.

Knowles, David. *The Religious Orders of England*. Cambridge: Cambridge University Press, 1961.

Ladner, Gerhart B. "The Concept of the Image in the Greek Fathers and the Byzantine Iconoclastic Controversy," *Dumbarton Oaks Papers*, VII (1953), 1–34.

Latimer, Hugh. *Sermons and Remains*. Edited for the Parker Society by George Elwes Corrie. 2 vols. Cambridge: Cambridge University Press, 1844–45.

Laud, William. *The Works*. Edited by W. Scott and J. Bliss. 9 vols. Oxford: John Henry Parker, 1847–60.

Lees-Milne, James. *The Age of Inigo Jones*. London: B. T. Batsford, 1953.

Leeuw, Gerardus van der. *Religion in Essence and Manifestation*. New York: Harper Torch, 1963.

————. *Sacred and Profane Beauty, The Holy in Art*. Trans. by David E. Green. New York: Holt, Rinehart and Winston, 1963.

Letters and Papers, Foreign and Domestic of the Reign of Henry VIII, 1509–47. Edited by James Gairdner and J. S. Brewer. 21 vols. London: H. M. Stationery Office, 1862–1910.

Ludwig, Allan I. *Graven Images, New England Stonecarving and its Symbols, 1650–1815*. Middletown: Wesleyan University Press, 1966.

MacColl, Malcolm. *The Royal Commission and the Ornaments Rubric*. London: Longmans, Green and Company, 1906.

Maclure, Millar. *The Paul's Cross Sermons*. Toronto: University of Toronto Press, 1958.

Marchant, Ronald. *The Puritans and the Church Courts in the Diocese of York, 1560–1642*. London: Longmans, Green and Company, 1960.

Martin, Edward James. *A History of the Iconoclastic Controversy*. London: SPCK, n.d.

McConica, James K. *English Humanists and Reformation Politics*. Oxford: Clarendon Press, 1965.

Merriman, Roger B. (ed.). *Life and Letters of Thomas Cromwell*. 2 vols. Oxford: Clarendon Press, 1902.

More, Thomas. *The Dialogue Concerning Tyndale*. Edited by W. E. Campbell and A. W. Reed. London: Eyre and Spottiswoode, 1927.

Muller, James A. *Stephen Gardiner and the Tudor Reaction*. New York: Macmillan, 1926.

Neal, Daniel. *History of the Puritans*. 3 vols. London: Longmans, Hurnst, Rees, Orme and Brown, 1811.

New, John F. H. *Anglican and Puritan the Basis of their Opposition 1558–1640*. Stanford: Stanford University Press, 1964.

Nichols, James H. and Trinterud, Leonard J. *The Architectural Setting for Reformed Worship*. Chicago: Presbytery of Chicago, 1960.

Niebuhr, H. Richard. *Christ and Culture*. New York: Harper, 1956.

Oman, Charles. *English Church Plate 597–1830*. London: Oxford University Press, 1957.

Otto, Rudolf. *The Idea of the Holy*. Trans. by John W. Harvey. New York: Oxford University Press, 1958.

Owst, G. R. *Literature and Pulpit in Medieval England*. Oxford: Basil Blackwell, 1961.

Parker, Matthew. *Correspondence*. Edited for the Parker Society by John Bruce and Thomason Terowne. Cambridge: Cambridge University Press, 1853.

Pecock, Reginald. *The Repressor of Over Much Blaming of the Clergy*. 2 vols. Edited by Churchill Babington. London, Longman, Green Longman and Roberts, 1860.

Pendrill, Charles. *Old Parish Life in London*. London: Oxford University Press, 1937.

Perkins, William. *The Workes*. 3 vols. London, 1626, 31.

Pollard, A. F. *England Under Protector Somerset*. London: Kegan Paul, Trench, Truebner and Company, 1900.

Prynne, William. *Anti-Arminianisme or the Church of England's Old Antithesis to the New Arminianisme*. London, 1630.

————, *A Breviate of The Life of William Laud. . . Extracted. . . Out of his owne Diary, and other writings. . .* London, 1644.

————, *A Briefe Survay and Censure of Mr. Cozens His Couzening Deuotions*. London, 1628.

————. *Canterburie's Doome, or the First Part of a Compleat History of the Commitment, Tryall, Condemnation, Execution of William Laud . . .* London, 1646.

————. *Hidden Workes of Darknes Brought to Publike Light*. London, 1645.

————. *Histrio-mastix, the Players' Scourge, or Actors' Tragaedie*. London, 1633.

————. *Lord Bishops, None of the Lords Bishops. . .* London, 1640.

(Ram, Robert.) *Soldiers' Catechism*. Edited by Walter Begley. London: Elliot Stock, 1900.

Réau, Louis. *Les Monuments Détruits de L'Art Français*. Paris: Libraire Hachette, 1959.

Ridley, Nicholas. *Works*. Edited for the Parker Society by Henry Christmas. Cambridge: Cambridge University Press, 1841.

Rites of Durham. Edited by J. T. Fowler. London: Surtees Society, 1903.

Robinson, Hastings (ed.). *Original Letters Relative to the English Reformation*. Cambridge Cambridge University Press, 1846.

————, *The Zurich Letters*. 2 vols. Cambridge: Cambridge University Press, 1842.

Ryves, Bruno. *Mercurius Rusticus: or, The Countries Complaint of the Sacriledges, Prophanations and Plunderings, committed by the Schismatiques on the Cathedrall Churches of this Kingdomes*. Oxford, 1646.

————. *Mercurius Rusticus or the Countries Complaint of the Barbarous Outrages Committed by the Sectaries . . .* London, 1685.

Salerno, Luigi. "English Seventeenth Century Literature on Painting,"

Journal of Warburg and Courtauld Institutes XIV (1951), 234–58.

Scarisbrick, J. J. *Henry VIII*. London: Eyre and Spottiswoode, 1968.

Schoene, Wolfgang et al, *Das Gottesbild im Abendland* Witten, Berlin: Eckart-Verlag, 1959.

Scholes, Percy A. *The Puritans and Music*. London: Oxford University Press, 1934.

Smart, Peter. *Canterbury's Cruelty* . . . London, 1643.

————, *A Catalogue of Superstitious Innovations* . . . London, 1642.

Smith, Lacey Baldwin, *Henry VIII, The Mask of Royalty*. Boston: Houghton Mifflin, 1971.

————. "Henry VIII and the Protestant Triumph," *American Historical Review* LXXI (1960), 1237–1264.

————. *Tudor Prelates and Politics 1536–1558*. Princeton: Princeton University Press, 1953.

Sparrow, A. *A Collection of Articles, Injunctions, Canons, Orders, Ordinances and Constitutional Ecclesiastical with other Publick Records of the Church of England*. London, 1675.

Steele, Robert (ed.). *Tudor and Stuart Proclamations 1485–1714*. 2 vols. Oxford: Clarendon Press, 1910.

Stow, John. *Survey of London*. London: J. M. Dent and Sons, 1956.

Strong, Roy, "Edward VI and the Pope, a Tudor anti-papal allegory and its setting," *Journal of the Warburg and Courtauld Institutes*. XXIII (1960), 311–13.

————. *Portraits of Queen Elizabeth I*. Oxford: Clarendon Press, 1963.

Strype, John. *Annals of the Reformation and Establishment of Religion and other various occurrences in the Church of England during Queen Elizabeth's Happy Reign*. 4 vols. (in 6 parts) Oxford: Clarendon Press, 1824.

————. *Ecclesiastical Memorials relating chiefly to Religion and the Reformation of it, and the emergencies of the Church of England under King Henry VIII, King Edward VI and Queen Mary I*. 3 vols. (in 6 parts). Oxford: Clarendon Press, 1822.

Thomas Aquinas. *Summa Theologica*. 3 vols. New York: Benziger Brothers, 1947.

Thomas, Keith, *Religion and the Decline of Magic*. New York: Charles Scribner's Sons, 1971.

Thomson, John A. F. *The Later Lollards*. Oxford: University Press, 1965.

Tillich, Paul. *Theology of Culture*. Edited by Robert C. Kimball. New York: Oxford University Press, 1959.

Trevor-Roper, H. R. *Archbishop Laud 1573–1645*. London: Macmillan and Company, 1940.

————. *Historical Essays*. London: Macmillan and Company, 1957.

Tyndale, William. *Works*. Edited for the Parker Society by Henry Walter. 3 vols. Cambridge: Cambridge University Press, 1849–50.

Usher, Roland G. *The Reconstruction of the English Church*. 2 vols. New York and London: D. Appleton and Company, 1910.

Vallance, Aymer. *Greater English Church Screens*. London: B. T. Batsford, 1947.

Varley, Frederick John. *Cambridge During the Civil War, 1642–46*. Cambridge: W. Helfer and Sons, 1935.

————, (ed.). *Mercurius Aulicus*. Oxford: Basil Blackwell, 1948.

————. *The Siege of Oxford*. Oxford: Oxford University Press, 1932.

Waterhouse, Ellis. *Painting in Britain 1530 to 1790*. Harmondsworth: Penguin Books, 1953.

Webb, Geoffrey. *Architecture in Britain: The Middle Ages*. Harmondsworth: Penguin Books, 1956.

Wedgwood, C. V. *The King's Peace 1637–1641*. New York: Macmillan, 1956.

————. *The King's War 1641–1647*. New York: Macmillan, 1959.

Weiss, Roberto. *Humanism in England during the Fifteenth Century*. Oxford: Basil Blackwell, 1941.

Welsby, Paul A. *George Abbot*. London: SPCK, 1962.

————. *Lancelot Andrewes 1555–1626*. London: SPCK, 1958.

Whinney, Margaret. *Sculpture in Britain: 1530 to 1830*. Baltimore: Penguin Books, 1964.

Whinney, Margaret and Millar, Oliver. *English Art 1625–1714*. Oxford: Clarendon Press, 1957.

White, Helen C. *Tudor Books of Saints and Martyrs*. Madison: University of Wisconsin Press, 1963.

White, James F. *Protestant Worship and Church Architecture*. New York: Oxford University Press, 1964.

Whitehead, Alfred North. *Religion in the Making*. New York: Macmillan Company, 1960.

Whitgift, John. *Works*. Edited for the Parker Society by J. Ayre. 3 vols. Cambridge: Cambridge University Press, 1851–53.

Wilkins, David (ed.). *Concilia Magnae Britanniae et Hiberniae*. 4 vols. London, 1737.

Workman, Herbert B. *John Wyclif, A Study of the English Medieval Church*. 2 vols. Oxford: Clarendon Press, 1926.

Wyclif, John. *Select English Works*. Edited by Thomas Arnold. 3 vols. Oxford: Clarendon Press, 1871.

Yates, Frances. *The Art of Memory*. Chicago: University of Chicago Press, 1966.

————. "Queen Elizabeth as Astraea," *Journal of Warburg and Courtauld Institutes* X (1947), 27–82.

Zeeveld, W. Gordon. *Foundations of Tudor Policy*. Cambridge: Harvard University Press, 1948.

Zwingli, H. *Hauptschriften*. Edited by Fritz Blanke, Oskar Farn, Rudolf Pfister. Zurich: Zwingli Verlag, 1940.

INDEX

Church, 81, 82–83, 85, 89n, 93–94, 99–102, 114, 184; death of, 98
Edward the Confessor: shrine of, 72, 110; sculpture of, 144
Egglestone Abbey, 66n
Elizabeth I (Queen of England), 2, 90n, 91, 105, 140, 144n, 165, 194, 195; and the Church, 69, 112–113, 117–118, 128–132, 177, 183n; cult of, 119–121, 205; chapel of, 124–128, 161, 181; excommunicated, 132; Puritans under, 134. *See also* Elizabethan settlement
Elizabethan settlement, 109, 112, 113–118, 126, 129, 141; and the Puritans, 135, 171; result of, 139, 146; and the Laudian view, 153, 155, 157, 173, 176, 181
Emans, Thomas, 75
Erasmus, 42, 71, 72, 74–75; 79; views of, 35–39, 48; *Colloquies* of, 49–50; *Funeral*, 52n; "Pilgrimage of Pure Devotion," 37n; influence of, 52, 54, 63, 77, 108
Erkenwald, Saint, shrine of, 64
Essential and unessential, concept of. *See under* Melanchthon
Eucharist. *See* Communion; Mass
Excommunication, 30; of Henry VIII, 51; of Elizabeth I, 132
Exeter, 65
Exhortation to the people instructyinge theym to unitie and obedience, 51–52

Feckenham, Abbot, 106, 116
Fetish, defined, 3n
Fisher, the Jesuit, 153
Flemish weavers, ix, 66
Foxe, John, 78
Fountains Abbey, 66
Francis I (King of France), 78
Freman, John, 67
French Revolution, 4, 205n
Funeral, The, 52n. *Also see* Erasmus.

Gardiner, Stephen, 59, 110, 177, 209; as envoy to France, 78; and Henry VIII, 79; and the issue of images, 82, 90–94, 105; challenge to secular authority predicted by, 117–118, 194
Garrett, Christina, 111n
George, Saint, and the royal seal, 90, 92
Gibbon, Edward, quoted, 4
Glasier, Hugh, 103

Glastonbury: Abbey, ix–x, 64, 66, 70; holy thorn tree at, 24
Gloucester, diocese of, 167–168
God: creations of, and artifice, xi–xii; and the issue of images, 11–12, 16–17, 32–33, 48, 55, 86–87, 141, 163–164; representations of, 27; Wyclif's views on, 31; in Protestant ideology, 41–42, 56–57; in More's thought, 43–44; in Tyndale's thought, 46–47; in Zwingli's thought, 109; Richard Hooker on, 137; and the sanctity of the church, 139; in Puritan thought, 143, 189; destruction of images of, 186, 190; and the Reformation in England, 203–208
Goodman, Godfrey, 167–168
Goodrich, Bishop of Ely, 59
Gotely, Robert, 132–133
Gregory XIII (pope), 132
Gresham, Richard, 66
Grey Friars, church of, 67–68
Grindal, Bishop, 126, 131
Guthlac, Saint, bell of, 23

Hall, Joseph, 1
Haller, William, 79n
Hampshire, dissolution of monasteries in, 63n
Hampton Court, 199, 200
Haugaard, William, 115n
Haydock, Richard, 119
Hayles, abbot of, 76
Heaven, xi–xii, 81
Henry II (King of England), 70–71
Henry III (King of England), 72
Henry VIII (King of England), 37, 42, 48, 83–84, 91, 109; and the dissolution of the monasteries, 1–2, 21n, 61–66, 69, 204; and Thomas Cranmer, 7–8; divorce of, 50–51; as head of the English Church, 51–53; and the Pilgrimage of Grace, 55–56; injunctions of, 55, 58, 88; and the *Bishop's Book*, 56–58; uprisings against, 60–61; and the destruction of shrines and relics, 70–74; infant son of, 74; overview and effects of church reforms of, 77–82, 99, 202; heirs of (*see* Edward VI; Elizabeth I; Mary I). *See also* Henrician settlement
Henrician settlement, 83, 84, 87–88, 93, 99. *See also* Henry VIII